the pocket parent

the pocket parent

By Gail Reichlin & Caroline Winkler

Foreword by Burton L. White, Ph.D.

WORKMAN PUBLISHING · NEW YORK

Reichlin, Gail. The pocket parent / by Gail Reichlin and Caroline Winkler.
p. cm.
Includes bibliographical references.
ISBN-13: 978-0-7611-2182-4
1. Preschool children. 2. Child rearing. 3. Parenting. I. Winkler, Caroline.
II. Title.
HQ774.5 .R45 2001
649'.—dc21   00-069321

Cover and book design by Paul Hanson

The material presented in this book has been reviewed carefully and is
not intended to substitute for the professional advice of a pediatrician,
psychologist, or any other qualified therapist, education consultant, or
health-care professional. All children are unique, and while the book
offers suggestions and recommendations for parents and other child
caregivers, we encourage you to use your instincts and judgment to
determine when it's appropriate to seek professional counsel.

*Workman books are available at special discounts when purchased in bulk for
premiums and sales promotions as well as for fund-raising or educational
use. Special editions or book excerpts can be created to specification. For
details, contact the Special Sales Director at the address below.*

Workman Publishing Company, Inc.
225 Varick Street
New York, NY 10014-4381
www.workman.com

First printing, October 2001
10 9

With a "pocketful" of love and gratitude . . .
to my parents, Lovey and Phil Wernikoff;
to my husband, Ronnie; and to my amazing children,
Aaron, Rachel, and Joshua. Your love, lessons,
and laughter are my inspiration.—Gail Reichlin

To my parents, John and Ann Diamond, for their
encouragement and countless hours of child care;
my husband, Dennis, for his love and support;
and my three sons, Sean, Nolan, and Clark, for the
inspiration to write this book.—Caroline A. Winkler

Acknowledgments

Because we both have a firsthand understanding and deep compassion for all parents of two- to five-year-olds, we decided to write a book that addressed some of the most troubling issues they often face. Little did we realize this would become a four-year commitment! It has been a real challenge at times, juggling our busy schedules to meet our goals. But we never lost sight of our hope that the book would help parents make a positive difference in their daily lives. We have been fortunate to receive help and advice from so many people.

We would like to thank

All the moms and dads who shared personal parenting trials and triumphs through the Parents Resource Network lecture/discussions, telephone "warm line," and questionnaires; discussions with Caroline's Mothers and More chapter (formerly FEMALE); and daily chats and more formal conferences with parents of children in Gail's nursery school and moms and tots classes; as well as the parents of children in Caroline's Sunday school class. Please note that throughout the book all of their names have been changed to protect their privacy.

• Our dear friends, neighbors, and relatives whose stories are told throughout the book. Many of their names have been changed to protect their privacy.

• Nancy Crossman, our literary agent, for her savvy, creativity, support, and belief in our book.

• Carolyn Kott Washburne, who skillfully edited and proofread the book proposal and gave us a thumbs-up for our efforts.

• Jo Hansen for her perseverance, patience, and compassionate smile during the tedious revisions of editing the manuscript . . . just one more time.

• Martha Bullen for sharing her professional wisdom, insight, and encouragement.

• The Workman editorial team, lead by our editor extraordinaire, Suzanne Rafer, and her competent and ever cheerful assistant, Beth Doty. A special thanks to Paul Hanson, who designed a book that is truly pocket-size. Our publicist, Kate Tyler, and the marketing team working to get our book out there.

• All the psychologists, doctors, educators, child development specialists, and authors who are quoted in our book: Dr. Burton L. White,

Barbara Coloroso, Dr. Stanley Turecki, Alicerose (Sissy) Barman, Betty Weeks, Hiam Ginott, Nancy Samalin, Dr. Marc Weissbluth, Kay Willis, Dr. Marianne Neifert, Dr. T. Berry Brazelton, Fred Gosman, Dr. Ann McCartney, Nancy Bruski, Dr. Jane Healy, Jim Fay, Selma Fraiberg, and Dr. Patricia Greenfield.

• Robert R. Wilcox, Jr., Murray Gordon, David Zampa, and Mark Wiemelt for their sincere interest and legal advice concerning our project.

• Jan Pollack, the producer of our local cable television call-in show, *The Bottom Line for Busy Parents*.

• Laura Gordon for sharing her mothering and marketing knowledge and Louise Speck for her graphic talents, which helped create a meaningful focus group that identified many of the needs and feelings of our target audience.

• Authors Susan Hall and Anne Byrn for sharing their professional advice, experience, and words of encouragement.

• Joan and the staff at Kinko's in Skokie, IL, for their understanding of deadlines and caring attitude . . . even at 2 A.M!

A special thanks
from Gail Reichlin to . . .

. . . my awesome colleagues and friends who continue to nurture my spirit as a teacher, parent educator, and author by believing in me— Shelly, Steve, and Gigi Wernikoff; Inam Shalati; Elaine Leavitt; Jim Warda; Ed, Jo, Dana, Matt, and Sadie Joras; Bruno Lis; Judy Freedman; Cindy Schwab; Rhonda Rudolph; Mary Manning; Leonard Dubow; Estelle Greenberg; Meme Coryell; Susan Caplan; Deborah Leigh Wood; Blakely Bundy; Leticia Suk; Jim Reynolds; Eileen Goldberg; Paula Davis; Ricki Crown; Margaret and Jackie Quern; Beth Rosen; and Candy Reesh. And to my mentors, whose life lessons reside within my heart—Ann Reichlin, Grandma Ethel, Zadie Ben, Yussel Naiman, Betty Weeks, Fred Denzler, and Rich Jurica.

A special thanks
from Caroline Winkler to . . .

. . . all my special friends and "coworkers" from Mothers and More who offered feedback, advice, and their own personal words of wisdom, especially Mary Savitsky Ulowetz, Janet Olszewski Smith, and Meg Egan Hullinger.

Contents

Foreword

When you raise a child, especially for the first time, you'll have questions, lots of questions. Some will turn out to be unimportant. Some will resolve themselves through common sense and wisdom. But many more will continue to turn up, seemingly unanswerable, during your child's formative years. Where do you turn for advice?

Large numbers of books are written to provide child-rearing answers for parents in need, but perhaps it will come as no surprise that only a few of them are worth purchasing. Short-term fads, misinformation, scientific theories that fail to make the leap to real-life situations—these have been the common pitfalls of some child-guidance books.

In fact, so inconsistent and uneven has the field been that for years I have urged young parents to seek out mothers (and fathers too, of course!) who have done a particularly good job of raising their own children, and to use these parent-mentors as their principal source of information. Indeed, who better to consult about the difficulties of potty training a reluctant toddler than a mother who's succeeded in training her own children? Or where better to turn when faced with a three-year-old afflicted with the "gimmes" than a parent who's already been there, who's developed a successful strategy, and who can talk to you peer to peer?

Gail Reichlin and Caroline Winkler are exactly the kind of parents you would seek out with your questions. Knowing Gail for many years, I feel that she is unusually qualified to write a book about raising young children. She has a wealth of relevant experience, and she cares deeply about children. She and her coauthor, Caroline Winkler, two extremely capable women, are deeply grounded in personal experience (both are the mothers of three children), and they've used it to produce a well-written, accurate, trustworthy, and exceptionally valuable guide for parents and professionals who care for and work with young children. The book covers most anything a reader would need, and is written with intelligence, reliable knowledge, and real warmth. It's the next best thing to knowing Gail or Caroline personally, and it's there whenever you need it.

—Burton L. White, Ph.D.
author of *The New First Three Years of Life* and *Raising a Happy, Unspoiled Child*

parent to parent

When was the last time someone acknowledged what a great job you were doing as a parent? Think for a moment. Imagine what it would be like if your three-year-old gratefully exclaimed, "Mommy, thanks for reminding me to pick up my toys." Or, how about if your five-year-old uttered this unsolicited compliment at dinnertime, "Daddy, thanks for cooking all those healthy vegetables. You really take good care of me."

We can all agree—this behavior is *very* unlikely to occur in real life. In fact, in real life, most of us do a pretty impressive parenting job, even though we get little or no thanks—or for that matter, training—for it. Often, though, we find ourselves flying by the seat of our pants. And, with all the obligations in our daily lives, plus so many short- and long-term decisions to make, we can become confused, short-tempered with our children, and completely stressed out. And that leads to feelings of anxiety, guilt, and incompetence.

Gone are the days of generations past, when a neighbor had the time to listen to our hair-raising, child-raising sagas. You know the type of neighbor—slightly older, great sense of humor, ready with a cup of coffee, a kind, reassuring hug, and a confession that she'd been there, too. Her stories of what worked best with the kids made such good sense. But, today's hard working stay-at-home parents find that their neighbors are rarely available, and parents working outside the home find little time on the job to discuss family issues. So, when in the midst of a very bad day you find yourself approaching your wit's end, literally screaming out loud for help . . . where can you turn to restore your sanity?

Take heart, you're not alone! After working with parents and children for over thirty years, we know the questions parents ask, and we wrote *THE POCKET PARENT* as an upbeat, friendly adviser to provide the answers. Peppered with compassion and humor, it is here to help you deal more effectively with your child's occasional—or perhaps frequent—misbehaviors. After all, a two- to-five-year-old can present his or her parents with any number of challenges on a daily basis.

We've been there, too—embarrassing moments in public, feeling trapped in escalating no-win power struggles, losing our patience when our children tune us out. And, on a really bad day, talking to our kids in a way we'd never speak to our worst enemy— barking commands from morning till night like a frustrated drill sergeant. "Hurry up!" "Turn it off, now!" "Did you hear me?" "Stop that!" "You're hurting your brother!" "Say you're sorry!" "You forgot our rule again! . . . There's only love in this house!"

During our first years as parents, both of us found parenting advice everywhere, yet much of it was overwhelming, contradictory, and anxiety producing. We were looking for sensible down-to-earth solutions to our child-rearing problems. We eagerly read what the "experts" had to say. However, we often felt more confused, more inadequate, and more guilty and frustrated for our efforts.

Our book is literally written the way friends speak to each other. The topics we address range from the very practical— surviving morning crazies and assigning chores, to the more profound issues, such as explaining death, nurturing self-esteem, and teaching values. We chose a tone that is comforting and informal—that of a "neighborly chat." We have focused on building up your confidence in parenting. After all, *you* are the expert with your child. No one knows your child better than you do.

Our suggestions are just that: suggestions. They are not meant as things you *must* do or *never* do. There are literally no anxiety-producing "don'ts" or "shoulds" throughout our book.

If you're unhappy with the discipline methods you automatically use (like yelling, criticizing, spanking, nagging, threatening, bribing, or punishing), and you too often find yourself talking carelessly to those you care the most about, we're confident that our book can help you find some alternatives. We believe that in order to change your child's behavior, often you'll have to change *yours* first! Effective communication is the key to solving problems. Through hundreds of examples, we show what parents say and explain the messages a child receives. And we offer many options about how those conversations can change for the better, still enforcing the necessary limits, but responding with understanding and empathy for the child's feelings. Maintaining open lines in the early years is worth the effort, and we suggest many ways to do that.

THE POCKET PARENT approach to discipline advocates teaching right from wrong while respecting the dignity of both parent and child. Our book encourages you to think about not only what you need to say, but how to say it. The way we choose to communicate can encourage a child's cooperation, strengthen our general rapport within the family, and help us find more time to enjoy each other.

We believe that effective discipline consists of addressing the misbehavior as well as the feelings behind it. For example, if your child gets into a fight with another child, it is your job to stop the fight in the heat of the moment and give an appropriate consequence for that angry act. But we also suggest the importance of taking the time to get a handle on the angry feelings, when things have calmed down. The purpose of this approach is to try to understand why the misbehavior occurred in the first place. Then, by addressing the underlying problem that you discover, which may have nothing to do with the person your child has picked on (for example, it turns out she's jealous of the new baby), you are more likely to prevent the misbehavior from happening again.

You are your child's first teacher, and in the early years you really can help form his or her conscience and ability to self-discipline. Not only have we included a topic specifically on the process of teaching children values, but the themes of compassion and sensitivity are woven throughout our book. We illustrate how the most important lessons are taught by modeling the desired behavior for your children, as well as by expressing your own feelings appropriately. We include conflict-resolution skills and specific phrases that parents can use to help kids first identify their feelings and then to encourage them to express their feelings verbally rather than physically. We help you to lay the foundations of compassion and empathy early in your child, building his character for a lifetime.

Why so much focus, in the early years, on communicating and disciplining with dignity for both the parent and the child within the family? Because healthy family units are the primary building blocks for a healthy society. A family provides a child with his or her first feelings of belonging and acceptance, as well as lifelong relationships. During the early years, the family is the first place where children learn to control their impulses and live with respect and love for others. A family serves as a safe place where you and your children are allowed to fail and learn from mistakes made. And, although healthy families vary in structure (for example, nuclear families, blended step-families, single-parent families, families with two parents of the same sex, and so on), all successful family units serve as a never-ending source of unconditional love, understanding, and encouragement. During the early years, within this nurturing environment, needs are met, feelings are validated, a sense of humor is shared, and lessons are learned—helping boys and girls to grow into strong yet sensitive adults in the world at large.

the pocket parent designed for busy parents

THE POCKET PARENT follows a quick-read, A–Z format. It is not a coincidence that there are no "Z's" in the contents of this book. That's because most parents with two- to five-year-olds seldom get any! Instead, we carefully chose to end on "W" for "Wits' End," knowing for sure that every parent with young children has been there many, many times! We have designed this book to coincide with the very busy lives of parents today. Each of the topics can be read independently. Additionally, each topic has been organized into three main sections, and, depending on how much time you have, they can be read as separate units.

Question and Answer. We present a frequently asked question about a common concern on each issue, followed by an answer from us that offers a brief explanation of what is developmentally normal.

Sanity Savers. Every topic has a substantial collection of short tips that we hope will contribute to helping maintain your sanity. Each sanity saver is a complete thought. Some of the "hot button" topics—those where immediate action is needed—lead off with an Immediate Response box. These contain a list of things to do quickly, if, say, your child bites or hits another child, throws a tantrum in public, or uses unacceptable language in conversation with others.

The general list of Sanity Savers are our own carefully selected insights and practical solutions, as well as those from other early childhood experts, and from the *real* experts—moms and dads in the trenches of parenthood. Interspersed throughout are real-life anecdotes—again, some that we personally experienced and others from moms and dads who have shared their stories with us. Each anecdote relates to the tip preceding it. Keep in mind that no one solution works with all children or even consistently with the same child. That's why there are plenty to choose from. We've also included in this section what we call "Take Heart," a short "verbal hug" to help reassure you that you're not the only parent who occasionally regrets how you feel or act in a difficult situation. Hopefully you will take comfort in the fact that none of us is perfect!

The Bottom Line. Each bottom line is a carefully thought-out message that focuses on a positive angle of each difficult issue. These reassuring statements are meant to encourage you to let go of your anger, guilt or anxiety as you learn more effective ways to address a problem. You can choose to go directly to the bottom line (located at the end of the last page of each topic) and come away with a "nugget of wisdom" relating to the real crux of a worrisome issue.

Although this book is designed to address worrisome issues and arranged for quick troubleshooting, it embraces an underlying positive perspective and attitude for raising healthy, happy children. If you choose to use techniques from our book, we believe you will become more confident and successful in your approach to difficult issues. The entire family dynamic will also take a positive turn, leaving you more time and peace to notice and enjoy the precious moments.

Keep it handy, so it's there for you whenever you need some fast solutions, positive discipline strategies, a little "neighborly" advice, and of course, reassurance that you're not going out of your mind!

—GAIL REICHLIN and CAROLINE WINKLER

the cornerstones

It's a given that all two- to five-year-olds misbehave—some occasionally, some more frequently. And although we can't always know when our children's next outburst or misstep will occur, we do have control over how we choose to deal with it.

The following information is included to help you understand both the philosophy of discipline and the style of communication that guide the hundreds of tips in *THE POCKET PARENT*. We encourage you to filter the many suggestions that we offer through your own personality and parenting style, and use what seems to make good sense for your family.

discipline vs. punishment

Our philosophy of discipline is not synonymous with "punishment." Nor is it a wimpy approach that allows the kids to rule the roost. Based on unconditional love and firm limits, it is permissive with feelings but strict with behavior, with the goal of keeping the child's dignity and self-esteem intact. Our philosophy of discipline is a process of teaching right from wrong through a variety of strategies, including the behavior and attitudes you model for your child. Also important are planned discussions, either in private or with the entire family. Revisiting the misbehavior (often several times) to help teach kids the lesson that needs to be learned is done at the planned discussions. The focus of this philosophy is on solving the problem (rather than on placing shame, blame, fear, or guilt), within a clear framework of rules, values, and morals.

Punishment is actually quite different from discipline—as we just defined the term. Punishment is a type of consequence in which injury is inflicted or a penalty is imposed in order to cause the offender loss or pain. An angry parent who chooses, in the heat of the moment, to punish a child as a consequence of his bad behavior often seems to have the intention of "getting even." ("That'll show him who's boss!") Kids often respond with their own feelings of revenge, not remorse, thereby perpetuating the negative behavior. Although this is somewhat a matter of semantics, many parents and teachers agree that there is a huge difference between a "well-disciplined" child and a "frequently punished" child. In fact, when children experience firm and predictable limits, they feel protected, they feel safe, and they feel loved.

discipline terms

Parents deal with basically two types of discipline situations: getting a child to stop doing something wrong, and getting him to do something right. Our definition of discipline is twofold. First, in the short term, it means to control; setting and enforcing limits and immediately stopping your child's undesirable or dangerous behavior without hurting his body or self-esteem. Especially in the early years, you are accepting the responsibility to guide your child with wisdom, love, and limits by becoming his *external* control again and again until one day he can do it on his own (*self*-control).

Second, in the long term, it means the process of teaching your child right from wrong throughout his childhood as you continually impart the values and social mores that gradually help build his conscience. Over time, a well-disciplined child has learned to control his impulses, is able to negotiate and solve problems, and has developed empathy for others.

Positive Discipline Strategies: Techniques that use positive attention and communication skills to gain compliance rather than negative attention such as yelling, spanking, name-calling, criticizing, and threatening. All families are different, with different house rules and expectations, but there are many ways to approach a child's misbehavior from a positive perspective. Setting realistic expectations that match your child's developmental ability, temperament, and personality is important in choosing a strategy that works. For example, one parent may handle a situation by offering limited choices; another may use humor or distraction; while still another follows through with an appropriate consequence. All can be equally effective. No parent is perfect. Any parent may "lose it" sometimes, saying and doing things he wished he hadn't; however, it's never too late to change for the positive. Although it takes substantial thought, time, and effort, it's worth it.

Consequence: The result (good or bad) of your child's behavior, sometimes requiring intervention, sometimes occurring naturally by itself. Most of us have more often heard the term with its negative connotation, as in the common sayings, "Truth or consequences" and "suffer the consequences." Note that punishment is one type of consequence.

> *Natural consequence:* An outcome of your child's behavior that requires no parental intervention; a natural cause-and-effect relationship. For example, if your child doesn't wear her mittens when going outside during the winter, her hands will get cold. "Cold hands" are the natural consequence of "no mittens."

> *Appropriate consequence:* An outcome of your child's behavior that is deliberately chosen and that involves parental intervention without resorting to physical force, rage, or humiliation, while preserving the dignity of both parent and child. This is one type of positive discipline strategy. (The box on page 14 explains how to choose an appropriate consequence.)

> *Punishment:* This is a type of consequence in which the parent purposefully (usually in anger) causes a child pain, loss,

humiliation, or suffering as "payment" for an offense. The focus is on making the child "pay a price" for an infraction rather than on his learning why the misbehavior was wrong and should not be repeated. Furthermore, it often invites feelings of revenge rather than remorse. For these reasons, according to our definition, it cannot be considered an appropriate choice out of all the possible consequences.

Choosing Appropriate Consequences

How do you come up with an appropriate consequence when your child misbehaves? Try one of these responses:

→ **Immediate response:** Think of a consequence on the spot and go with it if it makes sense, is related to the misbehavior, and preserves the dignity of both parent and child; for example, taking a child out of the sandbox if he throws sand at another child, or going home or to some other activity where he does follow the rules.

→ **Predetermined response:** Establish the consequence of a certain misbehavior ahead of time, during a family meeting with your spouse and the children, or in a private, planned discussion with your child. ("Johnny, time-out! You remember, we decided in our family meeting, hitting always gets a time-out.")

→ **Delayed response:** Address and stop the misbehavior. Then buy yourself some time to come up with an appropriate consequence if you aren't sure what to do. ("Calling your brother a butthead was a bad choice. I need some time to decide what I'm going to do about that.") Note: This response is not recommended for a two- to three-year-old. Because of the way toddlers tend to live in the moment, they may not be able to connect the consequence to the past misbehavior.

→ **No response:** Deliberately choose to ignore the behavior because of the circumstances. If it's been a very long day, the kids are really tired, and you're on a short fuse for a variety of reasons . . . "let it go" without guilt.

communication

Many experts agree that communication is the key to solving all problems. We're willing to bet that many fights and frustrations that occur between you and your child are the result of miscommunication. So it makes good sense to think about not only what you need to say, but the way you choose to say it. Keep in mind that your choice of words, tone of voice, and body language can make the difference in being understood, thereby gaining your child's cooperation.

communication terms

"I" Statement: A sentence in the first person beginning with the word "I" that expresses one's own feelings, likes, dislikes, needs, or observations, without attacking the listener. For example, a parent can establish eye contact with a child and say, "I am really angry. I don't like to see toys all over the floor. I need some cooperation," while taking the child's hand and leading him to the task. Although our approach to discipline is permissive with a child's feelings, the way parents express *their* feelings is also very important and can make the difference between getting compliance or defiance from the child.

"You" (Attack) Statement: A sentence beginning with the word "you" that includes a character assault, and which almost invariably puts the listener on the defensive. For example, you shout at your child (who is already in another room), "You are such a slob! Why don't you ever pick up? Every single toy you own is on the floor! You get over here right now . . . or else!" Such a barrage is most likely to get no response at all from the child. Or you may get a full-blown tantrum, if the speech is delivered up-close and personal. This approach is one way to cause a child to tune us out or become defiant.

"Use words": A request encouraging a child to express his feelings verbally rather than by kicking, hitting, screaming, throwing things, or biting. You can start helping even a very young child to recognize and label his feelings by saying, for example, "I'll bet you feel angry when your sister pulls the toy out of your hands."

Hug Hold: From behind, embrace the child under his arms and around his chest, restraining him firmly but lovingly. This position allows you to get very close and whisper something calming in his ear and also lessens the chance of provoking kicking or punching.

Modeling: Demonstrating through your daily actions the kind of behavior you expect your children to learn. It is the most powerful teaching tool a parent has. Keep in mind, it's not just *what* you say; more important, it's *how* you say it; and most important, whether you *do* it. Remember, kids will do as you do, not necessarily as you say. You can count on your kids to let you know, often at the most inopportune time, just exactly what they have picked up by your example!

Family meeting: A prescheduled or spur of the moment get-together of the parents and the children to clear the air or just to connect. You can use this time to discuss various issues and problems, recognize exemplary behavior, organize chores and schedules, or plan special events.

How to Hold a Family Meeting

Family meetings can help the entire (often very busy) family feel more like a cooperative team, with children and adults working together to make decisions and solve problems. Regular meetings can clear the air of misunderstandings and annoyances that took place during the week.

We recommend regular family meetings as a way to address the feelings, needs, and concerns of everyone in the family. Everyone gets a chance to speak regarding a particular issue, as well as the opportunity to practice listening. Each person's input is initially validated; all suggestions or comments are written down on paper, without passing judgment. When all the opinions are recorded, parents review them out loud, one by one.

Maintaining a sense of humor is essential. Parents retain veto power, so they can nix unacceptable suggestions like, "Please have my sister move out of this house right now! She can live at Grandma's!" First, they acknowledge the child's feelings by saying, for example, "We can understand how angry you get with your sister when she goes into your room and destroys your things." Then add, "However, we love your sister too much to allow her to live with Grandma; we would really miss her. So we need to think of another plan to solve the problem. Any more ideas?"

Family meetings can also serve as an opportunity to plan for fun times together—long-range vacations or quick trips, picnics, and parties. These meetings can also be used as a time to decide what to do for a relative's birthday (for example, a huge, one-of-a-kind, handmade card designed by the whole family), or to talk about how upcoming holidays will be celebrated. There is often much more cooperation and enjoyment when the planning you do together becomes part of the event.

Last, family meetings can serve as a time where praise can be given for all to hear. Family members can be encouraged to share what went well during the week. Even a very young child can think of something that made him happy. You might decide to end the meeting with a favorite dessert, a family "high five," or a special family cheer that leaves everyone in a better mood. (Suggestions for when to call a family meeting can be found throughout the book.)

anger

Q: Am I the only parent who feels guilty that there are so many daily angry moments in our family?

A: The combination of the lack of a normal two- to five-year-old's self-control and the pressure on parents nowadays to "do it all" and "do it all well" can leave everyone feeling angry and frustrated much of the time. Communication is the key to resolving what's behind the anger.

sanity savers

Give a warning or status report when you feel yourself on the verge of an explosion.

> ■ *Caroline remembers saying one day: "WARNING! Mommy's patience is getting low. I only have this much left, about the size of a pea." Her son paused, gave her a big hug, and said with a smile, "NOW how much do you have? Is it as big as a grapefruit yet?" She admits she had to laugh, and the whole mood changed.*

Talk about *your* feelings (beginning your sentences with the word "I") without attacking your child's imperfect character. (See page 15 for more on "I" statements.)

> ■ *Becky, the mother of twins, said, "I am furious when I hear name-calling!" instead of saying, "You are a very bad girl! How dare you make your sister cry! There is only love in this house!"*

Resist the desire to give immediate advice to solve an angry child's problem. Just try to concentrate on listening to your child and acknowledging his feelings, so that he is better able to calm down and feel understood. Later that day, in a private discussion with you, he will be more able to talk about the incident and figure out (with your help) what needs to be done, so it won't happen again.

> ■ *Mandy's five-year-old came storming into the kitchen with tears rolling down his face. "M-o-o-o-m-m-e-e-e, Ari (his younger sister) messed up my race car track when I was in the bathroom." Mom stopped what she was doing, gently placed her hand on his shoulder, and looked her son straight in the eye as she responded, "Wow, you sound very upset." Jason said, "Yeah, I hate her!" "Hmmmm, I see," said Mom. "I bet right now you wish you didn't have to share your room with your sister." Jason began calming down as he nodded in agreement. Mom added, "I'm really sorry to hear that Ari's been such a pain today. Let's talk about this at bedtime and we'll figure out a plan to keep her away from your racetrack. Okay? Now, honey, how about a glass of juice?"*

Focus on the present situation; resist the impulse to dredge up all past wrongdoings to make your point.

> ■ *When her four-year-old got off the bus from preschool without his backpack for the fourth time that week, Gail had to bite her tongue to*

keep from blurting out, "Why are you so forgetful?
It was your coat last week . . . now it's your
backpack!" Instead, she sighed and calmly asked,
"How can I help you remember your backpack
tomorrow?"

Avoid physical punishments and threats. Do
what you ask your kids to do: When you're angry,
"use words instead of fists." Remember, in a
moment of anger, you may not know your own
strength and wind up regretting your actions.

Explore acceptable physical outlets for releasing
anger—your own and your child's.

■ *Yvette, a clever mom, appropriately channeled*
her need to yell. When she felt ready to explode,
she would go into another room and scream out
one word at the top of her lungs. The first thing
she saw worked just fine: "Toaster!" or "Bathtub!"
or "Bedspread!"

■ *At a family meeting, with the help of the kids,*
Ethel and Sol developed the following list of
options: "When you are angry, you may pound the
hammer on your play workbench; punch the
pillow; throw your ball against the side of the
house; go in your room, keep the door open, and
yell; jump up and down and scream; poke holes
in this paper with a pen; or draw a picture of how
angry you are."

Realize that even a well-meaning lecture
delivered "in the heat of the moment" usually falls
on deaf ears. Consider saving discussions for later,
keeping in mind that discipline is a process. Both
children and parents often communicate better at
bedtime, under the soothing cover of darkness.

Change your usual response; try using humor.
Kids often get so "infected" by the laughter of
others that they forget the power struggle.

> ■ *In the middle of a heated argument, Mick was
> suddenly struck by how cute his little boy's face
> looked as it turned beet-red with anger. Recalling
> a scene from his son's favorite movie, Mick
> extended his finger, tickled under his son's chin
> and said, "Coochie, coochie, just like the mother
> elephant's trunk did to baby Dumbo!" The boy
> couldn't resist cracking a smile, and both of them
> burst out laughing as they restored a pleasant
> mood. It wasn't long before the little boy learned
> the same technique to soothe his daddy when he
> was angry!*

Rely on nonverbal cues when you don't trust what
might come out of your mouth. Let pictures,
charts, and short notes get the message across
for you.

> ■ *Brad, a dad who's really into sports, developed
> a special "guy language" that worked much
> better with his sons than angry accusations. For
> example, when the kids were dawdling, he'd use
> the basketball hand signal for traveling to speed
> them up.*

Separate yourself from the source of irritation.
Parents at their wits' end can always choose to
leave the scene. With small children, you might
simply leave the room. Your two- to five-year-old
will not be far behind! Some parents do need to
literally leave the house to compose themselves.
(If you decide to leave the house, be sure a
responsible adult is on duty.) It's important to
make it clear to your child why you are leaving and
that you will be back.

■ *One day Barb, whose patience was worn out, told her kids, "Mommy's had it! I can't listen to you when you whine. I'm going to stay in my room alone until the timer rings." (Just one or two minutes can do wonders.)*

take heart

♥ *You're not the only parent who seeks refuge in the bathroom for a minute or two of peace.*

Work out a plan or secret code with your spouse so that you both know the cue to step in and take over when one of you is at your wits' end.

■ *When Mary screams "Code Blue," her hubby knows to take over IMMEDIATELY!*

Say "I'm sorry" when it's appropriate.

■ *At first, Caroline worried that she would lose her authority by apologizing to the kids. She now realizes it's good for the kids to know that everyone makes mistakes. More important, they can see how to take responsibility for their mistakes and make amends. Sometimes she even lets her kids hear her pray for more patience!*

Find your bottom line and stick to it. Focus on a few important house rules and periodically let the kids know that these rules are nonnegotiable. Once everyone understands you mean business, there will be less incentive to beg, plead, or push you over the edge. Establish a consistent routine and stick to it.

take heart

♥ *You're not the only parent who finds some situations (clean-up, bedtime, hair washing) difficult and frustrating. Grin and bear it; keep in mind, "This too shall pass." With the help of a relaxing bath or a good video relief can be yours sooner than you think!*

■ On Sunday Kate told her daughters that by nine o'clock they needed to have brushed their teeth and be in bed, ready for their story. On Monday, Tuesday, and Wednesday night, when the kids dawdled, Kate "stuck to her guns" and skipped the story. After a few days, the kids knew she meant business. On Thursday night, when Kate said, "Ten minutes until nine o'clock," she was pleasantly surprised as they scooted off to the bathroom immediately.

Address each objectionable behavior in a calm but firm manner, lest your anger escalate your child's anger and you both "blow up."

Jot down what triggers an angry response from you or your child; understanding the cause will help you address the situation more effectively in the future. (See "Tantrums," page 276, for more ideas on addressing your child's angry outbursts.)

■ Too often after a rough day at work, Brian felt overwhelmed rather than welcomed when he arrived home. The baby was usually screaming, for no obvious reason. David, the four-year-old, always wanted Dad's full attention immediately, and he took his place standing on Brian's shoe. His wife was usually shouting at him from another room, demanding that he come and fix whatever had stopped working that day. In order to meet these demands without losing his temper, Brian needed to find a way to "recharge his batteries" before he arrived home. Just sitting in his car a few blocks away from his house with his eyes closed for ten minutes or taking a brisk walk somewhere between the office and home did the trick.

Playing with puppets and toys can help encourage a young child to open up. Tell a story using the characters to get your point across. (See "Role-Playing" on page 25 for more ideas.)

Role-Playing

Role-playing is acting out a situation by the parent, the child or both together that can: teach a lesson or new skill, solve problems by sharing feelings, facts and opinions about situations that have already happened, or practice approaches to what may occur in the future. Try these techniques:

→ **Reversing roles with your child** can help teach a lesson or solve a problem. This is especially effective if you have a good sense of humor. The conversation might go something like this: Mom: (acting child's role): "Mommy, I didn't like the lunch you made today, so I threw it at our dog!" Child (as Mom, shaking finger): "That wasn't nice to do." Mom: "It was a big mess . . . there were Spaghetti-O's everywhere, but the dog licked up most of it." Child: "You wasted the food and food costs lots of money!" Mom: "I'm sorry, Mommy. If I don't like my lunch again, I'll tell you with words. Okay? Can I give you a hug now?"

→ **Ask, "What if . . . what could you do?"** questions to get a clearer picture of your child's fears and feelings. Find a quiet time when the two of you can practice what might happen under various circumstances. "What if you are staying overnight at Grandma's house and you are afraid just before you go to sleep . . . What could you do?" "I could bring Daddy's flashlight and keep it next to me in case I need it." "Good thinking. Here's another question. What if you really miss us while you're visiting Grandma. What could you do?" "I could call you on the telephone." "That's right, you could. But what if we weren't home? Then what could you do?" "I could go tell Grandma I was lonely." "That's good thinking, honey; I'll bet she'd give you a big hug and some hot chocolate!"

→ **You can play with "Good Choice" and "Bad Choice,"** two stuffed animals designated by you and your child for the purpose of talking about a bad behavior that has happened earlier. This works well at bedtime and goes like this: Your child holds the animal called "Bad Choice" and describes the bad behavior in a low-pitched voice, "I was very mean to my sister. I called her a dummy and pushed her out of my room because she was bothering me." "I see," says Dad. "What do you think 'Good Choice' would have done?" Child (holding the other animal and saying in a softer voice): "Kara, I'm playing with my racetrack now. Here . . . you can have these two cars to take in your room to play, okay?" (You can help by making suggestions if the child doesn't know what "Good Choice" could do.)

→ **Use puppets, dolls, or favorite stuffed animals to tell a story** that will help prepare your child for what is going to happen. Dad speaks to his son through Teddy the puppet, "Psst . . . I bet I can guess why you don't want to go to your cousin's birthday party. I know you love cake and ice cream and games. I wonder if you're worried about not knowing all the other kids. Daddy will make sure your chair is right next to your cousin's, and Aunt Meg will introduce you to everyone. And Daddy will stay in the room until you wave goodbye . . . okay?" (as puppet tickles the child's tummy).

Call a family meeting to discuss issues that are causing trouble, and brainstorm solutions. (See "How to Hold a Family Meeting" on page 17.)

Try some ways of soothing the body to alter the mood.

> ■ *When frustration was mounting and toys began whizzing through the air, Michael, a smart dad, came up with some ideas for redirecting that energy that worked. Sometimes he simply refocused everyone by whispering, "Kids, let's all sit down and have a super-delicious snack." Or he'd invite the kids to lie down and rest on his bed and they would take turns getting wonderful back rubs.*

> ■ *When things were going badly and tension was high, Diane, a sensitive mom, found that one of three questions usually worked to turn things around: "Who would like to snuggle up in a rocking chair with me?" "Who wants to listen to some soft music with me?" or "Who's ready for a nice, warm bubble bath?"*

When you are calm, write down ways you could have handled an angry situation differently, and try to remember them for "next time."

Expect most children to go through a period of defiance where they test the limits. Try to remain calm but firm as you "hold the line." Knowing that defiance is normal can help you remain calm and understanding as you continue to let the child know what is expected.

> ■ *Caroline was having a really rough day with her oldest child. He simply refused to come in from the yard to eat dinner with his grandparents, who were visiting. Then he blurted out what he had*

learned from another child: "You're not the boss of me!" Caroline felt her whole face redden. Grandma just smiled as she recalled one of her own favorite parenting stories. When Caroline was four years old, her parents had gone on a rare date, leaving Caroline's grandmother to look after the children. Caroline's mom was surprised when they got home late and found her still up. Caroline had refused to go to bed and had even told her grandmother, "You're not my mom! You can't tell me what to do!"

Have faith that angry situations will often resolve themselves without a reaction from you. Nancy Samalin, parenting educator, says, "The wonderful thing about saying nothing is that you never have to take it back."

■ *On vacation, Caroline's five-year-old was upset whenever they decided to eat somewhere that wasn't his first choice. Caroline's first reaction was a long lecture: "That's your choice. You'll be hungry later. You know as a family, we each take turns picking. Why can't you be less selfish?" and on and on, until she was all wound up. After a couple of angry incidents, she decided to try not responding to his remarks at all. Lo and behold, it worked! As soon as the waitress came to the table, Mom and Dad were amazed that Sean was the first one to order something to eat without a complaint.*

take heart

♥ *You're not the only parent who suddenly blurts out the very things you had sworn to your mother you'd never say when you had kids!*

Realize that your own responses to angry outbursts, good or bad, will set a powerful example for your child. If you respond to anger with anger, you'll soon be on the fast track to a major confrontation.

Think about your own childhood experiences, how they may affect your parenting expectations and frustrations, and how you can use this awareness to make things go better for you and your child.

> ■ *Ben found himself becoming first impatient and then irate over teaching his five-year-old to ice skate. Suddenly it dawned on him that he was acting just like his own father, who had often lost his temper in similar situations. So, without guilt, Ben realized it would be smart to ask his wife to take over while he cooled off.*

Take time to replenish yourself with the things that give you pleasure—a hot bath, a weekly massage, an evening out—and do it without guilt, so you can avoid burnout. The more refreshed you feel, the better place you'll be in emotionally for your kids and the less bothered you'll be by the everyday annoying incidents.

the bottom line

Consider angry feelings a useful warning that gives you a chance to regroup, think through your situation, and fix what needs to be fixed.

new baby

Q: My daughter has been acting up ever since we brought her new baby sister home from the hospital. What can I do to stop this?

A: All children desire 100 percent of a parent's time and attention. Kids are not fazed by your deadlines at work, your need to do the laundry, or the necessity of nursing a newborn. The feelings an older sibling has when there is a new baby in the house are akin to the feelings you might have if your husband were to bring home a new wife who was younger and cuter than you are. Even worse, the child is expected to immediately love this new rival for your affections and share everything with her! That's asking a lot!

sanity savers

Assume absolute responsibility for keeping your kids safe. Even a child who is not openly jealous of the baby may do inadvertent harm.

■ *When Caroline's friend heard she was having trouble with her three-year-old, he suggested a trick that he had used to keep his sleeping baby safe upstairs while he was busy elsewhere in the*

*house. An eight-inch-long hook was installed at the
top of the baby's door to keep it ajar while baby
slept. That way he could hear if the baby woke up
crying, and there was ample room for the siblings
to peek in but not enough for them to enter.*

Carry the baby with you rather than leaving him
and a young sibling (under the age of four) alone
together, even for "just a moment."

Use a baby sling or backpack when both kids are
screaming for attention.

■ *Caroline constantly carried her second son in a
front sling. That way, her hands were free to play
and cuddle with her three-year-old, and she was
still able to feel close to the baby.*

Redirect aggressive behavior with gentle words
and actions.

■ *Quick reflexes come in handy sometimes! One
day when Gail was nursing her daughter, her two-
year-old suddenly raised his arm as if he were
going to deliver a karate chop right through the
baby's windpipe. Gail gently but firmly grabbed his
hand and redirected it. Rather than scolding him,
she said, "Your sister loves to be tickled—like this!"*

Establish a few concrete rules, briefly stating
what is considered acceptable behavior. Toddlers
and preschoolers do better with only a couple of
rules.

■ *In Gail's house the family had three main rules:
"No hitting, no hurting, no bad names."*

Discuss acceptable ways for the older child to
deal with his anger. (See the sections titled
"Anger," page 19, and "Tantrums," page 276,
for more ideas.)

■ *Jeff told his daughter, "You may not hit the baby. Please use words to tell me how you feel, I may be able to help."*

■ *Once when three-year-old Sean got angry at the baby, Caroline stamped her feet and said, "Let's make angry faces. Show me how angry you are." At first he just looked astonished, but then they both burst out laughing.*

Be sure to give your older child your full attention at least a few times each day. This is easier said than done, but it's worth the effort.

Acknowledge your child's feelings, no matter how bad they sound. Tell him that it's okay to feel jealous, but not okay to hurt the baby.

■ *Daphne sat her three-year-old down, established eye contact with him, and said, "It's not easy having a new baby sister, is it?" Her son nodded. "Sometimes I think you wish your sister didn't live here," she added. "I understand your feelings, but it's not okay to hit the baby."*

Recognize that not all negative feelings are expressed aggressively.

■ *Two-year-old Cordelia had little to do with her new baby brother; however, she constantly "shadowed" her mom, even beating her into her favorite chair at just the right moment to interfere with nursing. Mom, realizing that her daughter was feeling jealous and left out, decided to make room for all three to be together on the couch.*

Involving your older kids in problem solving can help give them a sense of control.

■ *One day Caroline offered her three-year-old a limited choice: "While I nurse the baby, would you*

> *like to play with Daddy, or sit by me and read your book to the baby?"*

Focus on explaining *your* needs to the older sibling, instead of the baby's needs. This may help minimize her feelings of rejection and make her feel good about helping you.

> ■ *At nursing time, instead of saying "Baby needs me more than you do right now . . . you can wait!" Sandy explained, "I must go nurse now or my body will really hurt!"*

Model appropriate responses to anger. (See "Anger," page 19, for additional suggestions.)

> ■ *After her four-year-old son continued to complain about not being able to go the park during the baby's nap, Jackie responded, "Mommy's had it! I need a time-out in my room for a few minutes."*

> ■ *It had been a trying morning, and Jim's temper flared when his daughter demanded to know, "Why does that dumb baby have to sit in the stroller with me?" He replied, through clenched teeth, "I need to take a deep breath and count to fifty before I can answer that!"*

Assure, and reassure, your child that no one could ever take his place. (Kids need to hear this more than once.)

> ■ *Teresa, a mom from a close family, often explained to Patty, her three-year-old, "We love everyone in our family: Uncle John, Aunt Sally, Cousin Jane, Grandma, Grandpa, and the new baby. But there will always be a special place in my heart for you and you alone. You are my only special Patty!"*

Gradually, and gently, encourage the older siblings to become involved with the new baby.

A sudden barrage of constant requests to bring you diapers, shoes, and blankets may cause resentment.

■ *Ken, a thoughtful dad, asked his four-year-old, "Which outfit would you like to see your baby sister in today?"*

Encourage feelings of closeness and pride. This takes time, thought, and creativity.

■ *Caroline would stand behind Sean, where only baby Nolan could see her, and then would make funny faces and tell Sean, "See, Nolan is smiling at you! He must really think you're special." After a few months of this routine, she realized her efforts hadn't been all in vain. One evening, bursting with unselfish pride, Sean met Mom at the door and shared the happy news, "Guess what my brother can do now, Mommy? He can crawl up onto my bed all by himself!"*

Lighten up on your expectations for the older child "to grow up and set an example." Regression in such things as toilet training, thumb sucking, and baby talk may go away faster if parents don't make an issue of them.

■ *Sarah and Jack spent a lot of time turning the spare room into a nursery before the new baby arrived. Three-year-old Max seemed to resent their lack of time for and attention to him. One day Sarah caught Max intentionally ripping the wallpaper border by the crib. Rather than scolding him, Sarah took the cue and asked Max if he'd like to climb into the empty crib. Then Sarah wound up the mobile and asked Max which tune he thought the baby would like best. Max enjoyed the experience and hopefully felt more a part of welcoming his new sibling.*

■ *Caroline's girlfriend Jodi played a game with three-year-old Sean that he enjoyed. She would actually try to stuff as much of his body as would fit into a tiny baby sling in her lap. While Caroline nursed Nolan, Jodi would say, "This is my baby. His name is Sean. What's your baby's name? My baby weighs thirty pounds, how big is yours? My baby is beautiful." The delight in Sean's eyes indicated that this was one of his favorite games. Caroline realized that allowing Sean to indulge in silly, regressive behavior was often fun, and that he seemed to outgrow the need to regress when she stopped making a big deal out of it. On the other hand, comments like "You're the big brother, you should know better" bombed completely!*

Find ways to reassure your older child that staying home with the new baby is not all fun and games.

■ *Even though Marisa could have really used some time to nap, she decided to let Warren stay home from preschool for a couple of days when he objected to going. She suspected he thought she was just shooing him out the door so she could be alone with the new baby. Once Warren had sampled the sounds, smells, and constant demands of a new baby, he couldn't wait to go back to school.*

Help your older child protect his favorite playthings as the baby becomes more mobile.

■ *Nolan was already five and a half when Caroline's third son, Clark, was born. She was pleasantly surprised at how Nolan immediately welcomed his new baby brother. And Clark really enjoyed watching Nolan play while he sat in his*

baby swing. But when Clark learned to crawl, the
friction began. Clark seemed to be drawn as if by
a magnet to Nolan's most prized possessions,
including his precious baseball cards. Rather
than giving long explanations about how Clark
was just a baby and meant no harm, or pointing
out that Nolan shouldn't leave his stuff lying
around, Caroline came up with a plan. She and
Nolan decorated a box with stickers, and Nolan
was given his very own "big boys only" shelf in
the family room, where he could keep his special
things safely out of Clark's reach.

Arrange a special "date night" for your "original"
family, as it was before baby's arrival.

■ Three-year-old Richie's parents routinely made
a point of spending time together with Richie and
without the baby. They really enjoyed taking him
out for pizza. Even the high cost of baby-sitters
and the discomfort of missing a nursing session
were worth it! These outings helped Richie feel
that he was still special, and it gave Mom and
Dad a much-needed break from the baby.

the bottom line

When you are permissive with your child's
feelings but strict with his behavior, you can,
over time, help bring your kids closer together; a
little patience, a big sense of humor, and an
occasional baby-sitter will help smooth the way!

bad words

Q: Grandma nearly fainted when Jamie blurted out to Grandpa, "You are a stupid, lazy doo-doo head!" I was appalled! What can I do to curb his tongue?

A: Young children continually experiment with words and are very conscious of how adults react. A two-year-old may innocently parrot what he's heard from TV, his friends, or even you in a bad moment. A three- to five-year-old may start using bad words to express his anger, defy adult authority, get your attention, or just be silly with friends. Once you determine *why* your child is using inappropriate language, you will be able to choose how best to handle it.

immediate response

→ Take a deep breath before speaking, so you can use your normal tone of voice.

→ Call an immediate "time-out" in response to an angry insult.

→ Tell your child his choice of words is not acceptable.

→ Suggest acceptable substitute words to use.

➜ **Comfort the victim.** Say, "Your sister really hurt your feelings, didn't she? She knows better."

sanity savers

Avoid shouting back when your child is very upset and lashes out with his most powerful insults. By choosing not to fight this battle right then, a power struggle is avoided. You might simply say "Oh, sounds like you could use some time to calm down" and go about your business—but remember to discuss it later.

Use "I" statements to express your strong objections to your child's bad language. (See page 15 for an explanation of "I" statements.)

> ■ *Caroline told the boys, "'Shut up' is a rude thing to say. I feel angry when I hear you say that. I don't allow anyone to talk to me like that. Try saying, 'Excuse me. I really need to talk to you right now.'"*

Choose not to respond at all to bad language. If the kids fail to get a rise out of you, they might just give up trying to "get to you."

Ignore occasional "potty talk"; think of it as a form of innocent preschool humor.

Withdraw your attention by leaving the room when your child uses bad language. An explanation is optional.

> ■ *Leann told her children, "I won't listen to inappropriate words, so I'm going into my bedroom. Let me know when you are ready to talk properly, and I'll sit by you and listen."*

Consider responding to insults with humor to take the edge off of the child's anger and your own.

> ■ *Rachel, four, was upset that she could not go over to her friend's house before lunch. She got very close to Gail, her mom, who was stirring the macaroni, and with a distorted, angry face she snarled, "You wicked witch!" Gail chose to cackle a bewitching response right back: "I'm just boiling up a tasty pot of newts' blood and frogs' eyes . . . care to join me for a bite, sweetie? Cackle, cackle!" In spite of her anger, Rachel couldn't help but giggle.*

Compliment your child when you notice she chooses to avoid using bad language in a situation where she might have.

> ■ *Carol told Meg, "I liked the words you used to tell Jessica not to push you. You did a great job!"*

Establish a few simple rules, such as "no name-calling" and "no swearing," and take the opportunity to remind your child about those rules.

> ■ *When Joey started using bad words while talking to his brother, Dad would say, "Try telling your big brother that it's your turn to play with the toy now without calling him a bad name." Or, to the older child, "Tell your brother that you don't like being called names and that we don't use those bad words in our house."*

Take note of what might be influencing your child's vocabulary.

> ■ *One afternoon, Caroline sat down with her five-year-old and watched a couple of children's TV shows after school. She was appalled at the verbal abuse and name-calling. She calmly*

pointed out that in their family they do not talk
like that because it hurts people's feelings.

Realize, in an emergency, the "face-saving" power
of a little white lie. (Offer an apology to the child
later.)

■ Jack and Sue almost made
it out of the grocery store
without so much as a peep
from their usually cooperative
three-year-old son. And then it
happened. At the checkout
counter, Alec grabbed a
package of his favorite candy.
Sue looked over and said, "Put
that back!" Alec first placed
both hands on his hips, then
shook one finger at Sue and in
a deafening voice shouted,
"Don't tell me what to do,
bitch!" Suddenly, all eyes focused on the unruly
child's parents, who wished the floor would open
and suck them right out of sight. Instead, Sue
took a deep breath and, in a voice loud enough
for everyone to hear, turned to Jack and
exclaimed, "Honey, your nephew is simply
impossible today! He's going straight home!"

Allow yourself to tweak the rules occasionally; be
specific in what you suggest.

■ Caroline's five-year-old burst in the door and
said, "My teacher sucks!" Aghast, Caroline said,
"Sean! We don't talk that way." Sean whimpered,
"But Mommy, I've been good all day in school.
Can't I say it sometimes?" Caroline paused, then
said, "I'll tell you what, you can say anything at
all to the goldfish in your room, but not to me.

> When you're ready, let's talk about what's
> upsetting you without using bad words."

> ■ When three-year-old Zack called his dad a
> "poo-poo head," Len told him, "'Poo-poo' is
> bathroom talk. Bathroom talk belongs in the
> bathroom, not in the kitchen, not in the living
> room, not anywhere else. If you want to use
> bathroom talk, go into the bathroom and say it."

Notice that such words as "stupid", "dummy,"
"doo-doo head," "ca-ca," and "the F word" are
all bad words of the same degree to many young
children. Your response to any of them should
be even-handed, focusing on how bad words can
hurt people's feelings.

Plan a family discussion to talk about acceptable
words or behavior the kids could have used to
express their anger instead of resorting to bad
language.

> ■ The Cohens decided to make up a nonsense
> word that they would all use when they were
> furious. The kids were even encouraged to chant
> in public, "Doopee! doopee!"—and no one but
> Mom knew what it meant.

> ■ After Gail was embarrassed in public by her
> kid's inappropriate utterances one time too many,
> she came up with a foolproof plan. She told her
> kids that they could choose to use bad words, but
> they had to say them in their head, without
> moving their lips! Many times through the years,
> an angry kid would say to her, "If you only knew
> what I was saying in my head about you! La la la
> la la!"

Apologize if an occasional bad word slips out of
your mouth in the presence of your child.

■ *"Oops! I'm sorry, I shouldn't have said that,"* *Caroline told her son. "I know better than to use those words."*

the bottom line

Take comfort in the fact that many young children don't have a clue what swearwords and other rude words really mean; they are usually just trying out powerful words to see if they get a rise out of you. If you don't overreact, the behavior usually doesn't last long.

bedtime

Q: At bedtime, everyone is short on patience in our house; we are exhausted, and the kids drive us crazy with their endless energy and demands. Why don't we get any cooperation?

A: Many children protest going to bed on principle. Some keep getting out of bed because they are too "wound up." Others suffer from separation anxiety and want Mom or Dad to comfort them to sleep. Still others are afraid of the dark or worried about having nightmares. ("Fears at Night," page 100, addresses these fears.) While most kids can learn to stay in their beds, even the best parent cannot *make* a child go to sleep.

sanity savers

Sit down together as a family and set a few simple bedtime rules, such as what routine is expected, what you may do in bed if you can't fall asleep (such as look at a book or play quietly with teddy), and whether or not you may get out of bed.

Establish a consistent bedtime routine and stick to it.

Look for the beginning signs of a tired child: eye rubbing, yawning, dragging, or becoming irritable. Realize that the signs may come much earlier than you expect.

Put your child to bed when she is naturally sleepy. In many families, there is too long a time between the time at which the child first becomes tired and the established bedtime. This can lead to uncooperative, cranky preschoolers.

Move your child's current bedtime back by a half hour each evening, until it coincides with his natural peak of nighttime tiredness.

■ *Although many well-meaning parents think that missed naps or delayed bedtimes lead to later morning awakenings, just the opposite is usually true. In fact, pediatric sleep expert Dr. Marc Weissbluth says, "Getting in sync with the biological (circadian) rhythm of when the child is naturally tired in the 24-hour sleep cycle will actually lengthen the child's total sleep time per day." Weissbluth adds, "Sleep begets sleep."*

Create a bedtime routine that helps cue the child's mind and body to slow down, relax and ultimately fall asleep. (For example, consider giving a back rub, singing a lullaby, or reading a favorite story.)

Try to keep the activities low key for a half hour before bedtime to avoid having the kids get overstimulated.

■ *Mark, a conscientious dad, tried to "wear his kids out" by roughhousing with them before bed. He quickly learned that these activities only "wound them up"; they were actually too full of energy to settle down.*

Give a final warning about ten minutes before the bedtime routine begins.

Let an inanimate object (such as an alarm clock or timer) set bedtime.

> ■ *Margaret found that letting the clock announce bedtime removed one element of the power struggle. She would announce, "When the clock 'says' eight o'clock, it's bedtime."*

Use any props that you notice help the child switch from active to rest time, such as "white noise" from a fan or air conditioner, or the repetitive motion of a rocking chair. Try playing soft music, dimming the lights, or total silence.

Provide your child with a "lovey," like a "blankie" or stuffed animal, to stroke or hug as she learns to soothe herself to sleep.

Stay with the child who needs to be calmed by your presence, but set reasonable limits.

> ■ *Donna, a patient mom, said, "I'll stay in your room until you are no longer scared or until you fall asleep. But you must remember that after I say good night I'm going to sit in the chair and read my book. That means no talking, no hand-holding, no back rubbing, and no getting out of bed."*

Accompany the child back to his bed without reasoning with him *every time* he comes out—not easy to do, but it works. Studies show that as soon as the second night you will return him to his bed half as many times. By the third night, most children will stay in bed. (It is important to discuss ahead of time with the child exactly what is going to happen if he chooses to leave his bed. Emphasize that you will not talk to him.)

bedtime

Take turns with your spouse so that you avoid feeling trapped into putting the kids to bed every night (or marching them back to bed, as the case may be). This also gives the child the chance to relate to both parents and avoids casting one parent in the role of the "heavy."

Praise and compliment your child when he goes to bed willingly and when he stays in bed all night.

Be aware that any changes to your child's established bedtime routine may have repercussions.

■ *When Caroline's five-year-old started school, he begged to stay up later on the weekends. After they tried this for a while, Caroline found that when he stayed up more than an hour beyond his regular bedtime, it disturbed his sleep pattern. Come Monday morning, he was exhausted and cranky. She was barely able to get him to school before the bell rang.*

Realize that attempting to shorten a well-established bedtime routine may actually backfire and end up taking more of your time.

■ *One night when Gail was really in a hurry, she tried to shorten parts of the usual bedtime routine. She tried to get away with reading the shortest book, but her daughter protested, "That book was too short. I'm not sleepy yet. Read one of the ones you always read!" Then she tried skipping the song, but that didn't work, either.*

"You forgot to sing me the bedtime song and rub my back like you always do," Rachel said. Gail sighed, smiled, and resigned herself to being late for the appointment she was rushing to get to.

When you are away from home, bring along some familiar props—favorite stuffed animals or a lullaby tape. The more homelike you can make your surroundings, the more easily your child will fall asleep.

Take some time to sit on your child's bed (or even crawl right in with him) and chat calmly. Many children are more talkative under the cover of darkness; they will discuss the things that thrilled or bothered them during the day. It's also a good time to review family rules in a relaxed and nonconfrontational way.

■ *As Caroline snuggled right next to her five-year-old, he confided in her, quietly sharing details about his day at school: who teased whom on the playground, who had a crush on whom, and who got in big trouble. She found that the less she interrupted him, the more he talked. She came to cherish this special time together.*

Teach your child to respect the fact that Mom and Dad need some time alone at night.

■ *When Scott called his father back to his room repeatedly, his dad said, "I know you wish I could stay with you longer. But it's Mommy-Daddy time now. In the morning, you and I will have our cereal together."*

Consider giving rewards to recognize an accomplishment, like falling asleep without your constant presence. The younger the child, the shorter the time before he gets his reward.

■ *Ted told his son Matt, "As soon as you get five stickers on the chart, you will earn that new ball you told me you wanted."*

Do something each day that helps you feel replenished, so that you will have the energy you need to deal with your child at bedtime.

■ *When Caroline's boys were two and five, her husband worked very long hours. Occasionally at bedtime she was simply too exhausted to be patient, or even civil, with the kids. She found a way to give herself a breather and soothe her nerves during their bath time. She brought a big pillow and her favorite novel into the bathroom, then plopped the boys into a bubble bath and let them splash to their heart's content while she propped herself by the tub and read. She considered it a trade-off, her sanity for a few messy puddles of soapy water on the floor. Some nights, the kids were amazed at how wrinkled their fingers and toes were; but she assured them that they hadn't really shrunk and that they were both very, very clean!*

Consider the "family bed" that people in many cultures find comforting. This consists of the whole family sleeping together in one bed every night, not just when the kids are sick or are having bad dreams. Your local library may have a copy of *The Family Bed* by Tine Thevenin, which explains the concept in detail. This book can be helpful in deciding what is best for your family.

Realize the importance of parents coming to a mutual decision about the family's sleeping arrangements, lest your children decide for you!

■ *Sheila, a nursing mom, was so exhausted from getting out of bed at night that one day she actually fell asleep at work! Her concerned husband suggested that they let the baby sleep with them. Before long, they found their three-year-old right beside them every night, too. After a while they began to resent the intrusion of their kids; they simply had no privacy. The parents finally did what they should have done in the beginning: they discussed the situation and agreed on a plan. (1) Mom would put the baby to sleep in her crib while Dad tucked the toddler in bed. (2) On Sunday mornings, they would bring the kids into their bed to snuggle.*

Ask yourself whether having the kids share a room might be comforting for them. Although some families whose kids have to share a bedroom may wish for a larger house, the kids themselves may be comforted by each other's presence at night. Families fortunate enough to have a large house may be surprised at how well it works for the kids to bunk together and turn the unused bedroom into a playroom or den.

the bottom line

Find a bedtime routine that respects your needs as well as your child's; and however you "choose to snooze," feel good about it.

biting

Q: I was horrified when my two-year-old son bit into his best friend's arm. Is this the first sign that I'm going to be raising a bully?

A: Biting is a common behavior many two- and three-year-olds go through. Some children bite out of frustration, or simply to protect what they perceive as "theirs." Others may bite if they feel threatened, crowded, or inferior to others in terms of strength or verbal ability. The good news is that this phenomenon seems to have no lasting significance, although at the time it occurs, it can be extremely stressful for everyone involved. When a child bites, it's not the parents' fault, even though they may be feeling so guilty and embarrassed they suspect that everyone is talking behind their backs about their poor parenting skills.

immediate response

→ Address the behavior immediately by briefly but firmly stating the rule "Biting is not allowed."

→ Give your attention to the bitten child. Say, "Ouch! That hurts, doesn't it? Let's go wash it together."

→ If the biter is still angry, guide her to a place where she can cool off.

→ If the biter is totally out of control, give him a firm but gentle "hug hold." This often helps him to regain composure.

→ **Hug Hold** From behind, embrace the child under his arms and around his chest, restraining him firmly but lovingly. This position allows you to get very close and whisper something calming in his ear and also prevents him from biting or lashing out again.

→ Say "We'll discuss this later," rather than asking the child questions such as "Why did you bite your friend?" in the heat of the moment. (A furious child can rarely tell you why he acted out the way he did.)

→ Try to stay in control yourself when biting occurs; talk firmly, but avoid yelling.

sanity savers

If you notice that a child with a history of biting is getting wound up or frustrated, stay close and be prepared to intervene.

Comfort the victim, not the aggressor.

Invite the biter to help comfort the victim. Even fun, silly things can really help change everyone's mood.

■ *When three-year-old Louis bit Nancy, his baby sister, she burst into tears. Mom thought fast and said, "Honey, I think you can help Nancy feel better. How about we sing a song." Louis immediately replied, "She really likes 'The Wheels on the Bus.'" Mom said, "Great idea! Let's sing it*

together while I take care of your sister's finger."
(However, Mom admits she'd have been singing a
totally different tune on a really bad day.)

■ Barry, a thoughtful dad, said to his son, who
had just bitten Tommy, "Danny, come with me and
help me get some ice to put on your friend's
arm."

Keep in mind that the person who is bitten isn't
necessarily an enemy or even the source of the
biter's anger: he may just be the closest target.

Provide an out-of-control biter with the structure
he needs in order to calm down. This could mean
sitting quietly in a chair, going to his room alone,
or cuddling quietly with you. (See "Time-Out,"
page 299, "Anger," page 19, and "Tantrums," page
276, for ways to help your child regain self-control.)

Establish an appropriate consequence at a
family meeting, and follow through *every time* to
discourage repeated biting. (See page 17 for more
on family meetings, and page 14 for more on how
to choose appropriate consequences.)

■ Renowned child psychologist Dr. Burton White
found that holding a toddler very still for a short
time after a biting incident was quite effective. He
compares this technique to conditioning puppies;
young, active children simply don't like being
restrained. His research shows that within three
to four days of consistently using this technique,
most biting will stop.

Expect either no reply at all or a "tall (but often
very clever) tale" if you persist in asking questions
a biter can't be counted on to answer about why
the bite occurred.

■ *During her regularly scheduled conference, Johnny's mom received lots of praise about how her bright, capable son was doing in preschool. However, toward the end, the teacher said she wanted to share with her word for word Johnny's explanation of exactly what had happened the day he bit his best friend. The teacher asked Johnny, "How did this happen?" He thought very carefully before he lit up and gave his reply: "You know what, Miss Williams? I was just in the middle of a big yawn; my mouth was w-i-d-e open. All of a sudden I fell right on top of Andrew when he was crawling on the floor. My mouth must have just hit his butt and closed down on it!"*

Tell your child that biting hurts the victim every time it happens. Keep in mind that most two-year-olds do not yet have the ability to "put themselves in another's shoes" and know how another feels. Teaching empathy is a very slow and gradual process.

Let your child know that biting is not an acceptable way to get your attention.

take heart

♥ *You're not the only parent who's been tempted to show a biter "what it feels like" by biting the biter back! Remember, most toddlers cannot connect their own pain to the pain they inflict on others.*

■ *Fred reminded his daughter, "When Daddy is talking to someone and you need something, please take my hand and say, 'Excuse me, Daddy!' Biting my arm hurts me and is not a polite way to get me to listen to you."*

Help your child to understand that biting is *not* a game; it *really* hurts people!

biting

Learn to recognize the cues that your child is about to bite and be ready to intervene immediately.

■ *Gail noticed in class that Jason had a habit of turning red and puffing himself up, almost like a snorting bull, before biting. When he tilted his head a certain way, it was a sure sign that he was about to charge! Gail learned to head him off at the pass. Occasionally she was able to distract him by redirecting his attention to another physical activity, thereby totally avoiding a biting incident.*

Provide your child with something he *can* bite; even older kids go through teething episodes. Set out a handy "biting basket" stocked with "feel good" or "taste good" items: jelly-filled teething rings, iced washcloths, peeled apple slices, frozen bagels, carrot sticks, or chewy licorice.

Help your child express his feelings in non-aggressive ways. ("Hitting and Hurting Others," page 155, can give you specific ideas for helping your child channel aggression into acceptable behaviors.)

■ *When he told her it was time to turn the television off, Bob's daughter gave him a nip on the arm. He calmly but firmly said, "Biting hurts. Biting is not allowed. Use words to tell Daddy that you get mad when you can't finish watching your favorite show."*

Realize that biting can be very scary for the biter as well as the victim. A toddler's biting is more an instinctive animal reflex than a conscious response to a situation. The biter needs help in overcoming this instinct, rather than condemnation for having yielded to it.

Consider hugging the child who has bitten someone. This might help restore a sense of security to a child who is temporarily out of control or who may not even realize what he has just done impulsively. (Some children will refuse this.)

Try to get the biter and the victim together again soon, and focus on praising cooperative behavior when it occurs. If your child is the victim, understand that one incident doesn't necessarily mean repeat offenses are predictable. If your child is the biter, assure the parents of the child who was bitten that you will be watching your child closely to ensure the behavior doesn't continue at future play dates. If the two children seem to be locked in a pattern of pushing each other's buttons, however, it may be best to give them space from each other for a while without labeling or otherwise punishing the aggressor.

Biting is often a response to excessive stimulation or anxiety: respect your child's space and threshold for stress.

Refrain from demanding that a biter play with other children if he seems unwilling. Instead, provide similar toys for "parallel play" (side-by-side play, with each child doing his own thing).

Be aware that, if your child hears constant talk about his biting, or if he is labeled with a negative nickname, you may be setting up a self-fulfilling

prophecy. Excessive attention to the undesirable
behavior may actually reinforce it.

> ■ *When Nolan was a toddler, he often became*
> *frustrated by his older brother's teasing. Not*
> *possessing the vocabulary to effectively tease*
> *him back, one day Nolan gave Sean's tummy a*
> *big bite. After that, every time Nolan approached*
> *Sean, Sean started screaming, "Oh no! Oh no!*
> *He's going to bite me!" Most of the time this*
> *thought hadn't even occurred to Nolan, but when*
> *Sean drew attention to it, his eyes would twinkle*
> *mischievously and he would open his mouth*
> *wide, just as if he had decided what fun it would*
> *be to do just that!*

If your child is routinely biting at the age of four,
consider seeking some professional counsel to help
you evaluate and address any underlying issues
that may be causing the behavior.

the bottom line

A young child who bites occasionally is usually
going through a normal developmental stage;
take comfort in the fact that he is not destined to
become a bully or even a constant discipline
problem!

chores

Q: I need some *real help* around the house! Can I expect my young child to become responsible for doing some chores, or should I avoid the hassle and just resign myself to doing it all "properly"?

A: Studies show that 50 years ago, nearly all children helped maintain the house—free of charge! Today many parents (and their overscheduled kids) have very different priorities; they are too busy and are stressed to the max. It is also true that many families today have more money available to hire household help. However, pediatrician T. Berry Brazelton insists that having assigned chores makes children feel important. Although initially it's more work for you, in the long run your child will benefit from "hands-on learning" as he develops a sense of his worth in the family by carrying out his own special tasks.

sanity savers

Realize that having too many chores will usually overwhelm a young child. Involve the entire family in choosing both the chores and the appropriate consequences for doing, or not doing, them at a family meeting. (See page 17 for more on family meetings.)

Remind your child that everyone in your family has jobs to do that are important.

Help your children keep track of chores with visual aids such as charts or lists that use words, pictures, or stickers to record tasks completed.

■ *During a family meeting, the Millers, a family of six, chose to make a weekly chore chart with pictures that even the three-year-old could understand.*

■ *The Peters family used a "job jar" for additional chores that weren't part of the kids' regular*

Appropriate Tasks for Two- to Five-Year-Olds

→ Bringing in the mail and newspapers

→ Placing a napkin at each place setting

→ Getting fresh water for the dog

→ Sorting items to be recycled

→ Dusting the furniture

→ Picking up dirty clothes and putting them in the hamper

→ Helping fold laundry

→ Carrying the laundry basket of clean clothes to the bedrooms

→ Cleaning mirrors and windows with a squeegee and spray bottle filled with water (a big favorite with the kids!)

routine. In a family meeting, they all agreed that an appropriate consequence for failing to do an assigned chore was to draw a slip of paper out of the job jar. The offender then had to complete both chores before he could join the rest of the family in the den for games or TV that evening. The extra chores were very simple, like dusting one shelf, and might require your supervision.

■ *One regular house rule that the boys in the Wilson family often forgot was lifting up the toilet seat when going to the bathroom. In a family meeting, Mom, the only female in the household, expressed her anger about sitting on a wet toilet seat. She asked all "the guys" for their suggestions. The oldest quickly responded, "I've got it! The boys and Daddy will use the blue bathroom . . . we don't care if it's messy . . . you can use the bathroom upstairs." Mom responded, "I could use the upstairs bathroom, but in our house, leaving a wet, messy toilet seat is simply not an option." Dad thought a little sign, like he had seen in a public restroom, placed on the back of the toilet would do the trick. ("We aim to please, you aim, too, please!") The five-year-old said he would be more careful and suggested the family make some "pee-pee targets," tiny bull's eyes (biodegradable, of course!) that would float in the toilet. They all agreed that even if they were in a hurry or were just careless, they needed to take the time to wipe up after themselves.*

Be honest with your child, and admit that not everything we have to do is always fun. Emphasize how happy and proud *you* feel after completing a difficult task.

Schedule time to actually *teach* the child how to do the chore. Many young children will not automatically know how to do it properly.

Focus on giving a few simple directions at a time. Young children have trouble remembering more than three directives at one time.

Become a "hands-on" parent: Break the chore down into manageable steps, to help your child more easily understand and cooperate.

■ *On Monday, Gail called to her four-year-old daughter, "Come watch me set the table for dinner." On Tuesday, she asked her, "I bet you remember where we keep the plates. Let's see, how many do we need?" Rachel thought about it and carefully counted on her fingers, "Aaron, Rachel, Mommy, and Daddy." She reached for four plastic plates that Gail had thoughtfully placed in the bottom drawer, and Gail finished off the job with the napkins and silverware. On Wednesday, as soon as Gail called her, Rachel came skipping into the kitchen. Without Mom's asking, she counted out just the right number of plates and forks as she enthusiastically began arranging the table. Gail complimented her efforts by saying, "You remembered just how many we needed." By the end of the week, Rachel had mastered the task. On Friday night, as soon as Dad put the key in the door, she ran to share her accomplishment with him, "Papa, Papa, guess what? I set the table all by myself!"*

Take the time to praise a job well done. Try to make your praise specific, focusing on exactly what the child did well to help build his internal motivation to repeat those steps.

■ *Jerry told his two sons, "Without you, we'd never have gotten the table set before the pizza arrived. You remembered which side the forks go on, and to give everyone a napkin. Thanks for your help!"*

Many children cooperate better when everyone is working together at the same time—they find working as a group easier and more fun than having to do something alone.

> Giving her three-year-old an ultimatum for picking up his toys never seemed to work for Janet. But when she offered to join in the task and then let him "help" her, things went much better.

Appreciate how powerful routine can be; establish a weekly "clean-up" time. Once the routine is in place, the routine lays down the law; it takes the place of parents' constant reminders (also known as nagging!).

> One family of four agreed on a regular one-hour Saturday morning cleaning routine. Moving from room to room together, each working on his or her own specific chore, the family cleaned the house.

Set deadlines and goals to help get the job done.

> Sometimes Gail's kids were highly motivated to get a chore done before a deadline. She'd say, "I'll bet you can't put your dishes in the sink before I finish wiping the kitchen table" or "I'll bet you can't get your dirty clothes in the hamper before the timer dings!" When this worked, it seemed so easy.

> Caroline's family has become famous for their annual Super Bowl party. Entertaining more than fifteen families with dinner, games, and TV is a mammoth undertaking, especially since many are little kids who want to get in on the action. Every year they become better organized, making lists of what needs to be completed before their deadline, the time the party begins. Then they make sure they have everything they need and enough time to get everything done. One of

chores

Caroline's husband's jobs is to secure a TV for each room (even the bathroom!). The kids enjoy helping child-proof the house for the little ones, taking special care to make sure their favorite toys are out of reach!

Be consistent; when you decide on a chore, let your child know that she is expected to do it *every* time. Being inconsistent diminishes the importance of the chore in the child's mind and in turn decreases her motivation.

Respect your child's ability by resisting the temptation to "do it for him." This takes a lot of patience, but the result—a more confident, capable child—is well worth it!

Be firm but kind in your follow-ups. Resist lecturing.

■ *When Lynn noticed her daughter's plate still sitting on the kitchen table after lunch was over, she said, "Now, Brittany, what was our agreement about where your dirty dish goes?" Brittany smiled as she squealed, "Oops! I forgot!" and she ran to the table to clean up her mess.*

take heart

♥ *You're not the only parent who wonders why the same three-year-old who can operate the VCR complains that "it's too hard" to flush the toilet. A visit to your child's classroom will give you a sense of how much children really are capable of doing when it is outside of your own home!*

Acknowledge and praise your child's effort rather than criticize the quality of his work. Strive for completion, not perfection.

■ *"Thanks for putting all those heavy encyclopedias back on the shelf," Penny said. She chose not to point out the fact that the books were all out of*

alphabetical order and some were even upside
down.

Practice a new chore with your child, using
puppets or role-playing. What could be a better
way to teach a lesson than through play? (See the
box on page 25 for a discussion of role-playing.)

Kids get a kick out of using their very own kid-
size equipment whenever possible. Suddenly the
chore is so much more appealing.

■ When Sean noticed a child-size shovel in the
dime-store window, his face immediately lit up.
"Mommy, Mommy, if you buy me that shovel I
promise I'll help Daddy shovel the snow." She did,
and Sean was as good as his word. Every snowy
Saturday that winter, he eagerly shoveled right
alongside his dad, even before he asked for a ride
on the sled.

Consider your child's size and stage of
development when organizing your household, and
make things easily accessible for him.

■ Ed had just reached "the end of his rope"!
Even though he had put down all the groceries,
he still could hardly push the door back open
through the heap of coats, hats, and mittens
blocking his way. That night after dinner, he
called a family meeting to settle the matter once
and for all. Ed said, "I felt like a bulldozer trying
to come through the door today; your stuff was
all over the floor! How come your coats are
always hung up at school?" "Well, Dad," said four-
year-old Sarah, "Miss Murphy told the boys to
hang up their stuff on the yellow hooks and the
green hooks are for the girls." Ed said, "That's just
what we need. Let's go shopping together; you
can each pick out your own special hook and

*hang it right where you can reach it. Agreed?"
(The kids all nodded.)*

Realize that assigning chores contributes to the gradual development of a positive work ethic and a sense of personal responsibility, as well as pride and belonging.

■ *When Lanie came home from work early one day, she overheard her housekeeper asking three-year-old David to help fold the laundry. Mom was surprised by how eager her son was to help. "Let me fold Daddy's undershirt," he said happily. Even more surprising was what a good job he did!*

Decide whether or not you're comfortable giving an allowance for doing chores. Some families choose to give a weekly allowance to pay a child for his chores. Others pay per chore, while still others choose not to pay at all. Regardless of whether it is linked to chores or kept separate from them, children learn valuable lessons from managing their own money.

■ *By the time Sean was five, Caroline was tired of his endless demands for her to buy him something everywhere they went. So they came up with a plan. Every Saturday, Sean would receive a two-dollar allowance if all his chores for the week were done. The agreement was that he could buy anything he wanted as long as he had enough money. The first week, he couldn't get to the variety store quickly enough to see what he could buy. He carefully selected the two items he wanted most. Unfortunately, the ball and the bag of toy soldiers each cost two dollars. "Oh, I don't think I have enough," he quickly realized, and decided, "I'll take the ball now. It's two dollars, right?" Then he thought about it for another minute and said, "Oh no, that will take all of my allowance. I want to get something cheaper so I can still have some money left over to take home." Caroline was amazed at how much more discriminating he was with his own money.*

the bottom line

Beyond teaching your child important skills— such as time management and cooperation —that will serve him all his life, having assigned chores can help strengthen a child's self-esteem as well as lay a foundation for commitment to the community in general.

comparing and labeling children

Q: I tell my "hyper" son that he should calm down and be more like his sister, she's such a good girl. Why doesn't anything I say get through to him?

A: It's natural for parents to notice differences in children and tempting to use one of their kids, or even the child from across the street, as a comparison. But parents can make a conscious effort to not label traits in their kids that they're not proud of, especially in front of them. ("He's the family slowpoke.") Even well-intended positive labels applied to one child can discourage siblings from even trying to compete and make them feel limited by the roles assigned to them. ("He's our student, she's our athlete.") Think of the differences between kids as neither positive or negative but as a reminder that each child is truly unique, with his own particular strengths and weaknesses. (See "Self-Esteem," page 237, for ideas on how to focus on the positive to maximize your child's self-esteem.)

sanity savers

Appreciate that every person has his own strengths as well as weaknesses.

Identify the strengths of your preschoolers and guide each child to experience success related to those strengths. Become aware of a child's weaknesses as well, and expect and allow occasional failure. Failure often gives way to growth when it occurs within the security of the home or in the presence of parents or other supportive adults.

Change the topic when the neighbors get started comparing kids, even if yours is coming out the winner. Resist the urge to join in: It's the type of behavior that doesn't help you learn how to value each child as an individual.

Praise your child's specific actions rather than pointing out how well he fills a general role.

> ■ *Instead of calling her son, Aaron, "our family athlete," Gail said, "You really kept your eye on the ball! That catch was great!" She was afraid that if she locked her son into the "family athlete" role, her daughter might feel she shouldn't play because she could never keep up with him. And at the same time she didn't want to imply that athletics was his one and only road to success, either.*

Avoid setting the kids up against one another.

> ■ *When it came to eating, Dean's two sons were like night and day. Jimmy constantly picked at his food and ate very little, while Paul had a hearty*

appetite. One day Dad was so frustrated about
Jimmy's not finishing his lunch that he said, "Eat
your sandwich before your brother, the human
garbage can, gets it!" Unfortunately, this remark
backfired when "the garbage can" responded,
"But Daddy, I'm not hungry anymore!"

■ When Jenny said to her daughter, "Finish your
sandwich or I'll give it to your brother, the good
eater," both kids simultaneously lunged for the
food and began to fight. She found that a simple,
honest statement of fact worked better: "Let's eat
now because we have to leave soon."

Resist getting drawn into your kids' own constant
comparisons to each other.

■ Stuck indoors in the middle of a snowstorm,
Caroline turned on the stereo and encouraged
her bored, restless kids to dance. Soon the kids
were all sweaty and really caught up in outdoing
each other's fancy moves. Wiggling his hips,
Nolan said, "I'm the best dancer in our family. I'm
really good, much better than Sean, aren't I,
Mommy?" Realizing that both kids were intently
watching her face, waiting for an answer, Caroline
paused to collect her thoughts. "Let's see," she
said. "Nolan is really fast on his feet and twirls
around a lot. Sean is really strong and can keep
dancing for a long, long time without getting
tired. You each are good dancers in your own
special way."

Think about the impact of typecasting your older
child as "bully" and your younger child as "victim."
Although many parents are instinctively drawn to
defend the littlest one, sometimes that deprives
him of learning how to stick up for himself; or it
may encourage him to take the role of a
"tattletale."

Attempt to free your children from the roles cast upon them by their families, their peers, their teachers, their coaches, and even themselves.

> ■ *Carl and David's squabbling was really getting to Grandpa. Their mom, Liza, overheard Grandpa ask, for the third time that day, "Carl! Why are you being such a bully to your brother?" Liza said, "Carl can be kind. He likes to share when David asks politely."*

Strive for a home environment free from the pressures of the outside world.

> ■ *After a frustrating game of basketball, five-year-old Brent exclaimed, "I'll never make a basket! My friends are much better than me!" His dad replied, "Some of them do have good aim. But with your patience and a little practice, I'll bet you can shoot some mighty fine hoops, too. Let's practice after dinner at home, just the two of us."*

Solicit input from each of your kids, one at a time. Avoid assuming that the youngest or less assertive child can't contribute to the discussion. Make sure each child gets a turn to talk while everyone else listens.

> ■ *Jane took the time to ask her children's opinions, starting with her youngest: "Nathan, can you think of two places you'd like to go for our after-school outings this week?" Then she turned to her middle child: "Sarah, what do*

take heart

♥ *You're not the only parent who, on a very bad day, shatters the friendly atmosphere of the home and lets loose with a full-blown adult tantrum—comparing, labeling, and blaming everyone in sight for the current situation. Forgive yourself: you're only human! You'll do better next time.*

you think?" Then the eldest got a turn and Jane said, "Let's make a list." By planning the outings, she was able to satisfy each child's needs in a way that they could tolerate.

Reflect upon the influence of your own birth order and the impact of gender and other roles from your own past. This can help you gain an awareness of how you and your spouse might inadvertently be reinforcing certain stereotypes you grew up with and help you stop before the pattern becomes too entrenched.

■ *Nadine often found herself siding with her eldest child because of her own childhood memories. She often felt she had been wrongly accused as "the instigator," because her parents had always said Nadine was older and "should know better." Her husband, Harry, the youngest of five, quickly took the side of their youngest child. Nadine told her husband how her little sister had often "started things" just to get her in trouble. And Harry remembered how resentful his siblings had felt due to their mother's constant insistence that they "give in to the baby." (They responded by teasing him mercilessly as soon as she was out of sight.) Nadine and Harry were both able to laugh at how they had unconsciously empathized with the child whose birth order mirrored their own, and resolved to break the pattern in the future.*

Consider the possibility that you're asking your eldest to assume more responsibility, while your secret wish is to keep your "baby" from growing up!

■ *Caroline was embarrassed when she realized how she and her friends had enrolled their diaper-clad firstborns in toddler summer camp*

while they had lamented sending their "babies"
off to preschool at age four!

Try not to get hung up on "boy things" versus "girl things" or to favor a child because he or she is the only boy or only girl in a family of many siblings.

Constant attention to your kids' problems might actually reinforce a negative self-image and perpetuate the behaviors you want to change.

> ■ *Janie painfully recalled how her parents had fought about her sister's excess weight, while at the same time they had tried to force "skinny Janie" to eat more. When Janie's own kids came along, she didn't talk about how Brian's doctor had put him on a diet, nor did she complain about Nathan being a picky eater. Instead, she concentrated on adding more fruits and veggies to everyone's diet.*

Look carefully at what you consider your child's weakness; what may at first appear to be a weakness may actually be a strength for that particular child.

> ■ *Al was a big sports enthusiast, and he really enjoyed coaching his oldest son, George's, softball games. George shared Al's love of sports and was well coordinated and very athletic. All of the other kids on the team looked up to George. Al had to admit he was disappointed that his younger son, Peter, showed no interest in playing sports: He seemed to be more interested in watching other kids play than in joining in their ball games. Al was worried that Peter wouldn't have a chance to experience the success and popularity that George enjoyed. However, when Peter's preschool teachers frequently pointed out how much he loved inventing contraptions that*

*fascinated the other kids, Al began to regard
Peter in a new light.*

It's often hard to accept the fact that your
children are different from each other as well as
from you; learn to appreciate that everyone
succeeds best using his or her own particular
strengths.

Keep in mind that what you perceive as a
weakness at this young age may be the result of
a slight developmental delay that will disappear
without any intervention at all.

■ *Even though Matt's friends had no problems
tying their shoelaces, Matt did. So Frank, his
understanding father, bought Velcro-strap shoes
for Matt whenever possible. Trying to teach his
son how to tie his shoes had simply been too
frustrating for both of them. Frank was confident
that eventually Matt would "get it," so he decided
to wait until Matt was more coordinated to try
again. One year later . . . success!*

Discuss with your spouse the expectations each
of you places upon your children—to excel, to
share your interests, maybe even to pick up where
you left off.

■ *Dale recalls sharing with her husband an
insight from child development specialist
Alicerose (Sissy) Barman, who has defined the
expectations parents place on their children like
this: "Each parent would like his child to have,
do, and be everything that he enjoyed as a child.
Each parent would like his child to avoid
everything he found painful, difficult, and
unpleasant. And, each parent would like his child
to have, do, and be everything he has wished for
and never experienced." It was interesting to talk*

to the husband and wife, to share stories about
their very different upbringings, and to discuss
how their own childhood experiences related to
raising their own children.

the bottom line

Although labeling and typecasting seem to come naturally, by consciously focusing on and acknowledging each child's unique strengths, we can boost his or her confidence.

death

Q: My child's elderly grandpa just passed away. How do I help her deal with his death?

A: Preschool children often become curious and ask questions about death when a pet, relative, or neighbor dies. Their parents' responses can either provoke anxiety or increase their understanding of a very abstract issue. As you answer their questions, keep in mind that young children think differently from adults. In general, they tend to be very concrete thinkers and believe only what they can see. Although their perceptions are based primarily on their own experiences and therefore are limited, their comments can be surprisingly fresh and simple, but sometimes also profound and even comforting to their parents.

sanity savers

As a practice, set aside the taboo that discourages talk about death. Then your family will be more comfortable talking about it when someone close to you dies.

■ *After watching the animated classic* Bambi, *Bill opened a discussion with his five-year-old*

daughter by saying, "I felt so sad when Bambi
lost his mother."

■ Sonia hugged her son and said, "I'm so sorry
that your canary died this morning. Are you sad?
How would you like to say good-bye?"

■ Before he read Shawna a bedtime story, Ron
said to his daughter, "I noticed you heard me
talking to the doctor on the phone today about
how very sick Grandma is. Let's talk about how
she's doing."

Realize that your young child sees things through
"child's eyes." Focus your full attention on her
concerns; really listen to what she has to say so you
will know how best to comfort and reassure her.

■ Four-year-old Carla's grandpa had died recently,
and she had attended the funeral. Her parents
had talked to her about his dying and going to
Heaven, and she had said she understood. But
two weeks later, she was not herself, either at
home or at school—she was withdrawn and sad.
Finally her parents figured out what was upsetting
Carla. It seems she had noticed that Grandpa had
been buried without a coat, and with no food. It
was winter, and Carla had become very worried
that he would get cold and hungry. Her mom's
simple, honest reassurance satisfied the little girl:
"You know, honey, after someone dies he never
gets cold or hungry again." With that worry out of
her mind, Carla was relieved and her bubbly
personality returned.

■ Jeremy, always a very happy child, had
suddenly become withdrawn and quiet, and no
one knew why. With some well-placed questions
and a bit of patience, it all became clear to Mom
and Dad. Jeremy had seen his very sick neighbor

*get thinner and thinner, until one day he had
died. So when Jeremy's dad went on a diet and
began to lose weight, Jeremy thought it was a
sign that his dad was going to die. Once Jeremy's
fears were addressed, he returned to his old
happy self.*

Acknowledge your child's feelings and offer
suggestions for how to deal with them.

■ *Charlie said to his daughter, Jenna, "I see
you're feeling sad because our dog, Riley, isn't
around to play with us anymore. We'll both miss
him a lot and feel sad about it for a long, long
time. Sometimes, when we see Zach next door
playing with his dog, we might even feel angry
because we can't do that with Riley anymore." He
paused, then added, "I have an idea. Want to look
at the video Granddad took of you and Riley
running around together? It will help us
remember how happy he made us." Jenna smiled
and said, "Let's watch it now!"*

■ *At Grandma's funeral, Bob said to his young
daughter, "The funeral is taking a long time. I see
you are feeling antsy and don't understand why
everyone else is crying. I wonder if you feel
confused? Here's a little toy to play with quietly.
It should be over soon, and then we'll talk more
about why everyone is so sad."*

Be truthful, but not brutally honest when
discussing the death of a loved one.

■ *When Pamela was a child, her cat was killed
by a car when it darted across the driveway as
her dad pulled out of the garage. At first, her
parents couldn't bear to tell her the truth. She
remembers her futile search for her "lost cat"
before they finally decided to admit the cat was*

dead. As painful as it would have been for them to explain, an honest statement that poor kitty had died in an accident would have been more helpful to Pam in working through her grief than pretending the cat had run away.

Take one question at a time and keep the answers brief, concrete, and simple.

■ *When a similar incident occurred in her own family, Pamela was very careful to honestly but gently tell her kids right away what had happened. When they asked, she answered, "I'm sorry to tell you this, but poor Mittens was run over by a car." When asked where it had happened, she replied calmly, "Close to home." When they asked, "Where is Mittens now?" she answered, "She was hurt very badly, and Daddy took her to the vet right away. I'm so sorry, but the vet just called and said she died."*

Try asking your child, "What do you think?" when she asks you a difficult question.

■ *When four-year-old Luke asked, "What does Grandma's soul look like?" his dad replied, "That's an interesting question. What do you think?" Luke thought for a moment and exclaimed, "I know! God must have made souls invisible because I've never seen one." His dad responded, "That makes a lot of sense."*

Welcome a child's input; it will often surprise you.

■ *When four-year-old Donny caught his mom sobbing over the recent loss of her father, his mom regained her composure and explained to her son, "Although I believe Grandpa is happy in heaven, I'm so sad sometimes because I miss him and can't see him." He paused, then suddenly ran*

out of the room. He quickly returned, looking as if
he'd just saved the day. "Yes you can, Mommy,
here's his picture!" he said, holding it out to her.

Realize that concerned parents sometimes look
too carefully for trouble and end up misreading
the situation. Child psychiatrist Dr. Stanley
Turecki called this the "microscope effect," as he
related the following example in a lecture:

■ *Just after five-year-old Eric left for school one*
morning, his mom noticed that his pet goldfish
had died. She was so worried about her son's
reaction that she took time off from her job and
went to the library to read up on how to handle
issues of loss. Later that day the parents went
together to pick up their son and carefully broke
the news to him. They suggested going through a
little ceremony to bury the goldfish in a pillbox in
the backyard. Eric still seemed troubled the next
day, and his parents were worried that he hadn't
dealt with the loss properly. They took Eric to Dr.
Turecki and asked him to discuss the issue with
Eric. The child said he really didn't understand
what the fuss was all about. He told Dr. Turecki
his parents had kept carrying on and on, and all
he wanted to do was flush the dead goldfish
down the toilet and get another one!

Draw upon religious or spiritual beliefs, to offer
reassurance and comfort.

■ *One family was dealing with their eldest child's*
terminal illness. They had talked a lot about
Timmy's soul going to heaven after he died, but
his five-year-old sister was confused about the
relationship between the body and the soul. So
Dad thought of a perfect analogy to explain his
point of view. He slid on a leather glove that fit
his hand snugly, and said, "The soul is a perfect

fit to the body like my hand is to this glove."
Then, slowly wiggling his fingers inside the glove,
he continued, "When we are alive, the soul is
inside the body and they work together." As he
gently and slowly pulled his hand from the glove,
he said, "When we die, the soul easily slips out of
the body and goes up to Heaven. The body isn't
needed anymore and remains on Earth." This
illustration seemed to comfort the whole family.

Realize that your actions and reactions in the face
of death serve as a model for your child to follow.
(See page 17 for the definition of modeling.)

Observe and discuss with your child the life cycles
of nature and plan "hands-on" activities that
reinforce their learning (planting seeds, raking
leaves in the fall, visiting baby animals at the zoo).

■ *When Uncle Noel passed away, Caroline and*
her son planted perennial forget-me-not seeds.
When the flowers bloomed the following spring,
they brought happy memories with them.

Talk about your pet's ages and stages of life
(birth, growing, aging, and death).

Express your own feelings openly, rather than
trying to stifle them for your child's sake.

■ *Late one night, when Caroline thought Sean*
was in bed, she suddenly noticed him standing in
the doorway, staring at her with concern as she
wept. "Sean," she explained, "Mommy's feeling
sad right now because I'm remembering that
Uncle Noel isn't with us anymore. I could use one
of your great big hugs."

Accept grieving as a process that takes time to
run its course.

take heart

♥ *You're not the only parent who feels guilty about having broken down in front of your child, even weeks or months after the death of a loved one.*

Appreciate the fact that sometimes your kids can comfort you!

■ *The whole family was at the cemetery for the burial of Gail's grandmother. As the casket was just about to be lowered, Gail's four-year-old son tugged at her sleeve and whispered, "Why is Nana in a treasure chest?" His wondrous perception of the coffin caught Gail off guard. She even smiled and later talked about how precious Grandma had been—truly a family treasure!*

Explore the impact death may have on your child, as indicated by sudden changes in her behavior.

■ *Barb was concerned by her daughter's sudden fear of her first preschool experience. After discussing it with her during quiet time, Barb realized it wasn't really school that was upsetting her. The little girl tearfully explained why she didn't want to go. She was terribly afraid that Mommy might die, as their elderly neighbor had recently, and she simply wanted to stay close to her.*

Understand how painful it may be when a child learns that everyone will die one day; try to put your child's fears into perspective without lying.

■ *When five-year-old Brett constantly worried about his father dying, Dad knew just what to do. Although he didn't deny that everyone will die some day, honest reassurance worked for him. Dad told Brett, "I just visited Doctor Johnson. She checked everything over very carefully. My heart, my lungs, my eyes, and everything else are all fine. I plan to be around for a long, long time."*

Find the strength to discuss dying with your child. Realize that kids can read your body language and can sense when something is wrong. Your well-meaning silence may actually make things scarier for your child than talking about it would. It might even cause him to blame himself for what has happened.

> ■ Helen decided she would protect four-year-old Amanda as long as she could from the tragic news that Aunt Belle had been killed in a car accident over the weekend. Although not a word was spoken, Amanda kept asking her mommy, "What is wrong with you? You aren't listening to me." Amanda was "reading" the cold silences and her mother's distance and unavailability as signs that something was wrong. She even asked her mommy, "Are you mad at me?" thinking she had caused this unspoken tension. Finally Helen realized it would be best to tell her child the truth.

the bottom line

Young children don't yet have the discomfort so many older people have with the subject of death. Listen carefully to their questions and answer them compassionately and honestly, gearing your responses to their level of understanding.

discipline

Q: When I passed by my son's room I saw him pulling every single puzzle off the shelf and dropping them on the floor, scattering pieces everywhere. I totally lost it! When I yelled at him to stop he just turned, stared at me, then folded his arms across his chest and pronounced, "You can't make me! This is MY room!" Boy, I really wanted to let him have it, but I'm trying not to resort to negative reactions, such as threatening, punishing, and criticizing. However, I definitely don't want to let him get away with this sort of thing, either! What do you suggest?

A: Believe it or not, there are many effective positive discipline strategies that work in frustrating situations such as this, but they are skills that take practice and self-control on your part. They don't just come to mind automatically. The good news is that not only do these strategies stop the undesirable behavior, but in the long run they help enable the child to feel remorse not revenge, so that eventually he will become more responsible for his actions. In the heat of the moment, resist taking the bait. Instead of focusing on how you will "make" your child comply, focus on sorting out and cleaning up the mess. Keep in mind your tone of voice and careful choice of words can make a big difference in gaining your child's cooperation. Start by acknowledging your child's feelings ("Yes, this is your room") while remaining firm ("but it's part of our family's house and everyone in our family has to follow the rules"). Get your child in touch with the problem ("Remember how upsetting it is when the puzzle piece you need is missing?") Restate the rule ("That's why the rule is: Only take out one puzzle at a time." Solve the problem at hand together. ("It looks like you could use some help sorting out the pieces and putting them away. I'll find bear puzzles pieces while you work on the doggy puzzle.") Later on, perhaps at bedtime or during a family meeting, you can remind your child that you do not want to be spoken to rudely.

sanity savers

State *only* what needs to be done, rather than adding the not-so-nice thoughts about the child himself that might pop into your head.

Dee discovered that her son listened better when she said, "Coats belong on hooks," rather than, "You are such a slob! How many times do I have to tell you coats belong on hooks?"

Try talking less, and using single-word requests. Yelling and nagging tend to be tuned out by the kids.

■ *When Doug had to remind his daughter that she needed to wear mittens before going out in the snow, he simply said "MITTENS!" to get her attention. No explanation was needed.*

Start requests with the words "As soon as you" . . . or "When you . . ." These words make it clear that compliance is expected. Avoid saying, "If you . . ."

■ *Pat noticed that when she said to her son, "If you clean up your toys, we'll go to the park," she was giving him the message that she had some doubt whether he would choose to comply. (Emphasize that you assume you child will cooperate, a subtle point that can make a big difference.)*

Eliminate the usual negative impact that accompanies the word "NO"; instead of saying "NO," try saying "YES" without changing your rules.

■ *Earl, a dad with a temper, found it much more effective to say to his son, "Yes, you may go get a cookie, as soon as we clean the mud off your shoes," instead of raising his blood pressure by responding "NO! No way! Where do you think you're going, mister . . . making muddy footprints all over the kichen?"*

Show appreciation for cooperation (the good behavior); this is an important positive in effective discipline. Paying attention to positive behavior (without going overboard) can actually contribute to the process of teaching right from wrong, thereby minimizing bad behavior.

Look at things from your child's perspective; perhaps you can substitute some of your commands with incentives to gain compliance next time.

■ Caroline considered going to and leaving the park from her children's perspective. "Often my boys were so engrossed in playing and having fun, that to them, there was no reason to stop, even if it meant going to get ice cream. I started letting them know ahead of time how long we would stay in the park and gave periodic warnings before it was time to leave. Sometimes they would find a special surprise waiting on the carseat, like a sticker. I remembered to compliment their behavior without going overboard, saying 'Thanks for getting into the car so quickly without a fuss.'"

Set clear rules for your child that help you define and enforce the limits without attacking his character.

■ Sue was constantly attacking her four-year-old son verbally for hitting his little brother. Finally realizing her actions were totally inappropriate and were getting no positive results, she learned a new way to get her point across. One day she embraced her older son from behind, using a "hug hold," as she clearly stated in his ear, "Hitting is not allowed." This stopped the undesirable behavior. Then she took the time to redirect both kids humorously, by saying, "Let's all grab our coats and march like me. One, two, three, four . . . hear our shoes tap on the floor!

*One, two, three, four . . . march with me right out
the door!" The cool, fresh air changed the mood;
and there was no more hitting. Sue had changed
the behavior without yelling or using hurtful
words . . . and that felt good.*

Remind your child of important rules by
restating them at just the right time, in order to
prevent a mistake from reoccurring.

■ *As they approached the curb, Gail said, "We're
just about to cross the street. Now what do we
do? . . . Hold Mommy's hand, look both ways, and
walk carefully across the street."*

Follow through with appropriate consequences
that are directly related to the child's behavior,
that make sense to both you and the child, and
that can truly help a child feel remorse, not
revenge, for his misbehavior (this is not always
possible, but it is optimal).

■ *Although three-year-old Ethan knew he was
supposed to use his plastic cup at the bottled
water dispenser, he grabbed a glass instead. Just
as he managed to fill it, the glass slipped out of
his hands and shattered all over the floor. Mom
came running from another room and this time
chose to try an approach that didn't involve
yelling or name-calling. She said in a calm voice,
"Honey, don't move . . . there's sharp glass all
around you. I need your help to clean this up."
This smart Mom gave an age-appropriate job to
her son: "Here's a paper bag for you to hold open
for Mommy. Stay still while I pick up the broken
pieces of glass and then we will carefully take the
bag to the garbage can outside." Later that
evening, they talked about the incident again and
Ethan, without prompting, said he was sorry he
had taken the glass (he felt remorse). Mom*

repeated the rule, "Plastic cups for kid's drinks."
She was proud of the way she handled the
situation, and in turn Ethan kept to the plastic
cup rule.

Keep in mind that with very young children (two to five years old), consequences are usually most effective when they come as soon as possible after the misbehavior.

■ *The Kramer family planned to have a quiet*
Sunday breakfast at a favorite restaurant,
However, once everyone was served, Jenny, four,
and Chris, three, began to scream and throw their
food. Dad told them, "If you keep misbehaving
you're both going to bed at 7:00 tonight." Their
antics continued and soon Mom said, "That's it!
Now bedtime is 6:30!"

(Note: Unfortunately, in this case the consequence
was a distant threat and unrelated to the
misbehavior and therefore totally ineffective with
three- and four-year-olds. The parents might have
chosen a more immediate intervention, like
changing their seating arrangement, one adult and
one child on each side of the table, kids diagonally
across from each other. Or, if necessary, the family
could have even packed up and left or split up into
two groups, on opposite sides of the restaurant,
thereby finishing their own breakfast without
disturbing the other people eating!)

Establish appropriate consequences that relate directly to the misbehavior instead of physical punishment.

Think twice before you take away your affection as part of a consequence. A young child can't always separate her behavior from her person and therefore may feel she is being rejected for who she is, not for what she did.

discipline

take heart

♥ **You're not the only parent who has found himself in the midst of an angry confrontation, and been tempted to resort to giving your child a spanking. However, working toward using more effective, respectful ways to communicate results in more cooperation from your children and less guilt, fear, or feelings of revenge.**

■ *Lil saw how hurt and upset her daughter was when she said, "You made me so mad today, there will be no good-night kiss and no snuggle time!" and she vowed never to say that again. Snuggle time was one of the most enjoyable parts of their daily routine, one that reinforced her unconditional love for her daughter.*

When you make a connection between a restriction and the activity it applies to, young children are often more accepting of the rules.

■ *Sheila said to her son, "You may go outside, but remember, your jacket stays on."*

Choose your battles carefully. It will drive both you and your family crazy if you try to fight them all. Ask yourself, "Will this really matter an hour from now, a day from now, a week from now, a year from now?"

■ *After weeks of morning-time battles over mismatched clothes, one formerly embarrassed mom made her daughter a button that said "Dressed by myself and proud of it!"*

Look at what is "behind" the bad behavior and try to address the underlying issues. (Maybe the misbehavior can be avoided next time by an earlier bedtime, clearer directions, more one-on-one attention, or even a change in the seating arrangement.)

■ *Caroline told her suddenly defiant three-year-old, "I can see that you are really angry about having to stop playing to eat lunch. That's hard to do when you're having such a good time. After lunch I'd like to see the new baseball cards Daddy gave you last night." A very angry little face suddenly relaxed as they went downstairs to the kitchen together, talking "baseball" all the way.*

Buy some time to cool off when you're really angry and can't think straight. Honestly state your feelings by saying, "I need to think about that for a while" or "I really must leave the room to rest my brain!"

Remember, spanking carries the risk of injury to your child.

Try to explain "what's right" with the behavior. Kids are likely to pay more attention to words that don't include hysterical criticism.

■ *When Anne's four-year-old son ran quickly toward the street, it was tempting for her to scream, "What's the matter with you? Don't you know how dangerous it is to run across the street? A car could kill you! Are you trying to give me a heart attack?" Instead, she quickly grabbed her son's sleeve and calmly but firmly said, "Always hold Mommy's hand when we cross the street."*

take heart

♥ *You're not the only parent who tries to use positive discipline strategies only to find that what comes out of your mouth is not what you had practiced you would say. Not to worry! As Nancy Samalin, author of* Love and Anger, *says, "Remember, one great thing is that with kids, you'll always get another chance—sooner than you think."*

Give your child problem-solving opportunities.
When you invite the child's input, you are helping
him take responsibility for his actions. At a family
meeting, a child often has the best suggestions for
a consequence that really hits the spot, especially
for a sibling!

Be proactive by planning ahead for success rather
than reacting to failure.

> ■ *Rosie had to take her sons, three-year-old*
> *triplets, to her doctor's appointment. She knew*
> *the wait was sometimes up to an hour, so she*
> *took the time the night before to pack what she*
> *thought she needed. The next day at the office*
> *she was well armed to keep"the troops" happy*
> *(snacks, books, crayons, paper, and action figures*
> *for the kids). She was pleased when not even one*
> *sibling war occurred!*

Decide which issues are "never negotiable,"
which are "sometimes negotiable," and which are
"always negotiable." Your child will feel more
secure and confident as he learns that his world is
predictable, with consistent boundaries.

Stop the undesirable behavior with a time-out or
distraction. (See the section on time-out on page
299.)

Keep in mind that disciplining a child is a
process; realize that some of the most meaningful
learning takes place outside of "the heat of the
moment," over time. When both you and your child
are upset, it's harder to listen to each other.

Take advantage of quiet times like bedtime or
family meetings to go over with your child any
recent misbehavior, review the rules, and consider
options for next time, as well as possible
consequences that might occur.

Think about what it takes to raise a well-disciplined child with a healthy sense of "inner control." Try to recall the way you were disciplined and share your memories, positive and negative, with your spouse. You may both be able to "get a better handle" on the issues of discipline and punishment, and decide exactly how you will define those terms relating to your own family.

> ■ *Art and Denise remembered that as children they were threatened with physical punishment for misbehavior. They shared similar memories of feeling rebellious, inadequate, confused, and humiliated, and a strong desire to get even with their parents. They also discovered that they often complied with their parents' rules out of fear or guilt. Art recalled hearing, "Wait till your father gets home! You know what he always says . . . 'Spare the rod, spoil the child!' Oh boy! Are you going to get it!" Denise remembered being intimidated and shamed. "How dare you do that! God is going to punish you! You'd better shape up, young lady, or you'll never amount to anything!" They agreed that they didn't want to pass on these same negative messages to their children and talked about different ways to approach the same problems.*

Realize that punishment often invites children to defy you.

> ■ *Author Nancy Samalin says in her book* Love and Anger, *"Children who are frequently punished often become more devious, not more honest or responsible."*

Keep in mind that punishment can invite feelings of revenge and "getting even" on the part of your child. Punishment can also lead to a power struggle when your child refuses to comply. After repeated threats are ineffective, you may find yourself desperately searching for even stricter punishments each time your child repeats an undesirable behavior or escalates the battle. This leads to a lose-lose situation.

Heavy-duty punishment may actually prevent your child from feeling remorse for what he did wrong. A child who is beaten or otherwise punished may even feel that he has "paid his dues," because you "got even" with him.

> ■ *Selma Fraiberg, author of* The Magic Years, *has noted how some children welcome punishment to cancel the crime, thereby avoiding any feelings of guilt so they can misbehave again. She calls this behavior the "Bookkeeping Approach to Misconduct."*

the bottom line

View discipline as "giving" your child something positive rather than as depriving or taking something away from her through punishment; by using positive discipline techniques you are gradually giving your child the gift of inner control.

doctor and dentist visits

Q: My daughter hates going to the doctor. She is due for some routine shots and we're both dreading the appointment. What can I do to make our visit less stressful?

A: Many children (as well as many adults) develop anxieties about seeing a doctor. These fears are usually based either on past negative experiences or on an overly active imagination. Your child can't avoid these checkups, so why not help her develop a positive attitude about visiting the doctor. Discuss with her what to expect during the visit and plan something fun to look forward to for after the appointment.

sanity savers

Decide how much advance notice you should give your child lest you inadvertently cause her to worry for days ahead of time. Most pediatricians recommend telling a two- or three-year-old the day of the visit and a four- or five-year-old the day before. But it depends upon your child's temperament and personality too. Learn what works best for your child.

■ *Caroline thinks she overdid it trying to reassure Nolan about a follow-up visit to the dentist. "I wanted to let him know that we would be going back, so I told him a couple of days ahead of time. The morning of the appointment I reminded him where we would be going that day. Then the trouble started. He refused to get dressed and I literally had to drag him out to the car while he kicked and screamed. As soon as we arrived at the dentist, he got me in a choke hold and wouldn't let go. I didn't make the same mistake again. Next visit, I simply got him dressed that morning and told him we were going out. Arriving at the dentist's office, I calmly told him that we would have to stop in this morning but that it would be his last visit for a long time. Heaving a deep sigh, he resolutely took my hand and we walked in together."*

Realize that your child will often look to you for cues about a potentially frightening situation, such as a visit to the doctor.

Be mindful of the words you choose in explaining the visit. Well-intentioned parents who say "It won't hurt a bit" can actually add another dimension of stress for the child. The child probably wasn't even thinking about pain until Mom or Dad mentioned the possibility of it.

Try role-playing with your child, taking turns playing the roles of doctor and patient. Taking her puppets and dolls to visit "Doctor Teddy Bear" can also be a non-threatening way of imparting key information and discussing the feelings that go along with a visit to the doctor. (See box on page 25 for more on role-playing.)

Share funny stories about doctor visits and other memories of your own childhood experiences with your child.

Decide what is appropriate information for your child's age and encourage questions. For instance, if your child is scheduled for a shot, consider explaining to her that although shots hurt a bit, they keep us from getting very sick. Keep your explanations honest but simple; too much information may defeat your purpose and confuse or upset your child.

See if you can come up with a plan as to how you and your child will handle pain or discomfort.

> ■ *Virginia remembers how five-year-old Jerry was very impressed with Felice, one of the nurses at their pediatrician's office. Felice had taught Jerry a technique that helped him get through his shots. She asked Virginia to stand in front of Jerry and hold both his hands. Then, right before she gave him his shot, Jerry was to take a deep breath, blow into Virginia's face, and squeeze her hands tightly. While he was concentrating on following those steps, Felice quickly and efficiently administered the shot. Exhaling deeply also helped Jerry to relax while the shot was being given.*

Remind your child that everyone occasionally has to do something that they would really rather not do. From time to time give your child some examples of things you have to do that you really don't enjoy doing, such as washing dishes. (If they find this hard to believe, you're doing a good job of positive modeling!)

Expect some visits to be difficult, especially if your child has unpleasant memories of other visits.

Ask your doctor or dentist if administering a child's pain reliever prior to the visit might help your child better deal with painful procedures.

Many pain relievers take a while to "kick in." Administering one ahead of time, with your doctor's permission, rather than right after the visit, might be helpful.

Consider taking a very anxious child to the doctor's office once or twice ahead of time (without scheduling an appointment), just to play in the waiting room and look around.

Teach your child some simple relaxation techniques she can use in the doctor's office.

> ■ *While Carrie and her three-year-old daughter were waiting for the doctor, they enjoyed practicing the deep-breathing exercises Mom had learned from a Lamaze video.*

Acknowledge your child's feelings so she knows you understand.

> ■ *Alan, a sensitive dad, said, "I can see you're worried about going to the doctor. I'll be with you the whole time."*

Realize that your child's anxiety may be related not to fear of physical pain but rather to the doctor's getting too close physically and invading her "personal space." You can use this as an opportunity to reinforce your child's healthy instinct for privacy, while also explaining that this is one situation when it's okay to allow someone to touch her, and that you'll be right there with her.

Schedule something pleasant to look forward to after the doctor's visit.

> ■ *When Betty told her son he had a dentist's appointment, before he could protest, she asked if afterwards he would like to go to the fast-food restaurant that had the video racing-car game. He*

enthusiastically agreed, so Betty said, "Okay. Here, honey, let's put some quarters for the game in your pocket now. While you're at the dentist, you'll be able to feel them in your pocket and think about how fast you're going to drive that car!"

Take along some books, toys, or even a snack in case you have a long wait at the doctor's or dentist's office. These can distract your child from his anxiety and help him keep busy and calm.

Take your child's toy doctor kit and doll to the appointment. Many children are more comfortable when the doctor "examines" the doll first, while the child watches.

Approach the doctor in a relaxed manner and make some small talk to let your child see that the doctor is, indeed, a friendly person and that *you* are comfortable with him or her.

Ask your doctor to spend a few minutes reassuring your child about the purpose of the examination. Explanations like "It's my job to make sure you are well all over" may help.

Try to step aside and let your child answer the doctor's questions for himself. Communication between the doctor and your child may go very well without your intervention. Who knows? Your child may even come to think of the doctor as his friend!

If your child is anxious, ask the doctor if she can sit on your lap during the examination.

take heart

♥ *You are not the only parent who has trouble accepting the thought that your precious little 36-month-old "baby" is actually a bright three-year-old who is perfectly able to converse with the doctor herself.*

During an examination, talk to your child in a reassuring manner; or try stroking, hugging, or singing to him.

Address your child's concerns sensitively but honestly.

> ■ *When the doctor told Donna's son he was going to get a shot, she remembered a line she had read in a children's book and reassured him, "Yes, shots do hurt, but only for a moment. Like a quick pinch, and then it's over."*

Try not to create a power struggle by making angry retorts to an uncooperative child. Making a big deal out of "bad" behavior at the doctor's office is not only unhelpful, it's likely to make your child an even more reluctant patient next time.

As a last resort, restrain an uncooperative child in a "hug hold" (see page 16).

If your child becomes really upset, consider giving him a breather so he can calm down and compose himself, then try again. It might even be necessary to leave the doctor's office and reschedule the visit.

> ■ *After an unsuccessful struggle to get four-year-old Sammy to take his shot, Roberta, a thoughtful mom, came up with a plan. She calmly but firmly offered him a choice: "We can do this now and get it over with, or we can keep coming back here every day until you keep still for your shot. I know you don't like shots, but you have to have one now to protect you from getting sick." Seeing the determined look on Mom's face, Sammy reluctantly decided to try again.*

Sometimes it's best to let the medical professional decide whether it's really easier for both of you if you *don't* stay with your child for a very difficult procedure.

■ *During a dentist's visit, Nolan was being uncooperative and simply wouldn't let go of Caroline's neck. Caroline suggested that she sit in the chair with Nolan and hold him on her lap. The dentist asked her if she were pregnant, as she was about to take some X rays. Discovering that she was, she asked Caroline to leave the room and gently explained to Nolan that the X rays wouldn't be good for the baby in Mommy's tummy. Once Caroline left the room, Nolan was much more cooperative.*

take heart

♥ *You're not the only parent who dreads watching your child undergo a procedure. It's often so much harder on you to plan, anticipate, and finally witness it than it is to undergo the procedure yourself!*

Try to let go of your guilt; you simply can't always make every situation pleasant for your child.

Praise your child for being brave and cooperating so well.

the bottom line

L earning to deal with challenging or scary situations is a sometimes difficult but important part of growing up. Be supportive and understanding, and congratulate your child for being a "real trouper" at the doctor's or dentist's office.

fears at night

Q: My child often wakes up scared in the middle of the night. He tells us about the monster that lives in the closet and the one that sometimes hides under the bed. How can I convince him he's safe?

A: Such fears are common and normal for preschoolers and even older kids. Discuss these fears with your little one, letting him know that you understand what he's going through. Most children between the ages of two and five are still struggling to differentiate the imaginary from the real, so try not to over-react to the situation or make fun of your child. Instead, help him deal with the fear in a way that makes sense to him.

immediate response

→ Turn on the lights.

→ Comfort your child by saying, repeatedly if necessary, "I'm here now . . . Daddy's here now."

→ Look your child in the eye and listen to him with your full attention.

→ Respond to her fears in a calm, soothing tone.

→ Offer your child her favorite stuffed animal, doll, or action figure to keep her company when you leave her room again.

sanity savers

Acknowledge your child's fear: The *feeling* of being scared is real to him, no matter how silly or absurd it seems to you. Saying "I can see you are really scared" assures your child that you understand.

Although not every child is comfortable talking about a scary dream, some welcome it. You can, during the day, offer ideas that may help the child conquer his "scaries." You know your child best.

> ■ *Julia's son sometimes came into her bedroom in the middle of the night saying he'd had a bad dream. After trying in vain to coax him to talk about what had happened, Julia realized what would work for Ned. Repeating his bedtime routine, ending with a loving cuddle and kiss as she tucked Ned back into his bed, usually comforted him. When Julia asked if he was feeling better now his dream was over, he actually told her, "Let's just forget about it, but can you tell me another bedtime story?"*

If a child does want to talk about it, you can suggest the child try some magic powers in his dream, like flying or making things disappear or shrink, to help him out of a scary situation (like being chased by a monster). Kids have great imaginations, so give your child some direction in using it to his advantage right before he goes to sleep. Studies show this technique is very effective.

After offering your child comforting words, try helping him relax through reassuring touch.

■ *Mark knew his son Chase felt better after a bout of middle-of-the-night fears when he hugged him, snuggled, and rubbed his back.*

Find concrete solutions to give the child a sense of control.

■ *Rita found that her son felt much better if he could keep Daddy's flashlight in his bed with him.*

■ *Laurie was afraid of creatures under her bed. Her mom often took a broom and reassured her by carefully sweeping the "scaries" away from every corner before bedtime.*

■ *Gail often switched pillows with her son so he could have something of hers and smell her scent as he went to sleep.*

■ *Derek was afraid of the dark, so his parents taped a string of light blue Christmas lights to the ceiling in his room. He was comforted by the twinkling, "friendly" glow of his "sleepy lights" at bedtime.*

take heart

♥ *You're not the only parent whose first instinct, in the middle of the night, is to make your child walk into the closet to prove no monsters are there. Too late, you realize that what seemed rational to you only intensified his fears.*

Meet the child at her level of understanding, rather than trying to make her rise to your level.

■ *Cliff said to his daughter, "Did you say the monster's afraid of noise? Let's make a big noise to scare it away!"*

■ *Denise asked her son to help make a special label for a bottle of "magic water" they used to spray away the "scaries."*

If you feel the need to help your child distinguish between what is real and what is not, try offering comfort without validating the presence of the "scaries."

■ *Ellen said, "I've checked the corner and I do not see any monsters, only shadows. But if you feel scared, you can sleep with the lights on."*

Encourage the child to choose a "lovey" that brings her comfort in bed. One special item, such as a blanket or stuffed animal, works better than a crib full of toys. Even a flashlight or a photo of a parent can comfort older kids.

■ *By the time Colleen had her third child, she was older and wiser. She encouraged her son's attachment to a simple piece of soft cloth (and kept extra pieces for replacement handy). She found it was also much less embarrassing to see her child drag this "lovey" around in public than the satin negligee her friend's son had become attached to!*

Go shopping together for a special "lovey," if you don't already have one.

Use role-playing, books, and family discussions to help you address issues of nighttime fears during a calmer time of day and to help involve the kids in finding a solution. (See box on page 25 for more on role-playing and the reading list on page 337 for book suggestions.)

■ *Caroline's son got a big kick out of hearing the stories of her childhood "monsters under the bed," or so she thought! She later learned he had thought her story was silly only because he knew that monsters really hung out in the closet, not under the bed!*

Make occasional exceptions to the usual rules so everyone can get some sleep. In situations where the child is unable to be comforted or insists on coming into your bed, a sleeping bag on the floor of your room may be a good compromise.

Children can often surprise you by solving a problem using what they have experienced or learned about the beliefs and rituals of other cultures.

■ After they had admired a Native American dream catcher at a powwow, Mona's mom made a tiny replica and hung it on her daughter's headboard to "filter out" unpleasant dreams.

■ On a tour of a traditional Japanese garden, Nick could see the wheels turning in his son's head when the curator explained that evil spirits travel only in a straight line. "Daddy, can I run across the zigzag bridge to get rid of the monster that chases me at night?" he asked, adding, "He won't be able to follow me!"

If the problems are recurring or especially frightening, consult your pediatrician.

■ Caroline's son experienced a medical phenomenon known as "night terrors" that some doctors believe is related to changes in brain wave patterns. During an episode of night terrors, her son screamed and trembled uncontrollably, *yet did not fully awaken and did not seem to recognize her. Although he was not able to be comforted and did best when left in his bed, it was terrifying and painful for Caroline and her husband to watch helplessly. Caroline was reassured to learn that children don't remember these episodes and they eventually outgrow them.*

the bottom line

An honest explanation that there are no "scaries" often doesn't work because the child is *really* frightened; acknowledging the child's feelings, opening the lines of communication, and offering comfort are all very helpful.

fighting in front of your kids

Q: I felt so ashamed after a recent tiff my husband and I had in front of our sons. We really got carried away: yelling, swearing, and saying mean things to each other. Should I be concerned about the negative effect this may have on my kids?

A: A relationship between a couple that never involves disagreement is a relationship in which no one is communicating. It's simply human nature to experience bad moods, conflicting viewpoints, and misplaced anger within the family fabric. And it's virtually impossible to live your life as if your kids were scrutinizing your every move. The important thing after fighting in front of the kids is to apologize to each other and make up in front of the kids, too, thereby modeling appropriate conflict resolution skills. (Sometimes this is easier said than done!) It's not the occasional spat but the overall pattern of behavior in the marriage that most influences your kids. If your fights are an everyday occurrence, consider seeking counseling.

sanity savers

Realize the importance of maintaining a polite rapport with your spouse (or ex-spouse) and find ways to do so. This helps minimize arguments in front of your children.

Be conscious of what you say about your ex-spouse in front of the kids. It is helpful to your children's self-esteem to have a loving image of both of their parents.

Ground Rules for "Fighting Fair"

Outside "the heat of the moment" is the time to establish some rules to try and stick to next time a battle is brewing. It may not be easy to keep them in mind, but it is important—and worth it—to try.

→ Define what language you and your spouse consider inappropriate and agree to avoid it.

→ Take turns speaking and listening.

→ Ask to table the discussion temporarily if either of you begins to lose control in front of your child.

→ Refrain from dragging up the past.

→ Come up with a way, such as a nonverbal signal, to remind each other to stick to these ground rules.

State the problem, using neutral language, without attacking your spouse's character. General criticisms and put-downs are not helpful.

Tell your spouse what you would like to see done. Be specific. Explain your feelings, beginning your sentences with "I want" or "I feel" rather than using words that put your spouse on the defensive, such as "Why do you . . . ," "You always . . . ," or "You never . . ."

Stick to the current issue. Ask for your spouse's suggestions for solving the problem.

Try to temper your language in front of the kids. Resist the urge to resort to the type of name-calling and insults you wouldn't want your child to mimic. This takes practice—and on a bad day just might be impossible! But don't stop trying.

take heart

♥ *You're not the only parents who occasionally blurt out some really angry thoughts in front of the kids.*

■ *Carol had been working with three-year-old Steven on expressing his anger and strong emotions without hurting anyone or anything. She often plunked him into a kitchen chair and said, "Time-out until you calm down." Apparently, this technique worked better than she had ever imagined! In the middle of a tiff between Carol and her husband, Steven stepped between them and said, "Hey! No name-calling! Mommy, you better go sit in the time-out chair right now!" Carol was embarrassed to admit that he was right.*

Demonstrate your self-respect by being calm but assertive during a confrontation.

■ *When Jay's wife got carried away, he turned to her and calmly said, "I won't be spoken to disrespectfully. I won't listen to people who swear at me."*

Resist blaming your spouse and others; instead, focus on solving the problem. Instead of giving your child the impression that problems are always someone's "fault," say, "I hear you, but I don't agree. How can we work this out?" This approach helps kids understand the value of negotiation; at the same time, they gain a sense of control over problems that need to be solved. In this way, children won't feel that they are at the mercy of whatever happens to them.

Resist making empty threats that you'll never carry through, such as "If you do that one more time, I'll never speak to you again!" (not easy in the heat of the moment!). Be aware that what you say may be taken quite literally when overheard by "little ears."

When you're really angry with your spouse, take a much-needed cooling-off period. But try to remember to tell your child that you will be coming back soon. (See "Anger," page 19, for other useful suggestions when things heat up.)

If you're at your wits' end, consider writing notes to each other rather than engaging in verbal battles. This way you can "hear" each other's perspective without interruption. (And without involving the children.)

Remember to tell your children when a conflict they have witnessed has been worked out. Unresolved arguments can be the most traumatic for children.

Schedule a get-together with your spouse out of the house, if possible, to address certain issues in private.

Think twice before you deny that something is wrong when your child asks. Children will often sense tension in the atmosphere even when they are told that "nothing is wrong." Some well-meaning parents try to hide all conflict from their kids so as not to upset them. However, this can deny kids the opportunity to observe how relationships evolve and to learn that everyone must work at resolving problems. For many children, basic security can come from knowing that, even though they don't always agree, everything will work out between their parents.

Keep your explanations simple. Children may blame themselves for your anger if the true cause is not explained.

> ■ Janice said to four-year-old Allie, "I wonder if you heard Daddy and me arguing this morning? We were having a disagreement about whose turn it was to go to the dry cleaner's. At first we both said we were too busy, but then we worked it out."

> ■ Paul, a divorced father, found it helpful to tell his children from time to time, "Although Daddy and Mommy are no longer living together, it's not because of anything you did. We both love you very much and will always be there for you. Hopefully, now there will be a lot less fighting around you."

Tell your children that all feelings are okay (but add that that doesn't mean all behaviors are okay). Then show them you mean it by encouraging them to express their own feelings. Let your kids hear you say that you've had a tough day. Let them see you comfort your spouse when he's had a rough day. Kids can learn that home is a safe place, and that bad feelings can be worked out.

Minimize fighting by realizing it's not necessary for your spouse to do everything exactly the way you do, although it is good to be united on major issues. From an early age, it is good for kids to learn how to adjust to the varying styles of different people.

> ■ *Bonnie and Mike agreed on an eight o'clock bedtime for their two young children. However, they allowed for personal differences in the bedtime routine. Bonnie enjoyed sitting on the bed and snuggling with the kids as she read them a bedtime story. Mike, on the other hand, had a talent for storytelling but a bad back. He preferred to sit in a straight-back chair as he wove his own original yarns for the kids. Interestingly, the children protested loudly when Mike tried to read them a book or when Bonnie attempted to tell them a story.*

Be prepared for your kids to "play one parent against the other" in order to get their way.

> ■ *When Joan told two-year-old Mark, "No candy before supper," Mark's eyes twinkled as he replied, "Well, Daddy lets me eat anything I want." Mom's first instinct was to criticize her spouse, but she bit her tongue as her husband walked into the room laughing. "Nice try, Markie," said Dad, "but we both know that's not true. I know you wish we'd let you eat candy all day long."*

Make time for dates with your spouse. You deserve more attention from each other than a few harried moments at the beginning and end of each day. The two of you will benefit from time alone to enjoy each other's company and undivided attention, and your children will see that marital relationships can be close and rewarding.

Find calm moments for you and your spouse to discuss your individual coping styles. Is your spouse's style quiet and reserved, while you've been brought up to "let it all hang out" in the heat of the moment and make up later? Differences in coping styles can lead to continual misunderstandings and hurt feelings that your kids will pick up on.

■ *Sally just hated the way her husband paced around every time she got the kids ready for a trip. He usually tried to rush everyone out the door before Sally had made sure everything was ready. One day, Sally asked her husband what it had been like in his home, growing up. He sheepishly admitted that his father had usually been the first one out the door every family trip. His father had sat out in the car, beeping the horn furiously while his mother ran around (late, as usual!) desperately trying to get everyone out the door without any help. Sally's husband promised to try to be a little more helpful in future.*

Realize that you are not doomed to repeat the past. You can learn to control the way you behave in front of your own kids and can change the patterns you learned when you were younger.

■ *As a child, Mia traveled through Europe every summer with her sisters and her parents, wedged into a tiny car with their luggage on the roof. She vividly remembers the uncomfortable feeling in her stomach as her parents' tensions escalated over reading the map. Mia's mother claimed she just couldn't follow a map, while her father drove around red in the face, swearing loudly about the foreign street signs. As an adult, Mia continued the legacy, but after a few fights with her own husband when they got lost on the road, she vowed that she would spare her kids these terrible scenes. Now, before her family sets off on a trip, Mia studies the map ahead of time and discusses with her husband exactly which route they'll take.*

the bottom line

Although an occasional fight in front of the children is bound to happen, it is an opportunity for them to see that even when anger and hurt are openly expressed, families can resolve problems and restore loving feelings.

first days of preschool

Q: I'm afraid my child will cling to me on the first day of preschool while everyone else skips off without even saying good-bye. What can I do to help her adjust?

A: It's normal for the first days of school to be an anxious period of adjustment for many parents and children. Kids are often working through intense feelings of anger, discomfort, shyness, and even fear. Parents, too, may struggle with their own feelings of separation anxiety, embarrassment, anger, guilt, and disappointment. When things don't go as smoothly as you hoped, try giving it some time.

sanity savers

Visit the preschool with your child before school begins. Point out some of the things that will interest or excite him. Check out the toys, crafts, books, dress-up box, and play equipment.

■ *"Oh, look, Josh," said Gail. "This will be your classroom. Want to have a look around? Let's go find the washroom and where you can get a drink*

of water. And wait until you see the slide they've
got on the playground!"

Reassure your child that you can be called if
needed and show her the location of the school
phone.

Encourage communication with the teacher
before school begins.

■ Gail sent the teacher a little note that she and
Rachel had written together. When the teacher
responded, Rachel proudly hung the note on the
refrigerator.

■ At one school, three moms divided up the class
of 21 preschool children into three groups. Then
each mom hosted a get-acquainted lemonade
party at her home and invited the teacher to
attend. (Some preschools offer their own get-
acquainted arrangements.)

■ Sean and Caroline called Sean's teacher on
the telephone to say hello a few days before
school started.

Try to encourage at least one friendship before
school starts. Ask the school to tell you if there are
any children from the class who live nearby.

Let your child get acquainted with the various
places (the office, the supermarket, the gym) you
might be while he is at school. He may feel more
secure knowing what you are doing while he's
gone.

Acknowledge and respect your child's "first-day
feelings" while remaining firm about having to
leave. Then give him something special to look
forward to when school is over for the day.

take heart

♥ You're not the only parent who has more "tummy butterflies" on the first day of school than your child does.

Gail said, "Rachel, I can see you are feeling sad that Mommy has to say good-bye. I'll miss you, too. I'd love a big hug before I go. As soon as school is over, we'll go out to lunch together."

Try not to show your own mixed feelings, if you have them. Act confident, strong, and matter-of-fact, and save the discussion with other parents of your own separation anxiety for times when your child is out of earshot.

If possible, leave younger siblings with a sitter for the first day or so. Your older child will appreciate your total attention on his "special day." For some children, just the sight of Mommy and baby brother walking off together makes separation more difficult.

Ask the teacher if you can stay in the classroom until you and your child both feel comfortable and ready to separate.

With the teacher's approval, allow your child to bring a small reminder of home, such as a picture locket, a "lucky penny," or a special note from you to put in his pocket.

Establish a morning routine and encourage your child to help with dressing and organizing himself. (See "Morning 'Crazies,'" page 208, for more helpful hints on how to get out of the house without losing your mind.)

Realize the importance of sitting down with your child and eating a healthy breakfast together.

(Easier said than done!) Mealtime can be an excellent opportunity for communication.

Choose a reasonable bedtime and try to stick to it (not always easy when older kids stay up later or when *your* favorite TV show is about to begin).

Use "quiet times" to talk about the school activities your child enjoys. Kids are often more receptive to talking and listening under the cover of darkness or during a bath.

■ *As soon as he walked in the door after school, Felicia anxiously pounced on her son, seeking reassurance that he'd had a great time. "Tell me what you did in school today!" she urged. His muffled reply was always the same: "Nothin'!" Felicia began to realize that he hated being bombarded with questions, so she learned to bite her tongue and concentrate on just spending pleasant time together. As they played, information seemed to roll right out, unsolicited.*

■ *Caroline's middle son, who had picked up a handy phrase from his older brother, began answering all her questions with "You don't need to know," followed by a mischievous grin. However, at bedtime, he loved to tell her all about his day.*

Share your calendar with your child, or help her keep one of her own, so she knows what to expect each day. Predictability and routine help your child feel more secure and in control.

Discuss the pickup arrangements with your child. Let her know when she'll be picked up (after playtime, after snack time, etc.) and who will pick her up (you, the sitter, another mom). Consistency and routine are usually comforting to a preschooler.

Talk to your sitter or car pool mom about the school's rules and procedures for dropping off and picking up children.

Understand that neither you nor your child is a failure if you don't do well with carpooling. Do whatever works for you . . . but give it a chance.

Go to class with your apprehensive child the first time and show her where she will sit, where the coatroom is, the bathroom, and so on.

Ask the teacher to give you a progress report at the end of the week about how your child is dealing with your leaving.

Share your stories about your own first days of school with your children. Remembering and relating your stories can let your children know you really do understand their anxiety, while offering reassurance that everything will be okay.

■ *Gail told her kids stories about how she had felt on her first days at school and her fear of being left there. She said, "When my mom took me to school, she told me every day that she would be back and she did always come back; but just like you, I was still worried about it for a couple of weeks."*

Listen to and observe what your kids can tell you through their play. Role-play going to school, saying good-bye, and coming back home with them. It can be helpful to switch roles and let the kids play teacher and parent sometimes. Dolls, puppets, and drawing materials can also help kids convey their feelings and concerns. (See box on page 25 for more on role-playing.)

■ *Caroline found that an inexpensive card game showing pictures of school activities, such as story time and playground time, helped her kids know what to expect in school. She used a Creative Child Games' rummy card pack. Call Playmore, Inc., at (212) 251-0600 for purchasing information.*

the bottom line

Each child develops at his own pace in his own way; for every parent embarrassed by his clinging child, there is another mother worried that a quick departure means her child hasn't bonded closely enough!

friends

Q: My two older children had lots of friends even at a young age, but I'm worried about my four-year-old. He doesn't want to get "too close" to anyone outside the family. I really want him to be popular, part of the "in group." What can I do to help him feel more comfortable with his peers?

A: Most parents want their children to be socially well adjusted and popular. Keep in mind that all children go through different stages of development. For some that might include a clingy or withdrawn period. Others simply have a shy personality. Every child is different, even within the same family. The best thing parents can do is to help their child first feel comfortable with who he is. Then expose him to a variety of opportunities to make friends. Give your child time to let friendships grow, keeping in mind his socialization preferences (some children are more comfortable inviting kids over to their house than they are going out). Then continue with what works best. While you can encourage friendships generally by providing opportunities for socialization, when it comes to your child's choosing his own best friends, seek and respect *his* opinion about which is the "in-group" for *him*.

sanity savers

Schedule routine get-togethers—trips to the park, play dates, preschool, moms and tots classes, toddler gym, and visits to the neighbors—to create opportunities for socialization, particularly good for a shy child.

Prepare your child ahead of time for what is going to happen. Predictability leads to cooperation and security.

> ■ *Gail reviewed with her shy three-year-old the routine of the moms and tots class they had recently joined. "Remember, first the kids play at the water table, then we'll have a snack. Next we'll sit in a circle and sing songs, including your favorite, 'The Wheels on the Bus.'" Josh seemed more eager to go to class when he felt prepared.*

Notice whether your child is more comfortable in a group setting or with one-on-one play. Continue with what seems the best match. ("Separation Anxiety," page 247, also discusses how to ease your child into play dates.)

Allow your child to sit back and watch the other kids play if that's what he prefers. Realize that he benefits socially, and is learning, by simply watching.

Teach your child some useful phrases for entering into play with another child. ("Can I help you do that?" or "I want to do that too! Can you show me where I can go?")

Role-play social situations with your child to help her practice relating to other kids. (See the box on page 25 for more on role-playing.)

Remind your child of past social successes.

> ■ *Robin put her arm around her son, James, and said with a smile, "Guess what? Amy's dad just called and said Amy would like you to come over to play until dinnertime. Remember what a good time you had doing puzzles when you went there last week?"*

Helping Kids Learn to Share

→ Let the kids know you understand that it is not easy to share by verbally acknowledging it . . . many, many, many times. Remember to compliment even the smallest attempt to share.

→ Consider getting together (at least for the first play date) in a neutral place, such as a playground or park. It's often too hard, at first, for some toddlers to share their house, their playroom, and their toys with a new friend.

→ When your child is going to play at a friend's house, send him with one of his own toys from home that he would like to share with his friend. (And let the other mom know you are doing this.)

→ Before a play date, let your child select some toys he is willing to share with playmates and help him put away his most precious toys, so he doesn't have to share everything.

→ Supervise as needed to maintain the peace.

→ Try offering choices. ("Which toy would you like Trent to use first . . . the airplane or the dump truck?")

→ Compliance often depends on your choice of words. Try asking your child to "show" or "teach

Choose your words carefully, and resist labeling your child as shy. Such a label may become part of his self-image or provide him with an excuse to avoid mingling with other kids.

> ■ *Jane used a carefully worded response whenever someone new asked if her daughter Erica was shy. Jane said, "She's just like me. Erica needs a little time to warm up to people."*

Have realistic expectations about sharing that coincide with your child's age.

how to use" his toy, instead of telling him to "share" or "give" it to his friend.

→ Reassure your child that his friend will not take the toy home.

→ Encourage four- and five-year-olds to come up with their own ways to take turns. Talk about the various options: flipping a coin, drawing straws, or playing "rock, paper, scissors" to see who goes first often works well.

→ Set time limits. Say, "First Kate will have the doll, and when the buzzer rings, Beth will have her turn."

→ Help choose toys and games that encourage cooperation. A one-of-a-kind stuffed animal or a small toy that only one child can use at a time invites conflict. Legos, blocks, markers, dress-up costumes, cardboard cartons, and pillows encourage children to play together.

→ Encourage activities that involve taking turns, like going down a big slide or running through a sprinkler.

→ Supervise projects that involve finger paints or Play-Doh to minimize conflicts. The kids can be encouraged to talk about what they are making.

How Children of Different Ages Tend to Socialize

→ **Two-year-olds** can spend up to half their time just watching one another. They often play side by side ("parallel play") rather than directly interacting with one another. Expect conflicts when two- to three-year-olds are playing together. Although these flare-ups can be frequent, they are usually also short, like the kids' attention spans. Generally, these kids are still very egocentric and don't give in easily. They don't pay much attention to each other's needs or feelings and in fact are not very capable of understanding the concept of another person's differing point of view, even when it is explained to them.

→ **Two- to three-year-olds** often find that learning to share is a difficult process. Kids in this age group often think of their possessions as extensions of themselves. They have not yet learned that if they momentarily let go of a toy, it still belongs to them and it will be returned. With this in mind, parents can be more tolerant and realize that their kids are not "bad or selfish" but merely "acting their age."

Remember that it is difficult if not impossible for a three-year-old to be in touch with his friend's feelings or distress. Adult thinking and reasoning are much different from a young child's egocentric thinking; a child is often unaffected by the logical reasons given by adults, because they make no sense to him. (See box, page 181.)

■ *A patient mom tried to explain to her three-and-a-half-year-old son, "Tommy wants to play with your truck now. How do you think he feels when you never give him a turn?" Her son stood*

→ **Three- and four-year-olds** often build attachment by asking other kids their likes and dislikes and echoing them ("You like pizza? Me too!"). Their notion of mutual give-and-take is not yet well developed, and they often make statements of conditional friendship ("I'll be your friend if you invite me!").

→ **Four-year-olds** usually socialize better because they are better at sharing and have longer attention spans. However, they sometimes are more competitive and will often try to outdo each other.

→ **Five-year-olds** are beginning to contrast themselves and their activities to others ("I'm building a different kind of castle. I'm making a moat around it."). At this age, children can begin to cooperate with each other and understand that their differences can be used to help each other out (complementary roles). ("You get the buckets of sand and I'll dig the moat.")

→ **Note** that there are wide variations in social skills among children whatever their age.

quietly with a blank look on his face, totally missing the point, and replied, "Mom, it's my truck!" She would have been better off just focusing on solving the sharing problem by saying, "In our house we share toys. It's Tommy's turn now. When the timer dings, it will be your turn again."

Playtime can go much more smoothly when children of mixed ages (two- to five-year-olds) get together. Younger children often admire and learn from older kids.

friends

■ Gail's older son often enjoyed playing with his younger brother's friends: It obviously made him feel helpful and smart. She would overhear him say things like: "That puzzle piece goes right in this corner. I've got a great idea . . . let's put all the Legos here and build an airport." Then he would continue, excitedly, "Would you like to pet my ferret? Watch out, he's very squirmy. If he gets loose, he's very hard to find."

Encourage your child to help choose guests for their play dates. Notice if their temperaments and ages seem to be a good match and be prepared to make suggestions about where to play if your child's friends are on the wild side.

Notice which children your child gets along with best . . . that's *his* "in group"! Get them together when *you* need a break.

Keep in mind the old adage "Two's company, three's a crowd." You may need to structure the play activities more carefully when there are more than two children: for example, outdoor play, finger painting at the kitchen table with your supervision, and so on.

Reach into your bag of tricks when the kids are bored and whining, "What can we do now?"

Be aware that friendships and children's feelings about each other may change, quickly and frequently! This is normal.

Tips for Hosting a Play Date

→ Exchange important information with the play date's parents ahead of time. Discuss any allergies to food or animals, favorite snacks, fears (such as of pets or thunder), and emergency phone numbers.

→ Keep it short. An hour and a half usually works well for two two- to three-year-olds and most first-time play dates of preschoolers.

→ Give children time to get comfortable with one another. Leave out a dollhouse or basketball hoop to help kids get started and "break the ice."

→ Stay close by until the kids seem comfortable together. (It may take more than one get-together for this to happen.)

→ Discreetly leave the room when things are going well, but stay within earshot.

→ Consider letting the kids choose what toys they will play with or what activities they will engage in for the next half hour. For example, decide whether or not video or computer games will be made available. In some cases, they may get in the way of kids interacting directly with each other; in other cases, they may be a shared enthusiasm that can help kids relate to each other and play together.

→ Build in some "downtime" for play dates if the kids seem tired. Offering a snack gives them a good break and helps restore energy levels. Even a short video or TV show may be okay if the kids are really pooped and need to relax. (They may need help agreeing on a choice.)

→ The courtesy that "the guest always goes first" may upset very young children. If so, consider suspending it.

→ Recognize that some conflicts are unavoidable and give the kids a chance to work out their differences.

→ If arguing or fighting continues, try playing soothing, quiet music or reading a story to help the children calm down.

→ When things aren't going well, try changing the environment; invite the kids to play outside for a while and see if they get along better. Sometimes a change in the temperature, the activity, or even the amount of light in the room does the trick.

→ Organize supervised activities like painting, Play-Doh, coloring, and cooking, which promote cooperation and discourage fighting.

→ Give a five-minute warning, or consider using a clean-up time to help in the transition, so that parting isn't too abrupt and kids have a comfortable sense of closure.

→ Involve your child in thanking guests for coming over and saying good-bye.

Leave some room for your child to choose friends, but explain that excluding others can hurt feelings.

Be reassured that many children, at one time or another, have an "imaginary friend"; this is a normal, creative way for a child to deal with emotions he might otherwise not be able to handle, such as loneliness, jealousy over a new sibling, or fears. (See "Lying," page 179, for more on imaginary friends.)

■ At the end of every school year, Gail handed each child in her preschool class a hand-painted smooth stone that she had collected along the beach. She told her students that these were magic stones with special powers and added, "Keep this stone in a special place. When you get bored, all you have to do is hold it in your hand and rub it gently with your thumb. It will think of something for you to do." Since no kid is going to stand in one place rubbing a rock for very long before he takes off, this trick really works. So go ahead and believe in magic!

Realize the power of your child's friendships with other adults. Children can gain great comfort by confiding in adults other than their parents whom they like and trust. Aunts, uncles, and grandparents often enjoy listening to a child and are less likely to judge, overreact, or punish.

the bottom line

Respect your child for who she is. Provide socialization experiences that seem to be a good fit for her unique personality and her current developmental stage, and introduce them at a comfortable pace.

"gimmes"

Q: My kids have a bad case of "the gimmes." They are so ungrateful for all our blessings. How can I teach them to appreciate what they have (and believe me, they already have a huge pile of toys at home) and not be constantly expecting more?

A: There's no doubt about it: kids nowadays seem to have so much more "stuff," and they seem to have little appreciation for it. American society today is very materialistic. And because kids are so easily influenced by images, they have become prime targets of mega-marketing campaigns. Although, as parents, it seems as if you have a lot working against you, by modeling good old-fashioned virtues (such as "waste not, want not") you can still make an impression on your children. (See "Values," page 317, for helpful ideas on how to encourage feelings of empathy and appreciation in your children.)

sanity savers

When your child sounds ungrateful, let him know just what you would like him to say instead.

■ As soon as Eliza's five-year-old daughter, Millie, ripped the wrapper off her gift, she loudly asked Grandma, "Did you bring me anything else?" Eliza quickly reminded Millie to say "thank you" to Grandma for bringing her a present. At bedtime that night, Eliza reminded Millie how nice it was of Grandma to remember them while she was on vacation. Mom explained that the fact that Grandma was thinking of them was even more special than the present itself.

Resist the urge to buy everything your child asks for right away. Take some time to evaluate what he really wants; chances are, his fickle whims may have passed a week, a day, or even an hour later!

■ Caroline remembers her mother's frantic search for a toy garage that Nolan had raved about after playing with it at his friend's house. He told Grandma he simply had to have it. Ironically, what seemed to make it truly special was the fact that he didn't have one! Sure enough, as soon as he got one of his own, he lost all interest in it.

■ Caroline also remembers how her mother came up with a terrific idea when shopping with her boys. One day when they were making numerous demands, she decided to run her "magic pen" over the UPC symbol on the toy "to record it for their birthday wish list." Now when Caroline goes shopping with the kids, they still ask for every toy they see but most of the time, they say "I want this for my next birthday." She says, "We'll put it on your wish list," and smiles to herself, realizing they may not even remember it when their birthday rolls around.

Emphasize how hard you work to earn your money and let your child know you must make decisions about how to best spend it. Tell him that the amount of money you have is limited, and that even grown-ups can't get everything they want.

Make a wish list for each member of your family and display it. Point out to your child that in your family, "needs"—like food and warm clothes—will be taken care of quickly, but "wants"—like new cars, vacations, and toys—may take some time.

Let your child hear you talk about how you arrive at a decision to spend a sum of money.

Make it a point to remind your child that when you do choose to splurge, it is something very special that you don't do all the time.

Provide your child with an allowance or small budget and guide him in making choices about how to spend his money. (See "Chores," page 57, for more ideas.)

Decide as a family what will happen when toys get broken. Will the parents replace them at their own expense? Should the broken toys serve as a natural consequence of misuse? Do the kids save up and use their own money to replace them? (See page 17 for an explanation of holding a family meeting.)

Encourage your child to explore alternatives to buying everything in a store. If you enjoy making things, you could create your own greeting cards; if you've got a green thumb, let them see you "grow gifts" from your garden; and if you're handy with a needle, let them watch you darn their socks instead of buying new ones.

Use humor to remind your kids that it's simply ridiculous to expect more and more of everything.

Remind your children that the constant quest for "more stuff" rarely makes anybody truly happy.

■ *Rory liked to read to his children the classic tale of King Midas, in which everything and everyone the king touched turned to gold, leaving him hungry and lonely.*

Be aware of the negative effects of advertising on your child (See also "Televison, Video, and Computers," page 283, for more on TV commercials.)

■ *Caroline was very aware of the power of advertising on young children, especially as they opened birthday presents. So she quickly disposed of the packaging that displayed the complete set of action figures available in the series. One year, she painfully recalled, her son gawked greedily at the pictures on the box of action figures as he simultaneously dropped the brand-new ones he had just received and demanded loudly, "I want this one, and the green one, and this brown one that Billy has. Can we go get them now? I really want them!"*

Especially at the holidays, try not to get sucked into the overall atmosphere of commercialism. Think of ways you can keep your family's preparations and decorations simple.

■ *For Nancy's family, the emphasis at Hanukkah is to reflect for eight days on the good things that have happened during the year, rather than on the eight days' worth of presents.*

■ *Some people elaborately decorate for the holidays up to a month in advance. Caroline prefers the low-key approach at her son's preschool. Celebrations there are simple—sharing*

*a treat or telling a story. The teachers also
minimize the frenzy of anticipation by not
discussing the holiday with the kids until a
couple of days before. In this way, there's not
such a big letdown for them afterward.*

Talk to your child about the "true meaning" of
Thanksgiving; make a list together of all the things
your family is thankful for, and have that be an
important part of your annual celebration.

Consider how you celebrate your child's
birthdays. Think about having a birthday party
with just the family and a few friends. You can
share cake and ice cream, memories, and photos
of the past year's highlights and still have fun.
Children who are routinely treated to parties with
clowns, pony rides, and magicians may take
elaborate celebrations for granted.

Some families give a big party every *other* year,
which is one way of simplifying everyone's life.

Consider going on a special family outing to
celebrate a birthday instead of purchasing the
latest "hot" toy as a present.

■ *Rosemary told her son, Seth, that either they
could have a party on his third birthday or they
could go on a special outing. If he chose the
outing, that would be his present. To this day, Seth
still keeps a picture on his wall of his first horse-
and-carriage ride on a chilly, late-November
evening. The family snuggled under blankets and
drank hot chocolate as they toured downtown
Chicago, admiring the enchanting, twinkling
holiday lights. To his parents' delight, the birthday
boy never uttered a single word about not
receiving any toys.*

Think about the appropriate number of guests for your child's parties. (Gail's rule of thumb is the child's birthday age, plus one.) This helps control the cost of the party, not to mention the toll on your nerves and your child's! Chances are, if you invite a lot of guests, your child will also be invited to a lot of elaborate parties; she may even come to expect a celebration almost every weekend!

Convey to the grandparents your concerns about "overdoing it" if you feel uncomfortable with their well-meaning generosity. (See "Grandparents," page 139, for useful suggestions on how to handle such issues.)

take heart

♥ *You're not the only parent who admits that six kids are all that you and your child can manage for his birthday. Although it takes a lot of courage to go against the "unwritten law" of inviting the entire preschool class, you might be surprised at how positively your child reacts and how much fun the birthday is. (Maybe you'll even start a new trend.)*

Let your child know that it's polite to express appreciation for presents, even if they aren't exactly what she had in mind.

Involve your child in thanking people for their thoughtfulness and gifts. If you choose to send thank-you cards, your child can dictate a message, color a simple picture or put the stamps on the envelope.

Think twice about bringing a sibling "just a little something" when it's not *his* birthday. It's okay to begin teaching children early in life to work through their jealousy and to feel happy for others when it's "their turn."

22

2

Remind your kids that, in your family, material gifts are never more important than the gift of friendship and family.

■ *Around the time of their birthdays, Grandpa Phil tells his grandkids, "Remember, it's not just the things we get in life that we appreciate the most. It's the family and friends who help us celebrate that make us truly happy."*

Let your child experience the true satisfaction of getting something which she has worked hard for, saved for, and waited for. (Remember how sweet that feeling can be?)

take heart

♥ *You're not the only parent who's patiently explained that you have no money for treats today, only to be matter-of-factly informed by your preschooler, "Mom, did you forget? All we gotta do is go to the money machine (ATM) and press the buttons!"*

Help your child understand that different families have different amounts of money and set different priorities. It's helpful for children to learn early on that comparing themselves to "the Joneses" is not a worthwhile pursuit.

■ *One afternoon, Aaron came running home from the neighbor's house with a new catalog in hand and whined, "Jimmy just ordered the best Halloween costume. I want one just like it." Gail calmly said, "Let's check the price in the catalog. Looks like all the pieces add up to $32. I can't afford that right now, but you have some birthday money you were saving, right? It's not quite enough, but if you decide to use it, I'll give you some jobs so you can earn the rest you need to buy that costume all by yourself. But remember, if you use the money for the costume,* you'll have to start saving all over again for that spaceship you wanted." As Aaron was considering this, she added, "We could make you a homemade costume that won't cost any money at all. Think about it . . . and then you decide."

Make a conscious effort to model practicing delayed gratification, even if you are in the fortunate position of having enough money to cover all your wants.

■ Although Larisa had enough money to purchase an entire ski outfit all at once, she didn't make the purchase because she understood the positive impact of her kids hearing her say, "I figured out that I have enough money to buy the new ski jacket now, but I need to save up $75 more for the ski boots. I'm going to put a picture of the boots I want on the refrigerator, next to a chart where I can keep track of the money I save."

Talk about how grateful you are for what you have. (This is not too hard to do, and it sets a very powerful and positive example over time.)

Draw upon religious and family traditions that may help you teach the kids to express gratitude. (And see "Gimmes" in the list of children's books for more support.)

■ Every night when Caroline and her boys pray together, they take turns thanking God for something good that has happened and picking a special person to bless.

Discuss the need to respect and take care of everything around you. Involve your child in volunteer opportunities such as cleaning up the local park on Earth Day or planting trees on Arbor Day.

Be aware of your own behavior; are you really modeling the behavior you desire to instill in your children? (See page 17 for more on modeling.)

Have patience with your children—developing an appreciative attitude is a process that takes time.

the bottom line

Through your actions, and with the benefit of your reminders, children can learn to appreciate what's really important in life.

grandparents

Q: My kids just adore their grandparents and our extended family is very important to me. But I feel like I'm a good mother and I don't need a lot of advice about my parenting. How can I deal with my in-laws' unsolicited remarks without hurting their feelings—and still remain true to myself?

A: Try to approach well-meaning but sometimes meddling grandparents with many of the same skills you would use to tenderly handle an irritable toddler. Keep in mind that being polite does not mean you have to embrace their advice. When all's said and done, you can do what *you* think is best for your own family.

sanity savers

Listen to grandparents' advice without arguing. Acknowledge their feelings and thoughts (even if you don't agree with them). Try saying, "I can see that's really important to you." Then take a deep breath and buy yourself some time by adding, "I need to think about that for a while."

Gift Giving

If the grandparents' generosity has gotten out of hand and you fear they're spoiling your kids, try the following suggestions.

→ Give grandparents a practical list of suggested gifts well ahead of time.

→ Offer to go shopping with them to choose gifts for your children.

→ When the grandparents come for a visit loaded down with gifts, limit the number of gifts your children can open at one time so they won't be overwhelmed.

→ Help the grandparents see that simply spending time together can be the most special gift of all; handmade coupons with pictures redeemable for nature walks, hugs and kisses, and baking cookies together can do the trick!

Take into consideration that each generation perceives things differently. Just as today's parents often don't see eye to eye with the ways of their parents, many of the grandparents consider today's lifestyle of rushing around to soccer practice, karate lessons, and birthday parties to be totally dysfunctional!

Bring to your child's attention the fact that the rules at Grandma's house may be different from your rules at home. Let the kids know this is acceptable, and make it clear that neither household needs to change its rules. When this is repeatedly explained up front to the kids, they won't be as inclined to use manipulation to get their way ("You're so mean! Grandma lets me do it.").

Help grandparents understand why you've set down certain rules by having them experience firsthand the consequences of their actions.

> ■ *Julie had pleaded with her mother for months not to bring the kids candy and gum when she visited. The loving grandma told Julie she just couldn't bear to visit empty-handed, because Kirk looked forward to her "special surprise treats." In desperation, Julie finally thought of a great idea. She simply invited her mother to come along to Kirk's dental appointment. After listening to the dentist's warnings about limiting sweets and watching him drill Kirk's cavities, Grandma resolved to change her ways. On her next visit, she thoughtfully presented a carton of fresh, sweet blueberries to her grandson as her "special surprise treat." To her surprise, he wasn't the slightest bit disappointed.*

Try to pretend that you are talking to a friend or colleague; this is one creative way you can find the emotional distance you need to make a point without being rude to a "difficult" grandparent.

Know when it's wise to stop talking; sometimes it's better "to agree to disagree." This will help you avoid setting yourself up for lengthy and painful discussions with those family members who seem to always drive you crazy.

> ■ *Joanne's stepfather was the family "know-it-all." He claimed to know just what to do about his grandson's picky eating habits and never missed an opportunity to expound on the topic. Over time, Joanne learned to respond to him like this, "Your point is well taken, but I don't agree with you. You know what? I'll take time to think about it. We can talk about it again later." When he persists in offering unsolicited advice, Joanne quickly excuses*

herself and makes a beeline for a "time-out" in the bathroom, where she can cool down.

Give yourself permission not to love, or even like, your kids' grandparents, but do try to be polite to them.

■ *One well-meaning but very critical mother-in-law was always bragging about how early her son had been toilet-trained. Finally her self-assured daughter-in-law cleared her throat, smiled, and carefully chose her words, "Wow! I don't know anyone nowadays who toilet trains at eighteen months!" she said. Meanwhile, she was thinking to herself, "What a dingbat! All you really did was train yourself to put Floyd on the potty every hour! Didn't you have anything better to do with your time?"*

take heart

♥ *You're not the only parent who's been embarrassed to hear your recent diatribe about your father-in-law repeated by your child with amazing accuracy, at the most inopportune time!*

Try to be conscious of what you say about the grandparents within earshot of the kids.

Encourage the grandparent-grandchild relationship even if your relationship with your parents or in-laws isn't everything you hoped it would be. Grandparents can be the source of an abundance of unconditional love for children, and that is a wonderful thing for them.

Children are often comfortable confiding in grandparents, and especially when things are "out of sorts" at home, grandparents can act as their emotional safety net.

■ *Maria remembers that, as a child, she always felt so good about going over to her grandmother's house. Even with all her irrational childhood worries, she felt completely safe and happy there. From an early age, she remembers, her thinking process went something like this: She knew Grandma loved her more than anything. Maria felt that because Grandma was such a good person, God would never hurt Grandma by letting anything happen to Maria in her presence!*

Encourage your children to enjoy learning their family history from your family's own "living roots."

■ *Sean and Nolan love to hear their granddad's stories about his evacuation from London during the bombing blitz of World War II. As a child, Caroline's father was sent to the English countryside to live with his grandfather, a French immigrant to England and truly exotic to his little "city-boy" grandson. Caroline's boys are lucky to hear stories their grandfather shares about his grandfather, a man born over 120 years ago!*

Make a point of trying to communicate with grandparents regularly. Initiate contact at a time that is convenient for you. Your regular phone calls will set a positive tone and may in turn lessen their sometimes annoying, untimely calls.

■ *By scheduling a special monthly date at a restaurant, Lisa was able to avoid stressful additional visits from the grandparents. When approached, she would politely tell them, "I'm so sorry, we're busy for the next two weekends; but we're really looking forward to getting together on the fifteenth like we planned."*

■ *A loving grandmother who often took care of her grandkids was reluctant to "put her two cents in" on issues she noticed with the grandchildren for fear of being perceived as interfering. To her pleasant surprise, the following week, her son and daughter-in-law opened easy lines of communication by initiating a weekly discussion. They were seeking her input on trials and triumphs with the grandkids. It was so much easier for Grandma to address things as they happened, before major misunderstandings built up.*

Help your kids find ways to develop a special relationship with grandparents who are far away. Today's technology—e-mail, video cameras, tape recorders, cell phones, answering machines, and discount airfares—really can help. Even when the grandparents are no longer alive, photo albums, the stories you tell about them, and memorabilia can still give your kids a sense of knowing who their grandparents were.

No matter how packed your schedule becomes, remember to make time to visit Grandma and Grandpa.

■ *When Gail, her husband, and the kids had overlooked a scheduled call to Great-Grandma, she would leave them a voice-mail message, supposedly in a panic about not wanting to miss that week's "blue-light special" on toilet paper, paper towels, or tissues at the supermarket. Great-Grandma couldn't drive, and everyone knew how lonely she got. She knew that the family all knew her basement was neatly stockpiled with more paper goods than she could ever use in her lifetime! This was just her unique, funny, nonconfrontational way of getting to see her grandkids and great-grandkids.*

Help the grandparents realize that it's not necessary for them to shower the grandchildren with gifts throughout the year.

> ■ *Donna, a thoughtful mom, reminded her parents, "Do you remember the special tickets you gave me when I was growing up, each good for one walk in the woods with Dad? Those are some of my fondest memories. I still remember walking hand in hand while Daddy patiently explained each different kind of tree, flower, and bird song. I'll bet my kids would enjoy a hike in the woods with you and Dad just as much as I used to, and it wouldn't cost a dime!"*

Plan how you will spend your time over the holidays in advance, to avoid hurt feelings. Many families find themselves faced with the pressures of wanting to be in two places at once. Working out a plan ahead of time relieves a lot of stress on the holiday itself. Having a plan is especially important for divorced, remarried couples. Accept the fact that you can't please everyone, but you can let them know that it's important to you to do the best you can. Try alternating holidays or celebrating before or after the real date. What child would mind three Christmases or two birthday parties?

Imagine what it must feel like to be a grandparent yourself.

> ■ *Blakely Bundy, one of Gail's friends, recently admitted, "The best thing about being a grandmother has been watching my sons become wonderful, caring, nurturing, very hands-on fathers who are absolutely crazy about their baby daughters."*

Accept the fact that grandparents often have a lot of something important that parents often lack . . .

TIME! Notice how special the undivided attention and love of a grandparent can make a child feel.

Realize that some less aggressive grandparents would love to help out, but are shy about suggesting it for fear of seeming too pushy.

> ■ *Sandy, a very busy mother with three small children, was having a really bad day. Swamped with errands, she found herself in a nervous tizzy. When her father called, he found Sandy at her wits' end. She began blurting out the list of everything she had to do, including yet another last-minute invitation to a birthday party. Just the thought of going to the toy store was simply the last straw! Sandy's father calmly responded, "Why, honey, I'd be happy to help you out. I'll swing by in an hour and pick up Travis; I'll need his help choosing just the right gift. We'll buy a couple extra gifts too, so next time you'll be all set!" Sandy was astounded that what had been a burden for her had actually become a pleasure for her dad. All she had to do was ask!*

Remember, most grandparents are worth their weight in gold as trusty baby-sitters (so be patient with them and bite your tongue, especially if you don't want to miss that big office party!).

the bottom line

When you're confident knowing *you* will ultimately make the decisions concerning your family, it's a lot easier to listen to the grandparents without arguing; remember, for every parent wishing the grandparents would just "butt out," there's someone else wishing they were still alive!

"i hate you!"

Q: Yesterday when I wouldn't let my preschooler go outside to play right before dinner, she screamed, "You're the meanest mommy! I hate you!" I felt like yelling back at her and then collapsing into tears! How could she say such a thing?

A: Sooner or later, almost every parent hears those dreaded words *"I hate you!"* Although this is extremely upsetting, keep in mind that your child may still be at the developmental stage of struggling to express herself. Even this verbal attack shows a measure of control beyond hitting, scratching, or kicking. What your child is probably telling you is that she is angry about something you've done or, more likely, about something you won't allow her to do. Just as it's your job to provide her with the security and consistency of firm limits, realize that it's your child's "job" to test you in any way she can think of. Try not to take this kind of attack too personally. Think of it as another opportunity to teach your child that although it's okay for

her to be angry, you don't like being spoken to
rudely.

sanity savers

When your child screams out she hates you, try to
resist "going for the bait" in the heat of the
moment. To avoid a power struggle, respond calmly
with a noncommittal response like "Hmm,"
"Ahhh," "Oh, my," or "Ohhh."

■ *Nellie's two older children ages 3 and 5, were
feeling jealous of the new baby. At one point when
they couldn't get Mom's attention, they lashed out
with some angry insults, including "I hate you so-o-o
much!" Nellie responded, calmly, "Oooo," and
nothing more. The kids seemed a bit miffed by the
lack of confrontation, and they repeated the
insults louder, only this time Mom said, softly and
slowly, "I see," with a hurt look, and turned her
attention back to the baby. The kids stared briefly
at each other until one of them broke the silence,
saying "I'm hungry." Then the other one added,
"Me too!" They ran into the kitchen to raid the
refrigerator. Jealous thoughts of the baby were out
of sight, out of mind! (At least for the time being.)*

Try ignoring your child's hateful words the first
couple of times she utters them; perhaps she'll get
the message that they're not going to "work" on
you.

Change the subject. Take a deep breath and
redirect the child's attention.

■ *Emmy was having fun playing tag with the
neighbor kids in her backyard. When Bruno
interrupted the fun by telling his daughter it was*

*time to leave for her dentist appointment, Emmy
yelled, "We can't leave now! I'm playing with my
friends!" When Bruno repeated the need to stop
playing and get ready to go, she cried out, "You're
so mean! I hate you, Daddy!" Ignoring Emmy's
outburst, Bruno took her hand as they walked to
the car together, and said, "Did you see the new
daffodils that popped open in our garden? Aren't
they pretty? Which one do you like?" Emmy
smiled and said, "I like this one!" "Let's pick a
bouquet for Mommy when we get home from the
dentist!" Daddy said.*

Acknowledge your child's true feelings; you
might also talk about what you think is the reason
for her angry words. Telling her that she mustn't
hate anybody won't change the way she feels.
Being allowed to state the reason she's angry helps
your child connect her intense feelings to the
situation.

■ *Tamara responded just right to her demanding
daughter. "I can see you're really angry," she said.
"You know, it's possible to have two feelings about
people. Sometimes we like them a lot and other
times they can really make us mad. I'll bet you're
mad at me because I didn't let you go outside
before dinner."*

Use an "I" statement rather than a "you"
statement to let your child know how you feel
when he says hurtful things. (See pages 15 to 16
for an explanation of "I" statements and "you"
statements.)

■ *Rather than blurting out her true feelings in a
character attack like "You're such a bad boy, you
should be ashamed of yourself! You make me so
angry . . . you're never to talk to your mother like*

that!" Mary learned to say, "I feel so angry when I hear you say that."

■ Caroline told her son Sean, "I'm sorry you feel that way. I feel upset when I hear you say that. Maybe later you'll feel differently." Then she intentionally walked away to finish the dishes, calmly ending the conversation.

■ Roger told his irate three-year-old daughter, "I feel badly when I hear you say that, because those words hurt people's feelings."

Let your child know what language is not acceptable to you and teach him alternative ways to express himself.

■ It had been a pretty good day, until five-year-old Nick blurted out a hateful, rude response to something Gary, his dad, had asked him to do. Gary calmly but firmly said, "Nick! I won't listen to rude words like that! I would feel much better if you simply said you were mad at me, even extra-super-mad, instead of saying you hate me."

■ Alicia told her son, "Let's think of a better way for you to tell your friend how upset you feel without saying 'I hate you!' and other mean things. How about telling Lonny that you don't like it when he snatches toys away? Tell him to use words and ask you for a turn."

Tell your child you are willing to discuss things further (if you truly are) when she can talk to you more politely.

Reassure your child that you still love him even if he says he hates you. (Although this is true, it may take some practice until it feels natural.)

■ Kathy sighed loudly and reminded herself that Sonny was only four years old. "Honey," she said,

> *"I'm sorry you feel that way. I want you to know that I'll always love you . . . but you still may not use my computer right now!"*

Stand your ground no matter how your child's hateful words test you. (This is not easy to do on a bad day, but stick to your guns!)

■ *Gail said to her son, "I see how angry you are, but I need you to tell me that without using mean words. And, by the way, Josh, you still have to hold my hand every time we cross the street . . . that's our safety rule!"*

■ *Olivia, a smart sitter, told five-year-old Annette, "No matter what you say to me, I am not going to change the rules, so you might as well be polite!"*

"Give" your child in fantasy what he cannot have in reality; it is often a magical way of changing the mood.

■ *One evening, Evan, an overtired three-year-old, said, "I hate going to bed, and I hate you, too, Daddy." Vic, his understanding father, acknowledged Evan's feelings without shaming him. Choosing his words carefully, he said, "I can see you wish you made the rules in our house instead of me and Mommy." As he continued to undress his son, Vic tried to change the mood by saying, "If it were up to you, what time would bedtime be?" His son's eyes lit up and a smile came over his face as he eagerly responded, "Nobody would go to bed until midnight!" Vic said, "Oh, I see . . . and what would you do until midnight?" "We'd watch videos and eat popcorn, of course, Daddy!" the delighted child responded. "That really sounds like a lot of fun," Vic replied. "How about doing it this Saturday?" "Yes, Daddy, I want to do it Saturday!" "Okay, it's a deal!" Vic*

*agreed. "And now let's try to relax. Lie down and
I'll read you a story."*

Responding with "yes," "as soon as," or "wait"
instead of the emphatic and confrontational "NO!"
may actually head off an angry "I hate you!" from
your child.

■ *Alexandra, an energetic three-year-old, rushed
into the kitchen where Joe, her dad, was finishing
cooking dinner. She charged toward the back
door, asking, "Can I go to Daniel's house?" Instead
of saying "No! Can't you see we're going to eat
right now!", Joe intentionally flashed his sweetest
smile and responded, "Yes, you can go next door,
honey, as soon as we finish eating dinner."*

Immediately compliment the child who copes
well with a negative situation instead of blurting
out his usual "You're such a mean mommy. I hate
you so much!" (See page 240 for more on praise
pointers.)

Attempt to resolve your child's angry feelings by
giving her some control over the situation; offering
two acceptable choices often works well.

■ *In response to her daughter's declaration of
hate, Gail said to Rachel, "I know you wish you
could have a cookie right now, but dinner's
almost ready. Let's pick out a cookie you can eat
later for dessert." Rachel's face brightened as she
almost contentedly responded, "Okay, Mommy, I
want this big one." Then she darted back to the
family room to work on her puzzle until dinner
was served.*

Most children have an excellent memory for
certain things; they often repeat over and over
whatever they see gets a rise out of you. Kids will
even settle for negative attention (yelling,

screaming, criticizing, bribing, and threatening) if, on a bad day, that's all they can get from you.

Keep in mind that when you respond to your child with yelling, disgust, or mean words, even if you think he well deserves them, you just may lose control of the situation and find yourself in the midst of an escalating power struggle.

Watch out for the most common triggers of a hateful outburst. Your child may be tired, hungry, resentful, or simply overwhelmed rather than genuinely angry with you. Consider whether a nap, a snack, a brief time-out, or maybe in some cases a snuggle on the couch may be all that's needed.

take heart

♥ *You're not the only parent who finds that it's really hard to squelch an automatic, negative, retort when your child verbally lashes out at you. But, with a little practice and a few good deep breaths, you might be amazed at the positive approach you're able to come up with!*

Model acceptable responses to frustration. (See "Anger," page 19, "Tantrums," page 276, and "Bad Words," page 37, for more suggestions on how to handle angry outbursts.)

■ *"Caramba!," Ricky Ricardo's exclamation from I Love Lucy, became a favorite way of letting off steam when things went wrong in Carla's house.*

Ask your child how she would feel if someone said they hated her, and let her know that others may not want to play with her if she says mean things to them. Remember, however, that helping your child understand how others feel is a process that takes time. The ability to feel empathy is more developed in a four- to five-year-old. With a two- or three-year-old, you're just planting the seeds.

Be aware of your own choice of hateful words spoken in anger—when you least expect it, they may come back to haunt you.

> ■ *Nolan, Caroline's five-year-old, had assembled the train set his friend Mack loved to play with. After admiring his work, he began to get impatient waiting for Mack to arrive. Soon he was interrupting Caroline every two minutes, whining a refrain, "When is he coming?" When the doorbell finally rang, Nolan pushed past Caroline and swung the door open. She was simply mortified at what he did next. In a style she is embarrassed to admit is her very own, he first placed his hands on his hips, then wagged his index finger at Mack as he loudly proclaimed, "Mack! I positively* hate *you for being so late!"*

the bottom line

Your child doesn't truly hate you, but the limits you have placed on her. And placing those limits, after all, is an important part of being a good parent!

hitting and hurting others

Q: My child has become extremely aggressive—hitting, kicking, or scratching whomever seems to get in her way. What can I do to address the situation while we still have a couple of friends left?

A: Almost all young children at one time or another resort to aggressive behavior for various reasons. When toddlers get hostile, adult intervention is essential, but it's important to understand that many hostile acts are basically a reflex at this stage of development. Even kids who often demonstrate that they know better sometimes resort to aggressive acts to get what they want. Those kids who have a somewhat belligerent "short-fuse" personality require even more supervision as they learn to control their impulses.

immediate response

→ Stop the unacceptable behavior immediately, but gently; take one hand of each child, on either side of you. Have the victim and the aggressor take a deep breath with you.

→ Try to surmise what happened yourself by a quick observation; angry interrogations often get conflicting replies or no answer at all.

→ Bend down so you can look straight into their eyes; often no words are necessary.

→ Acknowledge the bad feelings that provoked the aggression, followed by clearly stating the rule that was broken. "Kevin, I can see how very upset you are that Max broke your flashlight, but punching and kicking are not okay."

→ The less you talk, the more likely the child is to hear what you say. Say, "Hitting was a bad choice. We'll talk more later."

→ Restore the peace by redirecting both kids to a parent-supervised activity, like preparing a snack or reading a book together.

sanity savers

Point out the misbehavior. Say, "Time-out for hitting" or "Kicking and scratching hurt" or "Use words, not hands, when you are upset."

Let your child know there is never a good reason for hitting, kicking, scratching, and pushing.

Resist asking your child why he hurt someone. Chances are she won't be able to explain why and will only be further annoyed by your question.

■ *Serena found it much more helpful to set the stage for a conversation with her quibbling kids when she said things like this: "Okay, girls, I see you're both very upset. It's not easy to play nicely inside the house on a rainy day." Interrogating— "Why did you take her doll?" "What's wrong with*

*you?" "Who started it?"—immediately shut down
the lines of communication.*

Explain how aggressive acts hurt others.

> ■ *Gail liked to use days on which no fighting
> happened to continue the process of teaching
> her daughter right from wrong. She asked,
> "Remember when Derek got really angry the last
> time we visited his house? He pushed you
> backward and your head hit the corner of the
> table. Remember how much that hurt? That's why
> we don't allow pushing and hitting at our house."*

Ask the aggressor to "make it better." Reparations
are better than apologies. This may involve
rebuilding blocks or rubbing the sore spot on the
victim's leg.

Point out the consequences that may result from
the misbehavior.

> ■ *Linda said to her three-year-old, "I can see how
> hard it is for you to wait in line to use the slide.
> Have you noticed that your friends don't like it
> when you push them? They may not want to come
> and play with you again if you're too pushy and
> they're afraid you're going to hurt them. I know how
> much you look forward to your friends coming over."*

Give an "out-of-control" child the structure he
needs in order to calm down. This could mean
sitting quietly in a chair, going to his room alone,
or cuddling quietly with you. (See "Time-Out,"
page 299, "Anger," page 19, and "Tantrums," page
276, for ways to help your child regain self-control
when he's lost it.)

Anticipate the situations that seem to provoke
your young child's aggressive behavior and try to
head them off.

■ Rob said to his son, "Your cousins are coming over in a little while. And remember, the toys in the den are for everyone to play with." His worried son responded, "But, Daddy, I don't want to share my new train from Grandpa." Rob said, "I understand how you feel. I'll tell you what. Let's put it under my bed until everyone leaves."

Be prepared to intervene and redirect your child's aggressive tendencies until he outgrows them. It is your responsibility to keep your child's playmates and siblings safe.

Help your child express her feelings verbally by giving her the words to use and acknowledging when she is upset.

■ Gail told her daughter, "Wow, you really look angry! Use words to tell Lauren how you feel. Say to her, 'I don't like being kicked out of the sandbox.'"

Give your child the time and room to use words to express himself. It's amazing how much better children understand the concept of taking turns talking and listening when the procedure is explained clearly.

■ Caroline borrowed a great idea from her son's preschool and used it at home. During a family meeting, she explained to her kids what she was going to do when she heard screaming and fighting. She designated one kitchen chair a "talking chair" and one a "listening chair." Then she described her plan: "One of you is going to sit in the talking chair, the other in the listening chair. Then we'll switch, so that you each get a chance to talk and a chance to listen to one another without any interruptions." The kids had fun practicing the concept using the chairs and

even made sure Caroline and her husband,
Dennis, took a turn.

Hold family meetings and one-on-one planned "talks" about the aggressive behavior and how to handle a similar situation the next time it comes up. Ask the child to repeat what he has learned before closing the discussion. (See page 17 for more on family meetings.)

Brainstorm some alternatives to "hitting someone back" with your child.

> ■ *"You know, hitting and kicking aren't the only ways to fix things," Mel said to his son. "How else could Batman have stopped the bad guy without punching him? I wonder what words he could have used?"*

Ask your child to "teach" her stuffed animal or doll how to behave properly and how to set the consequences for misbehavior. This practice in restating the rules is a very successful approach for many children.

> ■ *Jesse couldn't imagine who her son was talking to until she quietly peeked into his room, and saw him pointing his finger at his large stuffed dog. "Sadie," he said, "no jumping up on people, because that hurts! Time-out in the corner for two minutes!"*

Hugs are good not only for the victim. They may also calm an aggressor who is totally out of control. Being hugged helps some children to feel they are still loved even though you don't like their behavior. Other children may push you away.

take heart

♥ *You're not the only parent whose first instinct is to teach your kid "tit for tat . . . hit 'em back."*

Alternatives to Hitting Back

Your child needs to know what he *can* do when someone hits or otherwise hurts him. Here are some suggestions for ways your child can try to tame an aggressive friend without hitting back. Choose a quiet time to go over them, so your child can focus on alternatives.

→ Tell him to stop it.

→ Tell her you don't like that.

→ Tell him you feel like hitting him, but you won't do that because you can use words to talk about it instead.

→ Move away from him.

→ Ask the teacher or a parent for help.

→ Stop playing with him for a while.

Provide your child with things he *can* throw, kick, or punch. Tell him to hit his tetherball, punch a pillow, or pretend to be a kung fu fighter, kicking the air.

Keep in mind that children tend to be selective in what they hear, so beware of what you say. Your explanations and admonitions may backfire, serving only to encourage the bad behavior that you were attempting to stop.

■ *Ryan and Candy were very specific about telling Zach what was expected from him when they left him with a baby-sitter. On the way out one night, Candy said, "Zach, remember, don't jump up and down on the new couch or pull the cat's tail, like you did when Grandma was over. No*

*hurting anything!" Zach's expression said it all.
He might as well have said to his parents,
"Thanks for reminding me!" And he did exactly
what he was told not to do as soon as they
closed the door.*

Focus on the "good things" your child does,
rather than on what he shouldn't do.

■ *It would have been better if Candy's parting
words had focused on what Zach had done well
last time: "Zach, I liked the way you sat on the
couch and stroked the cat while you watched
your TV program with Grandma."*

Think through your approach
to discipline . . . what are you
teaching by your actions? Are
you sending a clear, consistent
message?

Set aside time to talk with
your spouse if you feel that
your child is simply too wild
and your discipline
techniques seem to be
ineffective. Write down,
together, the kind of behavior
you would like to stop as well
as where and when it is
happening. Then devise a plan
for dealing with it.

■ *At bath time, two-and-a-half-year-old Jamie was
hardly ever cooperative. She kicked and
screamed and complained almost every night. It
got to the point where neither Mom nor Dad
wanted to volunteer for the chore, so they
decided to take turns on a weekly basis. This
helped them stay calm and clearheaded enough*

to help Jamie. When Mom acknowledged her feelings by saying, "I know you don't like getting your hair washed. I can do it really fast; and as soon as we're done you'll be able to play with your sponge blocks," Jamie became more cooperative.

the bottom line

Although you can't stop your child from feeling frustrated, threatened, hurt, or angry, you can show him how to express these feelings in ways that don't hurt others.

interrupting

Q: Sometimes my kids seem to have no respect for what I am doing if it doesn't relate to them. They can be so rude! Whether I'm in the middle of making dinner, putting on my makeup, or talking to a neighbor who just dropped by for a visit, they feel I'm fair game to attack head-on for my full attention. It's so embarrassing! And heaven help the poor soul who tries to reach me on the phone! Sometimes I think my children have been programmed to drop what they're doing and bother me every time it rings!

A: You're not alone! This annoying behavior runs rampant in the two- to five-year-old population, when kids are still at a very egocentric stage of development. They tend to concentrate on their own wants and needs, totally oblivious to how inconsiderate their behavior is to someone else. Some preschoolers also go through a possessive stage, interrupting because they desire their parents' exclusive attention. Although many parents initially reprimand their children for interrupting, some choose to give in to their demands in the same breath anyway. If your child sees that constantly interrupting you gets her what she wants, you can be sure this tactic will continue.

immediate response

➜ Let your child know you will be with her soon, even as you are finishing your conversation with another adult, by holding her hand, stroking her shoulder, rubbing her back, or sitting down and cuddling with her.

➜ Buy yourself some time to finish talking to your neighbor by giving the child a task to do. Pause, look him in the eye, and say, "Honey, I'll be with you as soon as you close the gate." Then talk fast!

➜ Offer your whiny, impatient child the chance to briefly talk to the person on the phone. This can change his mood.

➜ Keep a three-minute timer near the phone, and calmly say, "Grace, when all the sand runs down to the other side, I will be off the phone and ready to listen to you." Then turn the timer and set it down so your child can see it. (Keep your promise!)

➜ Be creative. When your phone begins to ring, "answer" your child's toy phone first. Say, "Jenny, it's for you." Then answer your phone.

➜ Show your appreciation immediately when your child cooperates with your requests for him to wait. Say, "Nice manners" or "Good listening" or simply "Thank you."

sanity savers

Schedule daily one-on-one time with your child, when she can count on having your undivided attention. When she knows she'll have your complete attention later, she is less likely to interrupt you at other times during the day. As little as five minutes of true one-on-one time can be more satisfying to your child than an hour of constant interruptions.

Discuss which situations warrant an interruption—for example, emergencies (and talk with your child about what constitutes an emergency). Talk privately during a quiet time or discuss your wants and needs as well as your child's, together at a family meeting. Role-playing sometimes helps everyone get the message and usually is a lot of fun. (See the box on page 25 for more on role-playing.)

Practice saying "excuse me" with your child, and compliment her when she remembers to use good manners. But also let her know that repeated "excuse me"s are another form of annoying interruption.

Develop a secret code your child can use (instead of rudely interrupting) when you're busy or when you are talking to someone.

■ *The kids in the Spencer family agreed with their parents that they could either squeeze the parent's hand or tap their own noses to get attention. The parents agreed to respond back with the same signal to assure the child that he had been "heard" and that he would be responded to shortly.*

Realize that waiting for your attention is very difficult for a young child because he just can't help thinking about whatever is bothering him— thirst, a boo-boo, a broken toy.

Suggest something specific for your child to do while she waits. Studies show that the kids who were the least patient while waiting for a parent were still focusing their thinking on the object they wanted. The kids who were the most patient while waiting had been directed to another activity.

> ■ Melanie said, "While I finish putting on my makeup, you can play with the sponges in the sink or you can go to your room and draw me a picture with your markers. As soon as I'm finished, I will play with you."

Tell your child that people take turns talking and listening. Tell him that you want to finish your turn talking to someone else and then he can have a turn talking to you, while you listen to him. Then be sure to keep your promise!

Inform your child that you will be busy for the next few minutes before starting an especially important activity. Ask her if she needs anything before you get started. Afterward, compliment the child who refrains from interrupting or whose interruptions have decreased.

take heart

♥ You're not the only parent who wonders why your child can play so well by himself, right up until the moment he spies you picking up the phone!

Anticipate or head off possible interruptions by being prepared. Keep a special movie or toy for use only when you're on the phone.

■ *Caroline has a special "phone box" that she keeps handy. When she's about to answer the phone, she pulls it out so her child can pick a special toy, game, or video that is offered only during a "Mommy call."*

If you work at home, consider making a small stop sign to place on your desk when you are "at work" and don't want to be interrupted (this works for short bursts of time). Wearing a work hat on your head can add to your visual message.

Plan ahead, and turn to technology for assistance. Buy an inexpensive headset. Most cordless phone receivers have a place to plug it into (it's covered with a small rubber flap that lifts up on one side). Then put the cordless receiver on your belt, and you're now completely mobile, with hands free to play while waiting for an important call.

Consider making phone calls after the kids go to sleep or during a period of time when a baby-sitter is with them.

Use e-mail to contact your friends and business associates, even at 3 o'clock in the morning. At least it's quiet!

Try limiting the number of times you respond to the phone when you're with your child. Let him know he's more important than the phone caller by letting the answering machine take a message!

■ *One day when Becky called her best friend, another mom, the friend said, "Becky, please don't take this personally. I've been on the phone all morning and John just can't take it anymore. Can we please keep this really short?" Becky not only understood, she admired her friend for putting her child's needs first.*

Occasionally it's worth it to stop what you're doing and give your child the time he needs to get settled. Then you can go back to what you need to get done.

■ *Natalie found that three-year-old Kevin would keep pestering her whenever she was trying to accomplish a task. The more insistent Natalie was on finishing the task, the more insistent he was on whining and interrupting. Mom found that, in the long run, it was better to satisfy her son's requests first. It often took only a few minutes to get him started in an activity that could keep him busy and happy for a long time. He usually ended up so involved in his play that he didn't bother her again. For example, if she helped him set up his train tracks, he'd leave her alone for a whole hour.*

Look at the big picture. When your child interrupts you, ask yourself two questions: What does your child need? What do you need?

■ *Caroline remembers, "Even though I made a decision to leave my job to concentrate on raising my children full-time, I found their interruptions annoying when I was trying to complete some household task. I reminded myself that I was home to spend time with and enjoy my kids, not to be a housemaid! I began writing my daily to-do list (a holdover from my working days) from a different perspective, and began to include things like 'Make Play-Doh with Nolan' and 'Sing the ABC song with Sean' and 'Go to the park.' When I thought about how my day had gone, it was easier to overlook the laundry I hadn't done, because I was so proud of what I had done with the kids!"*

Try to respond to interruptions in a positive manner, both verbally and with your body language. Hopefully your child will feel he's getting through to you.

■ *Gail was tidying up the kitchen when her son, Joshua, began begging to play a game immediately. Gail found that Joshua was more patient when she momentarily stopped what she was doing, bent down to make eye contact with him, and responded, "I can play just as soon as I finish sweeping." She noticed, on the other hand, that when she kept sweeping and said, "No, I can't play now. I'm busy!" it just generated repeated whining and interrupting.*

Watch for signs that your child has had enough and really needs you before he starts a series of rude, embarrassing interruptions. Is he lying down on the floor or hanging on your leg like an extra appendage? If so, it's probably time to set aside your needs and tend to his.

■ *Tonya was jotting down a list of errands a mile long when the baby-sitter called to say she had strep throat. Needless to say, Tonya was upset. She now had to regroup for a round of errands with Mikie, her very active three-year-old. The first step was to wisely reduce her expectations and cut her to-do list in half. Things went quite well until their last stop, at the post office. Both mother and son were beat, and Mikie began to whine and pull on his mom's skirt. Instead of heeding the warning signs, Tonya continued standing in the long line. Then it happened: All eyes were suddenly on Tonya, who (from the waist down) was standing at the post office window in nothing but her underwear! Mikie had pulled his mom's wraparound skirt straight to the floor! And it worked: he finally got her (and everyone else) to pay attention!*

If you promise your child a time when you will be able to listen, be sure to keep your promise. (For example, "when I'm done washing the dishes," "right after I close the window," "when you talk politely"). Remember, kids take what you say quite literally. Before you promise you'll be there "in a minute," make sure that's exactly what you mean—not ten minutes.

the bottom line

It is difficult for young children not to be the center of attention; with lots of practice and patience, you can help them become more considerate of others as they learn that sometimes it's necessary to wait in order to be heard.

listening

Q: My daughter doesn't listen to me. She seems to ignore almost everything I say, even if I scream or threaten her. How do I get her to listen?

A: Almost all children, from time to time, demonstrate selective hearing. Young children don't do well with long, rational explanations. Logic simply isn't important to them, so keep it "short and sweet" when giving your child instructions, rules, requests, commands, and explanations. Set a tone that's conducive to compliance by putting yourself on your child's side rather than at his throat. By acknowledging his feelings, you let your child know that his opinions matter to you and that you understand his perspective. Then, he is more likely to really hear what you are saying.

sanity savers

When you have something important to discuss with your child, take advantage of spontaneous moments, when she seems relaxed and able to "tune in" to what you are saying. Bedtime, bath time, or even time in the car together all offer such opportunities.

■ *Although carpooling to school really seemed convenient, Katie decided not to participate. She recognized that she really enjoyed spending this ten-minute period twice a day with just her own kids. Over the years many good laughs and memorable moments occurred during that time.*

Realize that your choice of words and tone of voice can make a big difference in getting your kids' attention and cooperation.

■ *Gail was embarrassed to realize how she'd often overlook giving her kids the same simple courtesy that she would give to any stranger. As her five-year-old stumbled out of bed each morning, her first instinct was usually to bark, "Hurry up! It's late! Brush your teeth! Eat your cereal! Get dressed!" One morning, she consciously took the time to choose her words very carefully. As she stroked her son's cute, tired little face, she said, "Good morning, honey . . . still sleepy? It's toothbrushing time." He smiled back and yawned as he headed for the bathroom on her first request. It was amazing how this kinder approach set the tone for the whole day!*

Check It Out

→ **If your child seems to have consistent problems hearing (and not just hearing *you*), have a pediatrician check her hearing periodically to make sure there is no chronic infection, fluid, wax buildup, or other physical condition responsible for her "not listening."**

Get near your child and stroke her arm as you establish eye contact before speaking. While it may seem to you that your child is purposefully ignoring you, a young child often becomes so totally immersed in what she is doing that she really may not hear you at all.

State clearly and specifically what you would like your child to do.

■ *Keith, a caring dad, found it was a lot more helpful to replace general commands like "Clean up this messy room" with specific requests such as "Please put the dolls on the shelf."*

Rely on "I" statements to get your point across. (See page 15 for more on "I" statements.)

■ *When Audrey lost it and screamed, "Why are you so lazy? You'd better pick up those books!," her kids just got defensive and blamed each other instead of picking up. When she learned to calmly and honestly tell her kids, "I'm angry and disappointed. I asked you both to put the books away and they are still on the floor," she got more cooperation.*

Avoid starting your sentences with the three "red flag" words—"If," "You," and "Why"—parent educator and author Nancy Samalin suggests. "If" is threatening; "You" signals an attack on his character; and "Why" demands that a child explain himself, when he rarely can.

■ *Sally learned to say, "The room needs cleaning up now," instead of "If you don't start cleaning up, you'll be sorry!"*

take heart

♥ *You're not the only parent who, in the heat of the moment, angrily reverts to threats like "If you do that one more time, I'll . . . , I'll think of something!" We've all been there.*

■ *Instead of an angry accusation that got no response like "You are so clumsy! Look how you spilled your drink from the refrigerator all the way to the table!" Martin calmly suggested a solution to the problem and got cooperation by saying, "We've got a trail of milk on the floor; here are some paper towels to clean it up."*

■ *Jackie never got a satisfactory answer when she demanded to know, "Why did you punch your sister? Why can't you remember the rules?"*

Give a warning five minutes before asking your child to clean up, leave the house, get dressed, brush her teeth, or come to dinner.

■ *Cheryl got her kids' attention by saying, "Almost time for hot dogs! When the timer rings, please wash your hands before we all sit down to eat."*

Break tasks into smaller steps, give directions one at a time, and give your child the time to complete one request before you pile another on another.

■ *Kevin said to his son, "Time to go! Put your coat on!" His son replied, in frustration, "But I haven't finished brushing my teeth yet! You just told me to brush my teeth. Can't you see I only have two hands!" (a phrase he'd often heard Kevin say).*

Get your point across with fewer words.

■ *Dan found that the kids responded better to a short and simple "Shoes on!" than to a tirade of "Oh my gosh! Five minutes until school starts. Johnny, do you hear me? Where are your shoes? Get your shoes on this minute!"*

Use visual and auditory cues instead of words to get the kids' attention.

■ *The Mason family hung a chart in the front hallway with pictures of coats, hats, backpacks, mittens, and books to remind their kids of what they needed for school.*

Refrain from lecturing or long explanations. Very young children respond best to directions that are short, clear, and to the point.

Try a simple note (or even pictures) to convey your message.

■ *Geoff wrote the words "Let's go" next to a drawing of a car, folded it into a paper airplane, and whizzed it into his five-year-old son's bedroom.*

Try whispering or singing instead of shouting. Some children actually listen more carefully when they can hardly hear you. Singing silly songs, or even using a singsong voice, often captures a child's attention.

If you want to get your child involved in taking the initiative, try substituting a question for a command.

■ *Caroline found that calmly asking "Sean, what do you need to take to school today?" worked better than "Hurry up! It's Tuesday. Go get those library books right now!"*

When time is of the essence, see if your child will rise to the challenge of "Beat the Clock" by saying, "I'll bet you can't put your coat on before the timer rings." Or invite him to race with you (then, of course, let him win!).

Replace words with action. Take the child by the hand and lead her to the task that needs to be done. Kids sometimes need parents to help them get started.

Validate your child's feelings. Children are often more compliant when they feel understood.

> ■ *Dean told his kids, "I see how tired you are. You've been yawning all morning. It's hard to get ready to go when you'd rather stay home. Oh well, tomorrow's Saturday and there's no school, but right now you need to put your shoes on."*

Ask your child to repeat, in his own words, what you just said. This will let you know whether he has clearly understood you and will help him remember.

Use the "broken record" technique: In a calm voice, keep repeating the direction to the child, without raising your voice, until she gets the message and accomplishes the task.

> ■ *Inam was teaching Braille to an impatient blind child who couldn't stop asking, "What are we going to do next . . . huh? What are we going to do next?" Inam's student finally got the message after listening to the calm request four times, "Put the paper in the 'Brailler' and then I'm going to tell you what to do next."*

Stay close by to make sure that your child is on track; remember, young children get distracted easily. Commands shouted from another room are more easily ignored.

> ■ *Jan had no success when she sent her two boys, aged four and five, upstairs to wash their hands before dinner. If they made it into the bathroom at all, they often filled the sink with bubbles and started making a mess. Mom found that when she accompanied them into the bathroom and asked, "Now, what did we come in here to do?" the boys hopped straight to the task of washing their hands.*

Praise your child's effort as soon as he begins to do what you asked and compliment him when the task is done—be specific, and keep it brief! (See page 240 for more on praise pointers.)

Hold regular family meetings, in which everyone in the family gets a turn to talk while everyone else practices listening. (See page 17 for more on family meetings.)

Remember that listening is a two-way street, and model the desired behavior. Give your child a powerful example by stopping what you are doing and really listening to him when he talks to you.

Try to focus on what your child is telling you rather than on responding quickly. Try not to finish his sentences for him or correct his grammar.

> ■ *It was important for Wendy to get the dishes done right after lunch, but three-year-old Ned always interrupted her. He never seemed satisfied with her short but polite answers. Exasperated, one day she set aside the dirty dishes and gave him five minutes of her complete attention. To her amazement, after their little "eye-to-eye" chat, he wandered off contentedly and didn't bother her again for a long time. She got the dishes done faster by taking the time to really listen to him first.*

If you find you're repeating yourself over and over, your child may already have learned to tune you out. Change your communication style; it's simply not working.

If you must speak while your child is talking, use neutral, one-word responses. Often sympathetic silence is all a child needs to feel understood. Interjecting with questions and advice sometimes turns them off.

■ *Fran changed her communication style. She tried acknowledging the fact that she heard her child with a single word instead of asking questions and offering advice. She found that a simple "Hmmm . . ." or "Ah . . . " or "Oh . . ." really encouraged her child to keep on talking.*

Keep in mind the words of parent educator Kay Willis, a mother of ten children and the author of *Are We Having Fun Yet?* She reminds us that "God gave us two ears and only one mouth for a reason. Listen twice as much as you talk!"

the bottom line

Ironically, if you want your child to tune in to what you are saying, you will probably need to talk less. Remember—good communication involves listening as well as talking, so become a parent who sets the example!

lying

Q: My wife and I don't want to let our two-
and three-year-old daughters get away with
lying, but punishing them when they tell a fib
seems to do no good. How do we get them to
tell the truth?

A: Lessons in honesty are best taught
when you make it easier for a child to tell the
truth, rather than try to catch her in a "lie"
and punish her for it. Keep in mind that a
young child's perception blurs the difference
between reality and fantasy, and colors what
she says. A child often fantasizes to get around
what she can't have, do, or be in reality. And a
child's memory is not perfect; sometimes she
may get confused or forget what happened.
Many toddlers actually think that by simply
denying they did something bad, the misdeed
disappears and they are able to avoid any
consequences and remain "good." Although
telling untruths needs to be appropriately
addressed, it is important to realize that a
toddler is usually not lying in the premeditated
(or often malicious) adult sense of the word.

immediate response

➜ Confront a child's lie calmly and in a factual manner, without attacking his character. For example, if it is obvious that your child ate a brownie, but he or she denies eating it, say, "I'm disappointed you ate the brownie without permission."

➜ Say to the child, "Tracy, it's important for you to tell Mommy or Daddy the truth so we can help you solve the problem."

➜ Make it easier for your child to tell the truth by avoiding accusations and angry confrontations. If you're looking for a confession, it's not helpful to say, "Look what you did! You knocked the vase over again, didn't you?" You may have more success with, "Something happened to the vase. How did it get on the floor? I wonder . . ."

sanity savers

Address your child's lie by calmly stating the facts, without accusations.

■ At the checkout counter, Patrick slyly slipped a package of gum into his pants pocket. Although Pam, Patrick's mom, noticed it out of the corner of her eye, she avoided delivering an angry lecture. She simply said, "That gum does not belong to you." Patrick, caught quite off guard, responded, "Oh, this gum? I took it from home." Pam replied, "Patrick, the gum belongs to the store; we didn't buy it. Please put it back on the shelf." Then she calmly but firmly took his hand and physically helped him put the package of gum back in its spot on the shelf.

How Does a Two- to Five-Year-Old Think?

A young child's immature thinking is rooted in his perception of the world as directly relating to his own needs, desires, and experiences. He focuses on what he can see rather than what can be deduced. And, although *you* clearly understand a concept, there are some things, no matter how you try to explain them, that a young child just won't get.

The following examples illustrate specific facets of children's immature thinking ability:

→ **They believe that things happen just for them.** One child thinks that it started to rain just so he could try out his new umbrella. Another thinks that while she is observing the lion at the zoo, it roars for no other reason than to let her know it wants to eat her.

→ **They often take things very literally.** One four-year-old actually keeps looking for the "eyes" in the back of Mom's head!

→ **They display the beginning signs of empathy.** The two-year-old offers her bottle to her crying mother.

→ **They use their imagination to serve their own needs.** Sometimes a child will blame her misdeeds on an imaginary friend, thereby remaining "good" in her own mind.

→ **They have little understanding of the abstract words that quantify units of time** (such as minutes, hours, days, weeks, yesterday, tomorrow, soon, later). One child finally understood that Daddy would be coming home from his trip in two days when Mom said, "Your dad will be back home with us after 'two sleeps'" (a concrete activity the child could relate to).

→ **They often give an honest answer—but to a question that is not exactly what you were asking.** Right before everyone sits down to dinner, Dad asks his son, "Did you wash your hands?" The child replies, "Yes, Daddy, I did" (not a lie . . . however, it was done yesterday!).

→ **They determine quantity by how things look to them.** A three-year-old perceives that a row of ten gummy bears lined up touching each other has fewer candies than a row of ten spread apart.

→ **They give human feeling to objects.** One toddler worries that pulling shoelaces tightly will cause them pain.

→ **They often have trouble distinguishing between fantasy and reality.** A younger sister can become quite frightened thinking that her brother has actually turned into a bear after he puts on a full costume with mask.

→ **Many times if children see or hear something on TV, they think it must be true.** One child believes that Superman can really fly, and that Santa comes in and out of his house via the chimney.

→ **Dreams seem as though they really happened.** Monsters and other scaries feel quite real to a young child.

→ **They may blame themselves when someone is hurt, even when it's not their fault.** When Mom's back begins to hurt, one preschooler thinks it was all her fault for "stepping on the crack" on the way to school. Another child feels his misbehavior is the cause of his parents' divorce.

A two- to three-year-old can tell you a lie and be unable to comprehend that his parents know he's not telling the truth. A child this age is often unable to take into account the perspective of others. See the box on pages 181 to 182 for illustrations of how two- to five-year-olds think.

■ *When he was two-and-a-half years old, Stevie accidentally knocked a glass of milk over on the breakfast table, then dropped his head in thought for a few seconds. Mom, Dad, and his older sister, Missy, were at the table. Then all of a sudden Stevie sat up very straight and exclaimed, "I didn't do it! Missy did it!" At Stevie's developmental stage, his denial made it seem to him as if it had never happened. Furthermore, he was unable to comprehend that because his parents had seen what happened they already knew without a doubt that he was the culprit.*

take heart

♥ *You're not the only parent whose first reaction is to angrily burst out, "What kind of a fool do you take me for?" or even crack up in a fit of laughter because your child's story sounds so ridiculous to you!*

Resist the temptation to ask questions to which you already know the answers. Realize that most children (as well as adults) detest being interrogated, especially in a condescending way.

Is It Really a "Lie"?

What appears to be a lie may actually be a child's fantasy, imagination, or age-appropriate perception of the world. Listen carefully and try to determine whether your child is stating his beliefs or telling an out-and-out lie.

■ Tina was quite upset to receive a call from her daughter's preschool teacher, who shared some thoughts with her about Amber's misbehavior, making Tina extremely anxious. However, when Amber arrived home, Tina took a deep breath and composed herself. She realized that her usual litany of questions: "Did something bad happen today? Are you in trouble again?" often caused her daughter to lie about events. Instead, Tina chose an approach that worked much better. She began the conversation by saying, "Amber, your teacher told me that you punched Sam on the playground. It sounds like you must have been very angry to do that. Let's talk about it."

Avoid asking questions in "the heat of the moment" if you're trying to get honest answers; save the conversations for a family meeting or a private planned discussion with your child. (See page 17 for an explanation of how to hold a family meeting.)

■ It was not unusual for Sal to find an empty potato chip bag on the kitchen counter. Not surprisingly, he never got a straight answer when he screamed, "Who ate this entire bag of chips before dinner?" Finally, he decided to call a family meeting where this issue could be calmly discussed from all points of view. The meeting started with Sal expressing his feelings: "Guys, I'm kind of disappointed you didn't tell me you were hungry instead of eating snacks without permission. Let's make some rules about eating snacks in our house." Everyone had a turn talking until they had all agreed on a plan.

The way you phrase your questions may be setting your child up to lie. Threatening children with punishment gives them very little incentive to tell the truth.

■ *The only response Raul got from the boys when he said "Okay! Someone's in big trouble now! Who smeared the blue paint all over the wall in the hall?" was guilty faces and a round of finger-pointing.*

Acknowledge and praise your child for telling the truth, especially when the temptation to lie is great.

■ *When Carl found the broken vase on the living room floor, he asked his four-year-old son, Jason, if he knew what had happened. Jason admitted he had accidentally bumped into the coffee table and knocked the vase over. Carl responded, "I know it was hard to admit that you broke the vase. I admire the way you told the truth. Now let's talk about how we're going to replace Mom's vase."*

Consider it quite normal for a two- to five-year-old to tell some "tall tales." There is no need to call this storytelling "lying" if there is no intent to mislead someone.

■ *Eddie overheard his creative, wishful daughter whisper to her playmate, "Do you know what my daddy did yesterday? He brought home one hundred teddy bears just for me! And guess what? He's going to add a new room onto our house just for them to live in!"*

Denying the presence of a child's imaginary friend, though, is not helpful in distinguishing fantasy from reality, because the friend feels real to the child.

■ *Four-year-old Christina was usually accompanied by her imaginary friend Megan, and*

almost always blamed Megan for the "bad stuff"
she had done. Mom said, "I wonder if Megan
sometimes gets blamed for things you do. There's
'naughty and nice' inside everybody. Maybe
sometimes Megan does good things and
sometimes Christina does bad things but says it's
Megan." Then she asked, "Christina, what do you
think the consequence should be when Megan
makes a bad choice?" This approach opened the
door to a discussion of Christina's actions and
appropriate consequences.

As your child grows, and as the opportunities
present themselves, gradually and gently begin the
process of pointing out the difference between
fantasy and reality. Your child's fantasies may
seem very real to her, and she may genuinely
believe that something she tells you that happened
in her make-believe world is true.

Recognize that a young child's conscience
develops gradually. Until it does, you cannot
expect him to consistently tell the truth (or even
consistently remember the rules while out of your
sight).

■ While in his mother's presence, two-and-a-half-
year-old Jeremiah seemed to remember the rule
not to touch the brand-new TV. When Evelyn
stepped out of sight for a moment to answer the
phone, she returned to find the TV was on a
different channel. When she asked Jeremiah
about this, he confidently looked her straight in
the eye and said, "No, not me, Mama . . . no, NO!"

■ Sylvia called her dad over, pulled him down to
the floor, and carefully covered his eyes with her
chubby hand. Then, with her free arm, she

*grabbed a crayon from her pocket and scribbled
all over the wall! She really seemed to believe
that if her dad didn't see her write on the wall,
she had done nothing wrong, and she denied
doing it.*

Acknowledge a child's feelings as you help her distinguish between fantasy and reality.

■ *When Emma came home from Michael's
birthday party, she exclaimed, "Mommy, Mommy,
guess what? Instead of treat bags, we each got
our own puppy to take home!" Her sympathetic
mom responded by saying, "Oh honey, I can see
how much you wish you had gotten a puppy."*

Observe your child's body language for cues that he knows he's "bending the truth."

■ *Dr. Burton White, renowned child psychologist,
advises: "When you notice a curve in the corner
of your child's mouth that is almost, but not
quite, a full smile, your child's thinking process
has matured and he understands not only that he
did indeed misbehave but also that he isn't
telling the truth about it." (This often starts at
about three years of age.)*

Some children lie because they are afraid the truth will disappoint their parents, and they want to avoid punishment.

■ *When Mrs. Klein returned the worksheets to her
kindergarten students, Jason's heart sank. He had
red marks all over his paper indicating each
mistake. He thought his parents would be very
upset, so he crumpled his work into a ball and
shoved it deep into his pocket. When he got*

home, he chose to lie. "No papers today, Mom. We just played all day long!" Later that evening, while sorting the laundry, Mom found the incriminating paper. She carefully contemplated how she would approach the lie. Then she called Jason over to join her. As she put her arm around him, Mom explained, "Honey, I want you to know I found your worksheet. I noticed you did a great job on this part. You know, when I was your age, I often got red marks just like this on my paper. My mommy loved to show me how to fix them. Let's go over the red marks on your paper together, okay?"

Model responsibility for your children by taking ownership of your own mistakes and failures and by making amends when needed. Take the time to explain what you learned from them.

When you allow and acknowledge your child's negative feelings (but not his negative behavior), you will be perceived as an ally; then he will be more comfortable telling the truth. He will also have the great benefit of feeling understood.

Realize that your child has not become a pathological liar by telling a few lies.

Be aware that excessive lying is often the fallback of a child used to harsh punishment or the pressure to please adults who hold inappropriate expectations.

Avoid punishments that not only don't work but also tend to invite lying; focus on solving the problem by helping your child change his behavior.

■ *Moira's son kept forgetting to bring home his sweatshirt from preschool. Every day she would ask the same question "Jake, did you bring your sweatshirt home?" (Of course, she already knew the answer.) One day Jake lowered his head and mumbled defensively, "The teacher gave it to someone else." Moira controlled the desire to blurt out "That's a lie, just like yesterday. No TV again this afternoon and, in fact, no TV until you bring that sweatshirt home!" Instead, she got a grip on herself and calmly said to Jake, "You really need your sweatshirt. How about pinning a note on your backpack to remind you to bring it home tomorrow?" Jake thought for a moment, then responded excitedly, "Hey, Mom, let's tie a string around my finger to help me remember. Bert [from Sesame Street] did that when he kept forgetting to buy some oatmeal!"*

Concentrate on finding solutions instead of placing fault or blame.

■ *After taking a parenting course, Kathy learned to avoid saying to her daughter, "You told me you were putting away your toys, but you lied to me again! They're still out! I can't believe this . . . what have you been doing? Now we're going to be late, and it's your fault!" Instead, she tried this approach, aimed at immediate cooperation: she established direct eye contact with her daughter and said, "I notice the toys are still out, and we only have a few minutes left. I've got an idea. You put the videos on the shelf, and I'll put the action figures in the bin."*

Remember, kids usually take what you say quite literally. Even a slight change in what you promise may feel to a child like a "lie."

■ *Ray promised his daughter a trip to the toy store right after preschool. As soon as he turned left instead of right at the light, Patsy shouted, "Wait a minute! You're going the wrong way. You*

take heart

♥ You're not the only parent who, at breakfast, exuberantly promises to play floor hockey with your kids before bedtime . . . only to find yourself "too pooped to party" after a hard day at work. Squelch the guilt when your kids call YOU a liar! This is a great chance to say you are very sorry you disappointed them (a lesson that parents are not perfect), reschedule the activity, and keep that promise.

said we were going to the store." Ray casually replied, "We will. We're just stopping at the cleaner's on the way." Patsy turned red and sputtered, "You said we'd go to the store RIGHT after school. You lied!"

Think twice about totally letting the child "off the hook" for admitting to the truth. He still needs to be held responsible for his actions. Let him know you're available to help figure out a plan to make things right.

Share with your kids a time when it was hard for you to tell the truth. Explain how you decided to accept the consequences by being honest and telling the truth.

the bottom line

There are many reasons for a child to lie, but your positive example, thoughtful reactions, and understanding can help your child gradually come to realize that honesty really is the best policy.

manners

Q: My daughter isn't shy, but when I introduce her to new people she rarely acknowledges them with a hello. In fact, this often happens when we run into friends of mine on the street. I wonder if I should insist that she treat adults with respect?

A: Greeting adults respectfully is certainly something we'd all like our children to learn. While you wouldn't want to force your child to say hello, you continually have the opportunity to teach good manners. Such positive discipline strategies as modeling the proper behavior, role-playing a polite greeting, and occasionally speaking on behalf of a shy or uncooperative child really show your children what is acceptable.

sanity savers

Realize that learning to use good manners is a process that takes time and practice.

Work on just one or two matters of etiquette at a time with your kids. There's a whole spectrum to choose from, including how to greet adults and other kids, how to say good-bye, saying thank-you, using tissues, proper restaurant etiquette, as well as manners associated with receiving and giving gifts. (See "Gimmes," page 130, "Mealtime," page 198, and "Values," page 317, for more on manners.)

Treat even the youngest child with respect. Make eye contact, pay attention when the child speaks, and treat his belongings with care and respect.

Prepare your child by explaining in a noncritical manner what the expected behavior will be. It's a mistake to take for granted that a child knows the rules.

Avoid rude behavior by explaining to your kids what they *can* do in certain situations. For example, when you are temporarily busy, tell them they can draw a picture, look at a book, etc.

Agree upon an acceptable way the kids can get your attention if they really need you. (See the section titled "Interrupting," page 163, for more ideas.)

Teach your children to use polite words and phrases like "please," "thank you," and "excuse me." Realize that, if heard often enough, these phrases can become "second nature."

Compliment your children when they are polite.

Modeling good manners for your child is often your most powerful teaching tool. (Children tend to do what you do, not what you say.) It's even more difficult to teach your kids to be considerate when occasionally you or your spouse are not!

Rehearsing, role-playing, using puppets, and telling stories can reinforce lessons about manners for your preschooler in a fun way. For example, if you allow your kids to talk on the phone, teach them the proper way to do it. (See page 25 for more on role-playing.)

■ *Whenever Gail's mother-in-law called, she wanted to talk to her grandson for a couple of minutes. Although two-and-a-half-year-old Aaron eagerly grabbed the phone, he often put the wrong end to his ear and even thought that by holding it up, as if it were a periscope, Grandma could "see" what he was talking about. Aaron often got distracted and literally left poor Grandma "hanging." So from time to time, mother and son practiced together how to talk on a play phone. Gail taught Aaron how to say good-bye and hang the phone up just right.*

Encourage your child to show off all those manners he's been practicing at home when he's out. (See "Mealtime," page 198, for more on table manners.)

■ *Donna didn't expect her kids to have perfect manners at home; home is where they all relaxed and had fun correcting each other. However, they agreed as a family to really try to use their best manners in public. She knew things were sinking in when her friend raved about how polite her son was as a dinner guest.*

Pass on a compliment that you were told about your child to your child.

■ *"Kurt's mommy told me that she loves having you play at their house. She thinks you have such nice manners, especially when you help clean up the toys without being asked before you go home."*

Consider speaking on behalf of your young child if he is very shy or temporarily defiant. Chances are, a reluctant child who is forced to speak won't do a very good job of it anyway. In that case, it's better to model the behavior you hope to instill.

■ *Caroline's three-year-old son literally "bowled over" the toddler next door as he ran haphazardly with both arms stretched out, screaming, "Look Mommy, I'm an airplane!" Caroline's first instinct was to grab her son and demand an apology. Choosing to avoid a power struggle, instead she picked up the little girl and within earshot of her son said, "Are you all right? Oh honey, he's sorry. He knows better than to play so wildly around others."*

■ *Debra found it was a lot easier for her to simply say "thank you" to the hostess for both of them rather than to repeatedly demand that her sobbing, tired child utter the words herself.*

Be forewarned: Your kids will always notice if *you* slip up and do something you've asked them not to do, like not talking about someone behind his or her back. (At least they were listening!)

take heart

♥ *You're not the only parent who's ever been immersed in some really juicy gossip about the new neighbors only to realize that your preschooler is taking it all in . . . after all, we're only human.*

Teach your kids to respect the fact that families differ in style. Decide which manners are important in your family.

■ *Lucy noticed that when Tony, her neighbor's four-year-old, came over to her house, he kept telling her son, "Sam, I get to choose what we do . . . I get to go first . . . I'm the leader . . . remember, I'm the guest." After a while it really got to Lucy. Her son didn't understand the courtesy of "the guest always comes first" and was literally reduced to tears. So she sat the boys down and explained that, in Tony's house, the guest always goes first, but in their house, they take turns going first.*

Consider appropriate ways to address the bad manners exhibited by visiting children (especially tricky in the presence of their mother). You may decide to "let it slide" and discuss the undesirable behavior with your own children later. Or you may choose a more direct approach and have a heart-to-heart discussion with everyone about the rules and expectations in *your* house.

Discuss with your friends and relatives the names or forms of address they prefer. Decide whether words like "Aunt," "Mr.," "Miss," and "Doctor" are appropriate. Explain to your child that using certain titles can show respect or affection.

Keep in mind that young children are very self-centered and uninhibited. A child may need help to know when being courteous takes precedence over being honest. Learning discretion takes time.

■ *One day, in a packed elevator, three-and-a-half-year-old Ginny wanted to bring something to her mother's attention. Unfortunately, she chose not to whisper and instead blurted out, "Mommy, that man is really fat!" Carol felt her face flush with embarrassment. The truth was, the man was fat, and Carol just couldn't think of anything appropriate to say. It seemed like an eternity until they reached their floor. At bedtime that night, Carol and Ginny talked about the "fat man" incident. Carol explained that some words hurt people's feelings and "fat" was one of them. She told Ginny that her grandmother used to say,*

"Know it . . . don't say or show it!" to help her
remember that some things were best not to be
talked about in public.

Before you reprimand your unruly child in public,
consider your options. Realize that your reaction
to your child may create an even bigger
disturbance than he was creating!

■ *Mary used to be very uptight and demanding*
about the way her son behaved in church. She
insisted that they sit up straight without talking.
However, all eyes frequently fell upon her as she
loudly and frequently shushed him. So Mary and
her son agreed on a plan ahead of time. When her
preschooler began to whine and nudge her arm in
church, he would be allowed to lie down on the
pew and suck his thumb while Mary rubbed his
back. Mary realized that her being more flexible in
her expectations meant less disruption for fellow
worshipers and a happier child.

Realize that your child may need some time to
become comfortable with people he doesn't see
often. Think twice before you decide to disregard
his feelings in the name of manners.

■ *Caroline remembers, "I used to cheerfully go*
along with coaxing my reluctant, clinging toddler
into kissing my brother whenever he demanded
it. One day, though, I had a vivid flashback to my
own childhood. My dad used to take my sister
and me to the nursing home to visit my Dad's
great-aunt. Although she was a sweet old lady, I'll
always remember shutting my eyes when she
asked my dad to bring us closer to her so she
could kiss my cheek. She had a large mole,
sprouting three long silver hairs, and I just
couldn't bear the thought that it might touch me.
After reflecting on my own experience, I realized

it was actually disrespectful to my child to insist that he kiss his uncle. So, instead I encouraged Uncle Noel to be patient and to say 'Nolan, I'd love to get a hug when you're ready.'"

Praise your child when he uses good manners. (See page 240 for more on praise pointers.)

the bottom line

Good manners never go out of style. People always appreciate courtesy and respect; at the same time, your child will gain social confidence by knowing how to act in various situations.

mealtime

Q: Mealtime is a constant battle with my daughter! The eating part, that is. The food she loved yesterday, she hates today, but of course it manages to show up in her hair and all over the dog. How do I keep my child well fed while staying sane in the process?

A: From time to time almost every kid simply refuses to eat, and not just because he doesn't like the food being offered. Some kids lose it when you can't put their broken cookie back together. Other kids have a fit when the melting red Jell-O turns the edge of the hot mashed potatoes pink. While it's up to the parent to provide a child with nourishing food, accept the fact that you really cannot *make* your child eat.

sanity savers

Be prepared for messy eaters. They really "get into" their food. (This is where a dog definitely can come in handy!)

■ *The Goldbergs resorted to dressing their "hands-on" toddler in only a diaper at mealtime. When the meal was over, Mom carefully lifted her*

*son out of the high chair and put him straight
into the bathtub, while Dad and the five-year-old
cleaned up the kitchen.*

Consider serving a variety of foods, one at a
time, to keep a young child "tuned in" to eating.

■ *Belinda, a smart mother of four kids, stopped
giving her two-year-old twins each one plate of
assorted food, since they both usually dumped
them on the floor within five minutes. Instead,
when it looked like the Cheerios were about to go
flying, she'd take them away and give the kids
bits of cheese. As enthusiasm for the cheese
waned, she'd bring out the cut-up fruit; then the
small pieces of chicken. The curious twins spent
several minutes exploring the touch, texture, and
taste of each food as it was offered separately.*

Keep servings on a small scale. Kids often find
small amounts of food served on small plates more
appealing and manageable. And take a tip from
your toddler when it comes to planning meals:
Many people prefer to eat several small, healthy
meals or snacks a day, rather than three large
meals. Some nutritionists even say that's a
healthier way to eat.

Try a creative twist to make "everyday foods"
more appealing.

■ *Terri, a clever mom, found that her kids often
ate foods they had previously refused when they
were given chopsticks or were served food on
thin pretzel "skewers."*

Substitute fruits for "yucky" vegetables, or to
satisfy a sweet tooth.

■ *After Peggy heard her pediatrician say fruits
provided many of the same benefits as vegetables*

and were more attractive to most children, she began offering fresh berries, cut-up pineapple, and dried fruits to her children. Her daughter enjoyed them so much that Mom even convinced Grandma to substitute her usual candy bar treat with a carton of fresh strawberries the next time she came to visit.

■ Randy, a frugal dad, is known for his talent in the kitchen. He whips up any available overripe or leftover fruit into a healthy milk shake made with skim milk, yogurt, or low-fat ice cream. It never turns out exactly the same as the last time, but it's always yummy!

Watch your child's juice intake during the day; too much can really kill her appetite at mealtime.

Keep in mind that at most a fifteen- to twenty-minute meal is all you can realistically expect from a two- to five-year-old.

Establish a few basic rules about mealtime courtesy. Rules can include: eating only at the table, not getting up from the table until finished, asking permission to be excused, bringing plates to the sink, washing hands before or after meals, being kind to the cook, and not burping or slurping at the table.

■ Just as Rachel was about to put a forkful of food in her mouth, Aaron screamed "Yuck! This is disgusting!" Immediately, Rachel's fork, still heaped with food, dropped from her mouth as she repeated her brother's sentiments and refused to eat as well. Gail quickly responded, "You don't have to eat the food, but you may not say bad things out loud about my cooking. It hurts my feelings!"

Try to refrain from advertising the benefits of a new food. The more you talk about it (how healthy it is, how good it tastes), the less some kids will want to try it. They are often uncomfortable with change and quite happy with monotony.

Consider introducing your children to gourmet cooking or foods from other cultures, but include one or more of their favorite foods along with the more exotic dishes.

Realize that you may have to serve a new food several times before your child becomes interested in trying it.

Offer a limited choice to give your child some control over the food he eats.

Let the food pyramid help you introduce basic concepts of good nutrition to your kids. Young children understand concrete information best. If you check out the pyramid on the back of most cereal boxes while the kids are eating, they'll understand the concept better.

> ■ *When Julia's kids asked her if candy is "good for you," she took a cereal box that had a picture of the food pyramid and pointed to the small area at the top that shows we need only a little bit of sweets and fats each day to stay healthy.*

Leave yourself open to new ways to get your kids to enjoy nutritious meals.

> ■ *During a family meeting, Caroline's kids voted to have pizza for breakfast! She was appalled initially, but gave them a chance to convince her. Her oldest son spoke up with confidence. "Look Mom, it's got three food groups all at once . . . it's very healthy!" Caroline thought for a moment,*

then threw her arms up and exclaimed, "You convinced me! Pizza for breakfast!"

Help your kids understand how healthy food builds healthy bodies.

■ *Bart and Bonnie get a kick out of their parents' asking them to flex their muscles to show how strong the chicken is making them. They also enjoy smiling broadly to show their "pearly white teeth" when they drink milk. And from time to time, they look forward to marking their growth on a wall chart in the closet.*

Introduce a policy of zero tolerance for food throwing.

■ *When Colin grabbed a fistful of mashed potatoes and threw them at his sister, his dad said, "Your potatoes are for eating, not for throwing. Lunch is over," and removed him from the table.*

Help your child anticipate when it is time to eat by having a set, daily mealtime schedule.

Expect your child's appetite to fluctuate or even to completely disappear for a time. Children seem to go through cycles that are dependent upon growth spurts, moods, weather changes, or other transitions.

Children occasionally get "stuck on" certain foods. Examine at least a whole week's or even a whole month's eating habits before you allow yourself to worry about deficiencies and malnutrition. Studies show that young children tend to eat a balanced diet over the course of a long-enough period of time, such as a month; however, on a daily basis, they often pick at one or two things.

■ *For some time, two-year-old Drake refused all other food and actually ate nothing but bananas and scrambled eggs. Since both foods were quite healthy, his mom chose to "go with the flow" and reached for the frying pan whenever it was time to eat. In time, of course, he did move on to other foods.*

Accept the fact that sometimes, no matter how hard you try, you won't be able to duplicate even the simplest of treats like someone else can.

■ *To this day, Gail's grown children love what they call "Grammy" apples—Granny Smith apples sliced to perfection and arranged symmetrically, overlapping each other to form a "flower." Each slice is of uniform thickness and peeled in a way that only their grandmother has the patience to do. When Gail or her husband tried to duplicate this presentation, the kids would say, "Nope, that's not the way Grammy does it, it's not on the Grammy plate, and the apples taste sour!"*

Remember that silence can be golden.

■ *When Caroline's three-year-old came to the table full of complaints about the food, she ignored him, directing her attention as well as her body elsewhere. She had discovered that if she didn't remove his food or fix him something else, her hungry son would eventually sheepishly pick up his fork and nibble at his food, sometimes until it was totally gone!*

Recognize that the flavors and textures of some foods may be intolerable to highly sensitive children. These children are extremely sensitive to texture, color, smell, and taste. Even switching brands can totally freak them out . . . so bring on the cereal!

Realize that a child's love or hate of certain foods changes over time and often makes no sense to an adult.

■ *Three-year-old Benny tolerated just about anything if it had a squirt of whipped cream on top—even liver sausage!*

Encourage your child to "listen" to his body and express his appetite by saying "I'm hungry" or "I'm not hungry right now" or "I'm full."

Respect your child's appetite as well as his general likes and dislikes. Getting into the habit of eating only when you are hungry can help everyone stay slim.

Define what mealtime means in your family. For some people, the emphasis is on nutrition; for others, the family social interaction is equally important. If mealtime is unpleasant for everyone, consider changing the status quo to something that works better for everyone.

■ *Kristy, a confident mom, devised a plan that worked. She found peace as well as time to talk at dinnertime by allowing her young kids to eat at 5:30, when their hunger naturally peaked. It was agreed by the whole family that after Mom and Dad ate their dinner at 7 o'clock, the kids would join them at the table to socialize and eat dessert.*

There are lots of different ways to treat mealtime. Decide if it's important to your family that everyone eat the same food at the same time.

■ *One household became a "mini-restaurant." Lou, a laid-back, well-rested dad, agreed to make a hot dog for the youngest child, microwave pizza for the oldest, and prepare a gourmet seafood gumbo for everyone else. (Can he be cloned?)*

■ *"Short-order" cooking was simply out of the question for Lou's neighbor Vicki. Instead, she and her kids shopped together for a "stash" of acceptable alternatives. The kids put the food in an easily opened bin in the refrigerator. If they didn't want to eat the meal that was served, they could select something from the bin and place it on their plate at the table.*

■ *The Tate family served their meals family style. The kids were encouraged, but not forced, to try everything. Even the two-year-old helped himself to what he wanted. The rule was that what they put on their plate, they agreed to eat. If they chose nothing, they knew they could always have a bowl of cereal.*

Give a child a sense of control by allowing her occasionally to take part in planning how, what, and where she will eat.

■ *The Kellers had enjoyed a special picnic in the backyard so much that they continued having "picnics" in the winter on the same blanket, spread on their living room floor.*

■ *Caryn's family made Saturday's dinner "theme night." One week, all the food was one color. Another week, all the foods served were round: meatballs, new potatoes, peas, Brussels sprouts, melon balls, and grapes. It was amazing how most of the food was eaten: the rest must have simply rolled out of sight!*

■ *The Roth clan agreed that one "sweet" per day
would be the rule. When five-year-old Jacob
demanded candy at breakfast, Dad was ready
with a perfect response: "Are you choosing that
as your sweet today?" Jacob gave it some serious
thought and carefully replied, "I guess I'd rather
wait and have chocolate cake after dinner."*

Plan an occasional "formal" dinner to give the
family a chance to practice using their best table
manners.

■ *The Pedersen family discovered that focusing
on table manners and having a polite
conversation twice a month worked better than
when the kids were constantly corrected every
day at every meal. Every other Friday night they
all ate in the dining room, complete with candles
and cloth napkins. For the most part, the parents
used their best manners, but occasionally they
chose to "slip up." Dad would burp and talk with
his mouth full and Mom would forget to use her
napkin, just so the kids could catch them and
have fun reprimanding them!*

Take an honest look at your own eating habits.

■ *A well-meaning mother in Gail's moms and tots
class prepared a very healthy breakfast for her
three-year-old, but her daughter would never sit
and eat. She kept popping up and down from her
chair and snatching a bite every now and then as
she waltzed around the kitchen. When Gail asked
the mom if she, herself, ate breakfast, her emphatic
reply was "I don't have time! I'm always running
around dressing, cooking, cleaning, and organizing
to get everyone off in the morning." Remember—
kids do as you do, not always as you say.*

Fun with Food

Sometimes you can short-circuit the old power struggle by trying something new. Surprise your kids:

→ Freeze seedless grapes.

→ Make "inside-out" sandwiches. (Wrap a slice of meat or cheese around a bread stick.)

→ "Cookie-cut" sandwiches into interesting shapes.

→ Serve frozen "breakfast on a stick"—blend yogurt, fruit, and juice and freeze in Popsicle molds.

→ Offer a vegetable-fruit juice combo like carrot-pineapple.

→ Introduce exotic fruits and vegetables with funny names like ugli fruit (a cross between a grapefruit and tangerine) or okra.

→ Serve crunchy freeze-dried vegetables and fruits.

→ Make smiley faces on the food with ketchup, mustard, or even whipped cream.

→ Switch dinner and breakfast—have tacos for breakfast and pancakes for dinner.

the bottom line

Understanding young children's eating habits, establishing simple rules together, and asking the kids to help solve the problems that arise can keep you relatively sane during mealtime; and remember, this phase too shall pass!

morning "crazies"

Q: Mornings are like a war zone in my home. Everything's a battle! I've tried to stay calm, but cooperation is sparse . . . HELP!

A: Because parents' needs (to be on time, neat, and organized) and children's needs (to live in the moment, be curious, and have fun) are often in conflict, mornings are difficult. In addition, many young children have difficulty with transitions, period. Changing from one thing to another is difficult, even if the next activity is as pleasurable as going out for ice cream. Hang in there and try some of the following tips!

immediate response

→ Validate your child's feelings; children tend to cooperate better when they feel understood. "Jared, I can see you're really upset that we have to leave in the middle of your TV program. Let's record the rest on tape to watch when we come home."

→ Describe what needs to be done with a firm one-word request. Say "Teeth!" instead of "How many times do I have to tell you to brush your teeth?"

→ Have your child get dressed in the bathroom. Kids are so easily distracted by the sights and sounds of siblings, toys, and TV.

→ Play some "hop to it" music, like a march, as part of your morning routine to get everyone going. Or use more soothing music if your child needs to get going slowly.

→ The night before, let your child choose one of his favorite small toys. In the morning, as soon as he is all ready to leave the house, give him the toy to play with in the car.

→ Try to build into your schedule a few minutes for some cuddle time, soft talking, or a favorite song or story to help start the day without stress. (This is not easy to do, but it's well worth the effort.)

sanity savers

Describe the desired action with minimal explanation.

■ *When Anna, a working mom, gave her son a detailed explanation of why she absolutely couldn't be late for an important meeting with her boss, he replied, "I don't care. That's not important to me!" Mom got compliance the next time with a simple statement that related to his world: "Breakfast's ready! It's time to eat."*

Use your sense of humor to get the kids' cooperation. Be specific.

■ *Gail was amazed. As if by magic, just using a silly, funny voice got her kids to cooperate. They*

tuned in better to specific, fun requests like "Pop
your head out of your shirt like a turtle" than to
general hurry-up statements such as "Please get
dressed right now . . . it's very late!"

Engage your child's cooperation by using the
senses of sight, sound, and touch. Bend down to
establish direct eye contact with him and place
your arm around his shoulders before you speak;
chances are he will hear you the first time.

Try the when–then technique.

■ *Elise got quick, cheerful cooperation by saying,
"When you finish your breakfast, then you'll have
time to watch TV."*

Use fantasy and make-believe to gain your child's
cooperation. Relax . . . have fun . . . what seems
silly to you can really get results.

■ *Vera remembers, "It was amazing what my kids
would do for their 'talking' boots: 'Please put your
nice warm feet inside my tummy . . . ooh! That
feels so good!'"*

Offer a "surprise" as soon as the task is done. It
doesn't have to be anything remarkable. In fact,
your labeling it as a "surprise" is usually enough to
make it special.

■ *"Once you get your coats on, we'll look for a
surprise on the way to the car," said one creative
mom. Then she excitedly gathered a couple of
beautiful autumn leaves for each child. "Oh, wow!
Aren't these beautiful?" she cried. "Let's take
these with us and show them to your teacher."*

Avoid setting yourself up for conflict by asking
questions to which the answer "NO!" is not an
option.

■ *Bruno, who was on a tight schedule, told his two-year-old, "It's time to get dressed." He had learned that asking "Are you ready to get dressed now?" would provoke an emphatic "NO!" from the child.*

To speed things up, offer the child only two choices. Open-ended questions often get a blank stare or "I don't know."

■ *Elsa asked her daughter, "Which pants today, the blue ones or the red ones?" She discovered that worked better than asking, "What do you want to wear today?"*

Consider occasionally helping your child get dressed even though he is perfectly capable of dressing himself. When you are all in a rush, it usually isn't the best time to teach independence.

■ *One morning when things weren't moving along, Jerry said to his son, "I'll put on your right sock while you do the left. That's what I call cooperation!"*

Step away for a few minutes when a power struggle is brewing.

■ *Some mornings, Caroline's three-year-old just refused to get dressed. "I learned to walk away for five minutes and do something else that had to get done anyway, like pack a lunch. When I returned, I would bring a toy to distract Nolan while I got him dressed. To my complete amazement, he had forgotten all about the power struggle and easily cooperated." (Every once in a while, a kid's short memory comes in handy!)*

Try a three-step approach for difficult situations or transitions. First, acknowledge your child's feelings. Next, explain what cannot be changed.

Then give something positive for your child to look forward to after he complies.

> ■ *Laura told her kids, "I know you're angry and sad that we have to turn off your TV show, but Mommy cannot be late. I appreciate your helping me be on time. I have a special treat you can eat in the car on our way to school."*

Become an "early bird." Pulling yourself out from under the covers on a freezing, dark winter morning is really a painful thought! But getting up twenty minutes earlier can make a huge difference in how well things go.

Decide on one place to keep your morning "stuff."

> ■ *Caroline remembers, "No matter when we did it, the night before or in the morning, we were always ahead of the game when we put coats, shoes, homework, and briefcases by the door. My kids even started keeping their lunch boxes by the door."*

Be aware that hurrying may get you there on time, but sometimes you pay an unexpected price.

> ■ *Renee shared the following story in Gail's moms and tots class. "One morning when my elderly neighbor attempted to talk to me and my son, my little boy really embarrassed me by interrupting his greeting. 'My mommy said that we're in a big hurry! I just don't have time to be nice today!' he cried."*

Use regularly updated warnings to keep everyone on track. Many kids adjust better with verbal advance warnings than to abrupt departures. Timers can even do the talking for you!

■ Dave found that using a timer helped his son cooperate: "When the timer rings, your TV watching is over. Then please put your shoes on and grab your green jacket. . . . Agreed?"

Use visual and auditory tools to help little ones remember what needs to be done.

■ Five-year-old Seth colored a chart listing the things he needed for school (teeth brushed, shoes, coat, backpack) and hung it by the door. He took pride in getting himself ready without reminders.

■ Stephanie found a way to communicate a pleasant morning message and at the same time saved herself from shouting commands (that were never heard) over and over. The night before, she would tape-record a positive message such as "Hi, Allie. I'll bet you remembered today is library day and your book is all ready to go." Four-year-old Allie looked forward to pushing the button and listening to her mommy.

Put first things first.

■ Instead of wasting precious time and energy urging the kids on, Gail FIRST got herself completely ready to walk out the door. THEN she dressed the kids and they all left right away. It seemed that the less time the kids had to wait for Mommy, the less fuss there was getting out the door.

Do things together as a "family team."

■ *On the other hand, Magda found it easier to keep the kids on track when she washed her face and brushed her teeth with them . . . even singing silly toothbrush songs in the bathroom together made it more fun for everyone!*

Switch roles with your spouse once in a while for a refreshing change. It can be emotionally exhausting for one parent to always be responsible for getting the kids ready and out the door.

Pull a trick or two out of your sleeve!

■ *When all else fails, try Gail's trick of putting your child to bed in a clean, comfortable sweatshirt and sweatpants . . . voilà! Dressed for the next day the night before!*

■ *Stacy keeps all the clocks in her house ahead by ten minutes. Then when she gets in the car and looks at the dashboard clock . . . wow! She has found a welcome extra ten minutes!*

Make a conscious effort to part on a positive note, keeping in mind that some days get off to a bad start no matter what.

■ *After rushing around one morning, Gigi was upset when she realized how her kids must have felt when they got to school. The next day, with a bit of extra effort, they were able to leave early and had fun talking and playing "step on a crack" all the way to school.*

Undo the effects of those nightmare mornings
with an unexpected call home later in the day.

■ *After an especially hectic morning, Caroline
would call home from work and leave a silly
message on the machine for her kids at the time
she knew they had gone to the park. As soon as
they walked in the door, they'd check to see if the
red message light was flashing. They could play
her message over and over again, and their sitter
said it really cheered them up.*

the bottom line

Adults have a need to be on time, and children
hate to be rushed. But there's no need to rush
them when a little creativity and some advance
preparation can help everyone get off to a good
start.

picking up toys

Q: No matter what I do, there are toys all over the house! How do I encourage my child to put away the things he plays with?

A: Cleaning up is usually not a high priority for children ages two to five, at least at home. Most of the time children's imagination and their need to create and explore conflict with an adult's need to maintain order. However, they are capable of doing it: parents who observe a preschool class picking up the toys at dismissal often wonder, "Could this be my child . . . ?" When confronted with a big job, anyone (but especially a child) feels overwhelmed just deciding where to begin. Breaking cleanup down into small, manageable steps helps.

immediate response

→ **Be specific in your requests. Say "Baseball cards in the little wooden box on the shelf, please" rather than "Clean up this mess this instant!"**

→ Ask an inviting question that helps get the job done: "I wonder who knows where this belongs?"

→ When the job is overwhelming, pitch in yourself. We've all been there: every single bin and basket— *dumped!*

→ Challenge the kids to a race. ("I'll bet you can't put the Hot Wheels away before Dad pulls the track apart . . . ready, set, go!")

→ Use "props" to make the task more fun. The "toy train" (two laundry baskets) chugs along and toots into the room (you provide the "steam") to pick up the toys that need to be put away first.

sanity savers

Realize that constant cleaning up can drive everyone crazy! (If following this tip sounds impossible, maybe it's time to reevaluate your priorities.)

> ■ *Fern wondered how her baby-sitter kept the house immaculate all day. When she was home on maternity leave, Fern discovered the baby-sitter's secret. In fact, she left all the dishes in the sink a good part of the day and cleaned up dishes and toys only once a day, while the kids napped or watched TV later in the afternoon.*

Try setting a daily time to pick up toys. Once your routine is established, it takes the place of constant reminders.

Avoid threats.

> ■ *Caroline found calm specific statements like "Sean, please put the blocks in the red block container" more successful than a threat like*

picking up toys

> "If you don't . . . clean up this mess right now . . .
> you'll really be sorry."

Consider creating a "Ransom Toy Box." Collect
all the toys that are left out and place them in the
box. You then get to decide what happens to the
toys and if and when the kids can get them back.
Talk about this at a family meeting so the kids
understand the predetermined consequences.

Use a warning (such as a verbal announcement
or the buzz of a timer) to help kids get
psychologically ready for cleanup time. They will
clean up better and fuss less.

Help the kids focus on what needs to be done,
then help them get started.

■ *Melinda noticed her kids were much neater in
preschool, perhaps because the teacher was
right there, helping them keep on track. They
tried out the teacher's way and found that if
they took the time to get their kids started
cleaning up, they didn't have to participate the
entire time.*

Take a tip from the preschools and sing a fun
song while picking up the toys. Any simple words
and catchy melody will work.

■ *Here's a simple little gem Gail has used for
years that helps get students' cooperation: "It's
cleanup time, it's cleanup time, everybody help
us. It's cleanup time, cleanup time, let's put the
toys away."*

■ *Caroline's husband and kids enjoyed cleaning
up as they whistled the Seven Dwarfs' favorite
tune, "Whistle While You Work." They always
laughed at Caroline's pathetic attempts to
whistle.*

Play games. Children often find the simplest, silly things fun and motivating.

> ■ *Gail invented a talking garbage can that spoke to her preschool class in an Oscar the Grouch voice. It ate paper scraps and made funny comments the kids loved. "Yum! Good paper, that went straight to my tummy!"*

> ■ *Wayne, a patient dad, put a positive spin on his request: "I'll bet you both remember which color bin the puzzles go in."*

Redirect the attention of a child who is not helping. Point to the toys on the floor and to where they belong, while praising the child who is picking up.

Give a child a specific quota: "Please pick up five things." This is easier to manage than being told to clean up an entire room, and kids enjoy counting the items that they put away. (You may want to add more challenge and drama by counting out loud with the child, especially a two- to three-year-old.)

Say "thank you" to everyone for a job well done. Remember, young children feel no need to clean up . . . it's the parent who has the need for order.

> ■ *After a short discussion, Dawn realized how differently she and her son viewed the toy soldiers all over his bedroom floor. To her, it was a huge mess that he'd forgotten to pick up. To him, it was an exciting battle in progress.*

Consider making a chart where kids get stickers for cleaning up. You might also choose to give the child a special reward after he's earned five stickers.

picking up toys

take heart

♥ You're not the only parent who decides to toss out unmatched toy pieces or "kid's meal" trinkets rather than endlessly sorting them out. Remember, kids are rarely ready to let go of anything if you make a point of asking them, but they usually won't miss what's out of sight.

Don't sweat it if you find yourself quickly putting away the last few toys. Little kids have a limited attention span, and if they've helped you with most of the job, they've done well.

Consider purchasing some inexpensive clear plastic containers to help kids spot the toy they want without pulling everything out and making a mess.

With the kids' help, make picture labels for containers or drawers to help identify what's inside.

Get your spouse involved in the cleanup process so he or she understands the challenge firsthand!

■ Caroline remembers, "When I phoned home while I was out of town visiting my mother, who was sick, Dennis complained, 'I'm really beat! All the kids do is run from room to room making a mess. As soon as I've picked up one room, they've already trashed the next one.' It really helped both of us that he understood just how hard it can be to maintain any kind of order."

Realize that there are different ways of cleaning up; each has its own pros and cons.

■ Some families enjoy quick cleanups, often using one huge toy chest to throw everything into. However, keep in mind that when everything gets thrown in together, toy pieces can get tangled up, broken, or lost.

Try simplifying cleanup by temporarily storing some toys in a big garbage bag out of sight. Your kids will welcome their old "long-lost" toys back (if they even notice any have been missing!).

Keep in mind that your child may have too many toys. Consider giving some away to needy children. (See "Gimmes," page 130, for more on this.)

take heart

♥ *You're not the only parent who agrees with author and pediatrician Marianne Neifert ("Dr. Mom"), who says, "Cleaning up is a cinch . . . as long as your standards are low enough!"*

Use your sense of humor, and resort to handy-dandy warning signs when you just can't keep up.

> ■ *Julie's mother-in-law often just showed up unannounced on her doorstep. Julie would quickly pull the doors shut on any messy rooms. After a while, she got so comfortable doing this, she decided to hang a variety of signs on the doors . . . "Cleanup in progress. Enter at your own risk," "Warning, perfectionists need not enter," or even "Condemned!"*

the bottom line

Teach your kids to help with cleanup. You might also consider redefining just how tidy things really need to be; hopefully, by lightening up a little, you'll find more time to enjoy your kids!

potty training

Q: My friend's two-and-a-half-year-old daughter is completely toilet-trained, but my son, of the same age, doesn't seem at all interested. Is there a "window of readiness" where I need to initiate the process, or can we wait until he's ready?

A: Toilet training in American society has been a controversial issue for a long time. It's a fact that you can't make your child want to use the potty, let alone go on command. However, even if you believe waiting for your child to initiate training is the best method, it's not always easy on *your* nerves. Well-meaning relatives and friends may urge you to "train" your child the way they did theirs. Or you may feel pressured to get potty training over before the birth of another child or before your child starts attending a preschool that simply does not accept students in diapers. This issue can involve feelings of competition, guilt, shame, and embarrassment and can lead to unnecessary power struggles between parent and child. Try to be patient and consider letting your child take the lead, and anticipate some ups and downs along the way.

sanity savers

Note that many experts recommend waiting until your child is at least two and a half before you initiate training.

Look for signs of readiness before you begin potty training. (See box below.)

Discuss with your child ahead of time how "big boys and girls" use the toilet instead of diapers.

Listen to your child for cues about readiness. The training period may be much easier and shorter when the child is motivated to get out of diapers.

Signs of Potty Readiness

→ Your child dislikes being in wet/soiled diapers.

→ Your child announces when he is about to urinate or have a bowel movement.

→ Your child understands the purpose of a potty or toilet.

→ Your child stays dry for a couple of hours between diaper changes or wakes up dry after a nap.

→ Your child has bowel movements at regular, predictable times.

→ Your child is comfortable with and curious about how others use the bathroom.

→ Your child pulls his pants up and down by himself.

Keep in mind that there is a wide age range during which the child is expected to attain complete mastery; experts cite anywhere between two and five years to be normal. Children have different degrees of mental and physical readiness, including such things as muscle control and body awareness.

Invite your child into the bathroom as you or your spouse demonstrate "how to go" and calmly describe what you are doing. Letting a younger child watch older siblings, relatives, or playmates (with their permission) may also set an example.

■ *One little boy was frustrated because he was just a little bit too short to reach the toilet, but using a stool made him too high up. By simply standing on his father's shoes, he discovered he was just the right height to "make pee-pee" in the bowl standing up, just like Daddy!*

Shop together for a potty-chair or a smaller padded seat if you sense your child might be afraid of falling into the toilet. It's pretty scary when a "little bottom" has a sudden splashdown, and it can put the entire toilet-training process on hold for a while.

Dress for success; let him wear sweatpants rather than pants with belts, zippers, buckles, or overalls. It will be a lot easier for you and your child to pull these clothes on and off quickly.

In warm weather, consider taking your nude child and potty-chair into your private backyard. She can then become aware of the sometimes sudden sensation of "having to go" without the risk of peeing on the floor, furniture, or carpeting inside.

Let your child flush the toilet if he wants to. Some children perceive their waste as a precious part of themselves and need time to become comfortable with flushing away their "accomplishment." Others are just so proud they don't want to flush "until Daddy sees," a logistical problem when he's working late!

Help your child clean up after an accident "like a big boy." Have him stand up in the bathroom near the toilet and use toilet paper to clean him, rather than having him lie down to have you do all the work as if he were a baby.

Praise your child. Recognize or compliment such accomplishments as letting you know when he "has the urge," sitting on the toilet even if she doesn't "go," pulling his pants up and down without help, flushing the toilet paper into the bowl, and washing hands.

Sit your child facing backward, straddling the toilet, when no potty seat is available. This keeps him from falling in!

Use positive reinforcement. Chart progress and include rewards. Some families find charts and stickers helpful motivators, as long as they don't get too complicated.

■ *Darla told us of her friend Bonnie, who started potty training her little girl, Anna, quite early. Since she knew Anna was just crazy about sparkly stickers, she found herself buying reams and reams of stickers adorned with Anna's favorite cartoon characters. Over lunch, Bonnie proudly described the system she had devised: "Anna gets one sticker if she sits on her potty, two if she goes pee-pee, three for poo-poo." Then,* to her friend's surprise, Bonnie in all seriousness asked, "Now, how many stickers do you think I should give her if she just passes gas on the toilet?" Too stunned to answer, Darla left that decision up to her well-meaning but somewhat compulsive friend!

Try to "lighten up"—a sense of humor really helps!

■ Rex made little floating bull's-eye targets for his son to aim at. It worked like a charm! (Even a drop of liquid soap in the toilet makes a fun target for little boys.)

Give your child a feeling of control by letting him help decide when he's done with diapers; ask him to stack up how many more diapers he will use before he switches to "big boy pants." Then stack up a couple of pairs of training pants or underwear beside the diapers so he can see what he'll be using when the diapers are all gone. Keep the stacks in sight and remind him often of "the deal." (This idea won't work with all kids, but for a kid who is "almost there" it just might do the trick.)

Anticipate accidents, and when they happen, reassure your child it's okay; and expect lots of laundry for a while.

■ Caroline remembers, "My first instinct, when Nolan came up to me totally covered in poop, was to scream, 'Not again!' But as I looked into his eyes, I was able to compose myself. Taking a deep breath, I managed to say, 'You're doing fine, sweetie. Everyone has accidents once in a while. Pretty soon you'll get to the potty in time.' I noticed a look of relief pass over his worried little face. A couple of days later, he approached me, walking as if he'd been riding a horse for many

Resist punishing your child for an accident or keeping her in soiled clothes to "teach a lesson"; it simply isn't helpful and could be downright traumatic.

Realize that many children may become so enthralled in their play that they ignore the urge to "go," especially if they are outside, far away from the toilet. A timer set at regular intervals might help you remind them without nagging or making a big deal out of it by announcing, "It's potty-break time!" Some families find it helpful to have more than one potty-chair and to station them in different rooms, on each floor of the house, or even outside.

If your child becomes resistant to training, back off. Avoid power struggles. Many experts believe that pushing a child who doesn't want to be trained will only make the situation worse.

Be aware that toilet training, for some children, occurs in stages and requires some understanding and patience from parents. Some children become bladder-trained before they are bowel-trained (or vice versa).

■ *Rose remembers how her brother, Stuart,*
almost five, would use the toilet only to urinate.
"He knew when he was about to have a bowel
movement. He'd sneak off into his corner. If
anyone asked, 'Stuart, do you want to go to the
bathroom? Let's try sitting on the toilet,' he'd
whine, 'Go a-way, go a-way!' as his face strained
and changed color. Nonchalantly, but a bit smelly,

he would suddenly reappear as if nothing had happened, sporting a noticeable bulge." When his parents chose to stop making it a major issue, Stuart gradually, on his own, began having bowel movements in the toilet. Mom and Dad responded with only positive attention and complimented him on his success.

Expect daytime dryness to precede nighttime dryness, in some cases by several months or even several years. (Note: Experts say that "bed-wetting" is not even considered a problem until after age six. For further information, e-mail info@pocketparent.com or visit the web site at www.pocketparent.com.)

Girls usually train earlier than boys (but not always).

Be aware that regression is normal during stressful times such as moves, illness, deaths, divorce, or the arrival of a new sibling. Your understanding and compassion will help your child get "back on track" faster than anything else.

take heart

♥ *You're not the only parent who's ever wanted to strangle the lucky mother who smugly confides, "I simply don't know what all the fuss is about! One day, my daughter just announced, 'No more diapers', and that was that!"*

Consider bringing out the diapers once again if your child regresses. You're not a failure as a parent if you have to put away your daughter's "big girl" undies temporarily. After all, it's probably easier on you to change diapers than to clean up all those accidents.

Consider the pros and cons of "pull-ups." While some families find them to be a handy invention, they are quite expensive and you might wonder if your child is getting mixed messages. If they're really "big boy" pants, why is it okay to "pee" in them? Do they remind your child that he has had an accident, or do they keep him so dry that he rarely notices that he's wet them?

■ One of Caroline's neighbors put her fully trained son in pull-ups for long car trips just in case she couldn't find a rest stop. However, Caroline decided not to use them at all because of the inconvenient cleanup. "I'll never forget standing up in a public bathroom, trying to gingerly rip apart the perforated sides to avoid smearing everything in smelly, runny poop. After that feat, I realized that I still had to take off Sean's shoes, socks, and pants before I could put on another pull-up! What a pain! A conventional diaper would have made my life so much easier."

the bottom line

Stop worrying about it; no matter what, your kids will become potty-trained in due time—well before they "walk down the aisle."

power struggles

Q: My son isn't even five years old yet, and almost everything we do turns into a power struggle. When I caught him reaching into the jar of pretzels before dinner and told him, "No, it's too close to dinnertime. Pretzels will ruin your appetite," he said, "They're fat free!" I said, "It doesn't matter." He said, "When Alex was over, you let us have pretzels right before dinner." I said, "That was a special occasion," and he said, "Why was it a special occasion?," and on and on and on it went. I want to minimize the power struggles, but I feel like I'm dealing with a mini-attorney. Where do I begin?

A: Many common, everyday situations relating to sibling rivalry, mealtime, bedtime, toilet training, picking up toys, or even washing hair and brushing teeth have the potential to turn into real power struggles. As a parent, you have to "choose your battles." Is this an issue you need to address right now? Keep in mind that the words you use to make your wishes known can make a big difference in the way your child responds. When your child feels you're on his side, rather than on his back, tension, anger, and even jealousy can literally melt away. Acknowledging his feelings, even the negative ones, lets your child feel understood. That, in itself, may be comforting enough to avert a power struggle. However, parents also have to decide when to "play judge" with "mini-attorneys" and just lay down the law!

sanity savers

When your child shouts at you, try to avoid shouting back—it only adds fuel to the fire.

Describe exactly what you see . . . and no more!

> ■ *When Stephanie walked into the messy family room, she began fuming. She yelled at her daughter, Emma, "I can't believe you did that again! You're such a pig. Pick up those candy wrappers this instant or you'll be really sorry." Instead of helping, Emma said, "Not now, my program's on." Stephanie was furious. She took a deep breath and realized she had taken the wrong approach. So she left the room for a few minutes to regroup. When she came back into the den, she calmly said, "Emma, I see the candy wrappers are all over the floor. I wonder who knows where garbage goes?" Emma looked up, replied, "In the garbage can, Mommy!' and cheerfully skipped over to throw them away.*

When you state the situation in as few words as possible it's less likely to be tuned out.

Use "I" messages to describe what you feel.

> ■ *"I get upset when I see such a mess."*

State what needs to be done.

> ■ *"Wrappers belong in the garbage can."*

Consider posting notes, signs, or even rhymes to convey your message without all the preaching. Review them with the kids: you'll be amazed that the kids remember the words even if they can't read.

> ■ *"Candy is sweet and a real treat, but not for me unless it's neat," or "If you don't want me to nag, please put the wrappers in the garbage bag!"*

Avoid a power struggle by saying "Yes, as soon as you . . ." instead of the usual "No!"—to get the same point across.

Help guide the child if you decide the job is not getting done to your satisfaction. But also be willing to temporarily lower your standards, in the interest of acknowledging the importance of "the process" rather than the finished product.

Try counting as a way of letting your child know you "mean business" (one-two-three or up to ten). This will not work with every child every time, but it sometimes comes in handy. (It's most effective after you've tried it once already and followed through with a consequence.)

Giving notice or warning before a transition takes place can help to minimize power struggles.

Try not to ask "yes" or "no" questions of your child if a "no" answer is unacceptable (If you do, you've just set yourself up for a power struggle.)

Allow your child to fantasize about what she cannot have in reality.

■ *Hoping to avoid the usual tears and tantruming when it was time to leave the park, one day Nancy tried a new approach. She calmly said to her child, "Janey, I'll bet you wish you could stay at the park all day long!" Janey nodded, with a big grin. "Honey, I can see if you had the time, you would build many sand castles . . . maybe even one hundred, all around the edge of the sandbox!" Taking Janey's hand, as they walked without a struggle to the car, Nancy continued, "You are such a wonderful artist!" (It feels so easy and good when a strategy works!)*

Give your child a way to undo the wrongdoing.

■ *When a frustrated Nolan began screaming because he couldn't make the tower on his castle higher, Caroline calmly gave him a time-out to calm down and added, "I'll be sitting here at the table waiting. When you calm down and can speak to me without screaming or using bad words, come on back and we'll finish working on our castle." As soon as Nolan returned, with a sheepish look on his face, Caroline greeted him warmly, deliberately not mentioning his previous behavior.*

Find a way to help yourself disengage from the beginnings of a power struggle.

■ *One admittedly "hot-blooded" mom and her husband developed a system to help each other out when things started getting out of control with the kids. Whenever Dad noticed that the kids were really pushing Mom's buttons and a battle was brewing, he made a loud sucking noise, to let his wife know she was being "sucked into" a*

power struggle. Mom got the message and usually
stepped out of the room and let her husband
take over. When the situation was reversed, Mom
used the same technique to signal Dad and took
over for him.

■ Literally feeling that she'd been driven to her
wits' end, Laurie paused and said to her
daughter, "I just can't talk to you right now. My
brain is overloaded and needs a rest. I'm going to
lie down for a few minutes . . . alone!"

Barking orders and threats, calling names, and
placing blame usually adds fuel to the fire and
defeats your attempt to avoid a full-blown conflict.
Step back, regroup, and try to analyze the power
struggle objectively.

Keep in mind that when a child is very upset, he
may lash out with some of his most powerful
insults. Limiting his actions is necessary, but
permitting and acknowledging his angry feelings
let him know you understand and helps to defuse
the escalating situation.

Decide to address the issue at a calmer time,
rather than in the heat of the moment. By
choosing not to fight this battle now, a power
struggle is avoided. Hang on to the thought that
the real lesson is taught over time.

Talk about the power struggle later, in a planned,
one-on-one discussion with the child or in a family
meeting where you can revisit the situation and
brainstorm solutions. Remember, learning right
from wrong is a process that takes time.

Allow your child to have input in figuring out
how to correct the situation next time. This helps
her realize that her feelings and opinions matter.

However, keep in mind that you, as the parents, ultimately have the responsibility to make and enforce the rules.

Realize that a child's behavior is usually directed to get your attention. Sometimes it doesn't matter whether you are scolding, screaming, threatening, or criticizing; if the child's need for attention is great enough, the behavior will often persist even though the attention gained is totally negative.

Ask yourself on a daily basis if you are giving more negative than positive attention, and if you are, make every effort to reverse the proportions. Acknowledge those behaviors that you wish to continue and avoid overreacting to those behaviors that you wish would simply go away.

Become aware of your child's temperament and yours. Do your styles complement each other, or do they tend to clash?

> ■ At a lecture, Dr. Ann McCartney, a child psychologist, asked parents to consider "How does your temperament or style fit with that of your child's? Can you see ways that this perhaps makes you more or less tolerant of certain characteristics or behaviors? Be mindful of your parenting 'hot spots' based on your history, and how they impact your expectations."

Think about your own emotional investment in common childhood issues. For example, if it's very important to you that your child be toilet-trained at a certain age, be aware that he may interpret your "enthusiasm" as pressure. This can ignite a "whopper" of a power struggle.

Realize that children go into and out of many developmental stages (in such areas as language,

take heart

♥ *You're not the only parent who's ever felt out of control and found yourself temporarily trapped in an escalating no-win situation with your child.*

small and large motor coordination, and thinking ability); many troublesome issues simply disappear on their own over time.

If you've been using a particular strategy—yelling, bribing, explaining—that just doesn't seem to be working, it's time to try something else!

the bottom line

Remember that in a power struggle there is no winner. As difficult as it can be, when neither you nor your child is thinking rationally, it helps to show some understanding of his perspective in the heat of the moment rather than letting the situation escalate.

self-esteem

Q: What can I do to help nurture a responsible, well-adjusted child who feels good about herself?

A: Over time children develop a sense of exactly who they are and how they "fit into" their world. Children come to value themselves by first feeling valued and loved unconditionally by those who are most important to them. When parents create an environment in which children are loved and valued just the way they are, as they grow up, they become more comfortable voicing their opinions, making decisions, taking chances, and dealing with life's difficulties.

sanity savers

Take the time to give each child your undivided attention for at least a few minutes every day. (See "Listening," page 171, for suggestions on ways to help you really focus on effective communication.)

Let your child know that you recognize and understand how he feels, even when you don't agree with him. Explain that two people can have different feelings. Neither person's feelings are right or wrong. But remember, acknowledging your child's feelings does not mean allowing unacceptable behavior.

> ■ *When George's three-year-old wailed, "But I don't want to brush my teeth," George's first thought was to respond by saying, "Of course you want to brush your teeth. You don't want huge cavities . . . do you?" Instead, he decided to try an understanding but equally firm approach. "I'll bet you'd rather go straight to bed; I can see how tired you really are. But teeth need to be brushed in order to stay healthy," he said as he took his son by the hand and led him into the bathroom.*

Whenever appropriate, ask your child for her opinion (if necessary, offer her a couple of choices that are acceptable to you). This will encourage her to think for herself and know that her input is valued, while giving her a sense of control. (This is especially effective with difficult questions, or when you need some time to consider your own answer.)

> ■ *When Caroline asked her child what he thought they should do next, Nolan enthusiastically responded, "Bikes, Mommy!" She replied with "TA-DA! . . . another good idea by Nolan Patrick Winkler!" After a while, her son felt comfortable saying "I have another good idea, Mommy!"*

Show your children unconditional love. Kids who feel loved and appreciated are more likely to be happier and better behaved.

> ■ *Gabe makes time every day for kind words and what he calls a "just because." Every now and then he gives his sons a hug or treat "just because"—in other words, for no particular*

*reason at all, except that they are lovable. His
love isn't earned or given for good behavior—it's
given unconditionally, even on very bad days.*

Set consistent, firm limits that enable your child
to learn that his world is predictable. This
includes following through with appropriate
consequences for misbehavior. Young children will
test the boundaries many, many times, but they do
actually feel a sense of security knowing that their
parents are in control. (See "Positive Discipline
Strategies" on page 12 for more on the importance
of limits.)

Address your child's misbehavior directly,
without attacking her character.

> ■ *Roberta, a patient mom, got her point across
> by telling her daughter firmly "Hitting is not
> allowed. Sit next to me until you calm down,"
> instead of "You're such a bad girl! In fact, you are
> the meanest kid in the park!"*

Use specific, rather than general, praise. When
your child feels that you really notice his good
efforts, he'll be more likely to repeat them.

> ■ *When his four-year-old son finally picked up all
> his toys, instead of shouting "Good job" from
> another room, Dylan took a different approach.
> He stepped into the playroom and had a good
> look around. Then he said, "Wow! Micah, I like
> the way you stacked up all the blocks. It must
> have taken a long time to arrange them so neatly,
> exactly where they belong. I call that organization!"
> Micah was beaming with pride that his dad had
> really noticed his good work.*

Keep in mind that indiscriminate or insincere
praise may cause the positive effects of true
compliments to be lost.

Praise Pointers

It's often quite an "eye-opener" to many parents that well-thought-out praise given over time can actually be a more effective discipline technique than punishment administered immediately after a misbehavior has occurred.

→ **Praise in moderation:** One of the most powerful discipline-teaching tools parents can use during the early years is to offer approval of their children's behavior. *Too little praise* early on often hinders a child's understanding of right and wrong as well as the development of his self-esteem. On the other hand, as the child gets older, *too much praise* can cause a child to expect and depend on attention from others in order to feel worthy, thereby stifling the development of his own internal sense of values. Reasonable praise goes hand in hand with reasonable expectations that most children can handle.

→ **Praise specifically rather than generally:** "I appreciate how carefully you put the socks in your drawer" is better than "Good girl!"

→ **Praise the effort rather than the overall performance:** Children who receive specific praise for their effort are more likely to repeat the behavior. "Thank you for working so hard at scrubbing the paint off the table." The fact that some paint still remained was not mentioned in this statement. Notice that if you were to add a "but . . . ," everything said before it would have lost its positive effect. ("Thank you for scrubbing the paint off the table, but you missed the corners.") However, you can make your point if you first pause after praising the child's efforts and then say, "Corners are really hard to clean; let's do them together."

→ **Praise with words that reflect your values:** This is one of the best ways you can teach your child the values you hold dear. For example, say "I noticed your patience and determination as you were building your fort just the way you like it. You must feel really proud of yourself," rather than simply "Good job." Again, this takes thought on your part.

→ **Praise with words that acknowledge your child's strengths:** "You're very good at drawing pictures. I'll bet you know just what colors to use on this paper." Your choice of words shows your confidence in your child's ability and often serves to help motivate him to do a job that he is proud of.

→ **Avoid praising with superlative words like "best," "smartest," or "prettiest":** Although these are positive words, if used often they can actually feel like pressure to the child as he tries to live up to the "perfection" or extraordinary expectations he feels you have placed on him. Although many parents think these words build a child's self-esteem, the effect is often just the opposite. The child who has been told constantly that she *is the best* often believes she is expected to *be the best,* all the time . . . quite a burden to carry around.

→ **Praise with words that your child has some control over, like "creative," "funny," "musical," "helpful," "kind," or "truthful":** For example, "I appreciated you being truthful in admitting how the window got broken." In this way a parent can guide a child in learning right from wrong without pressuring or criticizing him.

Role-play difficult or unfamiliar situations with your child ahead of time, to give her the confidence and comfort of knowing just what to do or expect. (See the role-playing box on page 25 for more ideas.)

Help your child learn some strategies besides enlisting the aid of an adult to solve a problem.

> ■ *Five-year-old Nate was having a rough time at kindergarten recess. It seemed that a bigger kid had begun making fun of him ever since he had admitted he still liked Barney. At bedtime, several nights in a row, Nate and his mom talked about various ways he could deal with the teasing. He could agree with the teaser, taking the wind out of his sails, by saying, "Yes, I do like Barney, a lot." He could say, "So?" which would let the teaser know that his put-down really didn't matter. Or he could flash a great big smile in response to the teaser as he said, "That's so funny. You make me laugh!" For over a week they practiced taking turns with these strategies. After Nate gained the confidence to actually use some of these responses, the bully stopped bothering him. At the end of the week, Nate ran into the house, beaming as he told his mom how he'd handled the situation all by himself!*

Respect your children's struggles; there's so much for them to learn!

> ■ *Losing patience as his four-year-old fumbled with buttoning her sweater, Frank's first instinct was to say, "Let me do it." Instead, he watched for a moment, collected his thoughts, and said, "Buttons can be tough for little fingers." His daughter paused. Encouraged to try again, she smiled at her understanding dad.*

Give your child tangible evidence of her developmental achievements. Show your child some of her artwork or play an old tape-recorded conversation or video to prove how well she has progressed in her small motor and communication skills.

> ■ One speech therapist had a great idea. She gave five-year-old Blakely a colored paper clip for each new word he mastered. At the end of the year, they strung the clips together and marveled at the way the chain reached all the way down the hall! "Wow! I'm really smart!" Blakely exclaimed.

Let your child know that everyone fails sometimes. The important thing to understand is that mistakes give everyone the opportunity to learn.

> ■ When Caroline's five-year-old became discouraged over learning to print his letters, she told him her favorite anecdote about Thomas Edison. "Remember, Sean, it took hundreds of tries before Thomas Edison invented a lightbulb that worked. Think of how dark it would be if he'd just given up and quit!"

Try focusing on the positive—not always easy to do, especially when you have a "challenging child." Although you may have to rack your brain to come up with something on some days, your effort is always worth it!

> ■ The Kelly family plays a "let's say something nice about someone" game at their weekly family meeting. They all take turns going around the table and saying one nice thing about the person next to them. No one is allowed to bring up anything annoying or bad about another person

*during the game. It's amazing how infectious it
can be—the sister is so amazed to hear her
brother say something nice about her that she
does her best to top his compliment.*

Help your child feel important at a young age by
giving him his own special jobs or chores to help
your family. (See "Chores," page 57, for more on
how to get started.)

Respect your child's individual temperament and
developmental readiness at various stages; let your
child set the pace.

■ *Caroline's son was shy and clingy as a toddler,
so when she saw the neighbors' children outside,
her first instinct was to literally pick him up and
dash across the street to help him socialize. But
Nolan just whimpered, "I don't want to go!" Instead,
he'd hide behind a tree, peeking at the kids. As time
went by, he managed a polite wave. It took about a
year until he wanted to join the other children.
Caroline really felt that had she forced him to
socialize before he was ready, he would have
become even more uncomfortable—and she would
have destroyed her own sanity in the process!*

Recognize and celebrate your child's strengths
instead of trying to constantly "fix" her
weaknesses. Providing your child with ample
opportunities to succeed at the things she really
enjoys and excels in can actually help build the
confidence needed to approach those tasks that
are difficult for her.

Avoid comparing your child (or yourself) to
others, favorably or not; let her know she is valued
just for being who she is. (See "Comparing and
Labeling Children," page 66, for more advice.)

Give your child a sense of roots; share interesting details about your extended families and your family history. Ask relatives to tell stories about their lives or even their grandparents' lives, including where they came from.

> ■ *One kindergarten class did a unit on families. The teacher asked each family to help their child learn a funny family story as a homework assignment. The kids proudly told their stories to the class the next day. They talked about the funniest things their parents or grandparents had done when they were kids. The children were so excited with the stories they had heard that they repeated them around their dinner tables at home. All of the families really enjoyed getting to know each other better. The teacher said it was the most fun her class had all year, and even the shy kids were happy to share their stories.*

Take time to celebrate and have fun together as a family. Establish some of your own family customs, rituals, and traditions that everyone can look forward to. If you're at a loss as to what to do, ask your kids. Chances are, if you've done something they enjoyed once, they'll let you know they want to do it again. Consider also celebrating little day-to-day things.

Invite your child into your world; share your passions, enthusiasm, and knowledge with him. There's a very good chance that the "quantity time" you spend together will truly become "quality time."

Appreciate your child's world; take her interests and concerns seriously no matter how trivial, boring, or repetitive they may seem to you.

Blow your own horn occasionally; let your child see you take pride in *your* accomplishments.

take heart

♥ *You're not the only parent who's ever been tempted to call your kid "knucklehead," "stinky-pants," "little piggy," or "slowpoke." Keep in mind that these words can easily be interpreted as harsh, hurtful insults by your child.*

Realize that "harmless" nicknames or playful teasing that seem funny to you may seem very different to your child. If he asks you to stop it, listen to him!

Try to see things through a child's eyes; remember that his sense of the world is based on his limited experience and thinking ability. (See page 181 for "How Does a Two- to Five-Year-Old Think?")

Expose your child to the diversity around her. Talk about how great it is that everyone is unique. Talk positively about cultural, physical, and more subtle differences in people. Hopefully she will conclude that no other person is exactly like her and that she is lovable just the way she is.

the bottom line

Within a secure structure of clear limits, encourage your child's input and value his strengths; as he experiences success, he will gain the confidence and good feelings that form the foundation of a positive sense of self.

separation anxiety

Q: My husband and I would really welcome a night out, and Grandma's all lined up to baby-sit. The problem is, whenever we leave our son, he screams bloody murder and then acts up again when we return. What can we do to help him handle separations?

A: Separation anxiety is experienced in varying degrees by almost all toddlers and preschoolers and is revisited later in life when your "baby" is going off to camp or college. Partly because all transitions are difficult and partly because he's had to "hold it together" all the while you were absent, it is also normal for your son to "act up" upon your return. Most children eventually grow out of this phase. In the meantime, you can continue to reassure your youngster that you will return, and try out some strategies to ease the transition times of your departure and return. (See "First Days of Preschool," page 114, for tips on how to help your child separate for school.)

immediate response

→ Try not to fall apart when your child carries on; accept the fact that your patience and understanding *will* be tested and hang in there.

→ Stay calm (at least outwardly), and speak in a matter-of-fact way.

→ Tell your child that you love him and emphasize the fact that you'll be back. Since young children have little concept of time, it may help to relate your return to his activities or schedule. For example, you might say "I'll be back as soon as your program is over."

→ Separation anxiety can often be eased by everyone leaving the house at the same time. For example, when you go to your appointment, your child and the baby-sitter go off to the park.

→ Engage your child in one of her favorite activities before you leave. Even though she may become hysterical when you leave, the sitter will have something already set up that the child really likes to go back to.

→ Acknowledge the child's feelings (but don't encourage the behavior). Then, no matter how difficult, pry those little fingers off your leg and go through your established good-bye routine, waving, smiling, and speaking comforting words. Then go! And don't look back.

sanity savers

Acknowledge your child's fears rather than trying to talk her out of them.

■ *Jan listened as her sitter struggled to reassure her teary-eyed daughter. "Becca, of*

course it's okay if Mommy goes out for a while.
You know how we always have lots and lots of
fun. I know how much you like playing with me."
Jan added, "Honey, I know you feel sad and don't
like to see me and Daddy leave without you, but
we'll be back."

■ When Gail's five-year-old daughter was reluctant
to go to a "drop-off" birthday party, Gail
understood. After all, what parent hasn't anxiously
approached an overcrowded cocktail party already
in full swing and wondered who on earth they might
talk to? When Rachel insisted she did not want to
stay at the party, Gail went and sat down with her.
After fifteen minutes, Rachel was having fun and
didn't mind staying at the party without Mom.

Give your child a chance to decide when he's
ready to separate from you and "join in."

■ Nolan seemed very hesitant to join the games
when he and his mom arrived at his cousin's
birthday party. Instead of joining the adults in
another room, Caroline gently pulled him onto her
lap and said, "Boy! That looks like fun. Want to
watch for a while? Whenever you feel ready, you
can join in."

Explain to your child that you will return and let
him know when you'll be back in a way he can
easily understand.

■ Caroline told Nolan, "Mommy needs some time
alone with Daddy, so we are going out to dinner. I
will be back before you go to bed." She was
afraid if she told him they would be back at eight,
he'd keep asking the sitter every five minutes, "Is
it eight o'clock yet?" Even worse, if they walked
through the door at 8:15, his older brother would
chastise them about being late!

Try leaving something tangible of yours with your child—a scarf, a photo of you, a card you colored for him—to help him deal with your absence.

Give your child something to look forward to upon your return, if possible.

> ▓ *Gail told Aaron, "I'll be home in time to tuck you in and read your favorite bedtime story."*

> ▓ *Reggie said to his three-year-old son, "I have to work late, way past your bedtime. But when you wake up tomorrow, we'll eat breakfast and read the sports pages together."*

Resist the urge to "sneak out" without saying good-bye to your child. Many experts believe your child may feel abandoned and betrayed if she looks for you and suddenly, without an explanation, finds you gone.

Leave immediately after you have said good-bye. Saying good-bye once can be stressful enough for some kids, without a long, drawn-out departure.

take heart

♥ *You're not the only parent who's ever left your parents' house with a big lump in your throat because your child is in tears, pounding on the door, while Grandma adds fuel to the fire by chiding you for not stealing away when your child was distracted with her toys.*

Try to project a positive attitude yourself lest your child pick up on your hesitation and sense that something is wrong.

Ease your own anxiety with a follow-up phone call to see how your child is doing. More often than not, you'll hear that your child stopped crying just as soon as you were out of sight.

Easing Child-Care Transitions

→ Set aside a little extra time to help your child go through a difficult transition.

→ Get to a play date, or Grandma's, or day care, early enough to stay and play with your child until he gets involved in his activities.

→ Ask the sitter to arrive early and get involved in a pleasurable activity with your child before you leave your house.

→ Allow your child some proper closure at her day care for a few minutes before you abruptly whisk her away. Sometimes it's helpful to pull up a chair and literally enter your child's world.

Develop your own family rituals for departure and use them consistently to give your child a sense of security.

■ *At the door, right before Eliza left, she blew three little kisses at her three-year-old. Her husband always asked their oldest son for "a big high five to get me through the day" just before he left for work each morning.*

Remind your child that he can hug his "lovey" (one special possession, such as a blanket or stuffed toy) when you leave.

Tape yourself singing songs or reading a story and suggest that your child listen to it when you are away.

Help your child gradually get used to the idea of going on a play date if he seems reluctant.

■ When kids started asking Nolan to come over after preschool, he simply refused. Suspecting that being in preschool without his mom was enough for one day, Caroline invited one friend and his mother over to their house. When they reciprocated with an invitation, Nolan didn't want to go alone. Caroline asked if she could accompany him on the first visit to his friend's house. This strategy worked. Nolan gradually became so enthusiastic that one day he literally burst out of the classroom and eagerly asked, "Can I go over to Brian's house now . . . can I, Mom, can I?"

Realize that it's not unusual for your toddler to have a hard time adjusting to change, including the transition from being with you to your leaving him, no matter how loving or fun his substitute caregiver is.

Prepare the child who must go back and forth between Mom's house and Dad's house. For a smoother transition, try using stickers on a calendar so that the child has some sense of control over his life by seeing what the schedule is. In this way, the visit is not a surprise to him. Try to understand the stressful feelings and issues your child must be dealing with in this situation. Resist talking badly about your "ex" in front of your child; remember, he/she is your child's parent, too!

the bottom line

As your child grows and becomes more self-confident and outgoing, separation anxiety will diminish; during the process, acknowledge your child's feelings and communicate in a way that is sensitive, honest, and reassuring.

sexuality

Q: When is the right time to talk to my four-year-old about sex? Sometimes he talks about things that I am not sure he really understands.

A: Parents want their children to feel comfortable with their bodies and to have an understanding of sexuality. Many children ages two to five naturally become curious and explore all parts of the body, although in a more innocent manner than we, as parents, often see it. Keep in mind that learning about sexual issues is a gradual process. The right time to address the issue is when questions are asked. Then try to answer them as simply and honestly as you can. You may very well discover your child is using words while having no understanding of their meaning. If you are caught off guard and aren't sure what to say, tell your child, "I'd like to answer that question, but I need to think about it for a while."

sanity savers

Model and teach privacy, respect, and personal boundaries. What is considered "normal" varies a lot from family to family. Consistency in your actions will minimize mixed messages and confusion for your child.

Respect a child's curiosity while maintaining adult privacy. Choose an approach that allows for your verbal responses to the child's curiosity but avoids his looking at or touching "private parts."

> ■ *When Tom went into the bathroom, his three-year-old daughter followed him in. He responded to Jenny's stare by saying, "I see you really would like to watch me, but I like to be alone while I am using the bathroom." As he took Jenny's hand to guide her out of the doorway, he added, "If you have a question, I'll be happy to answer it when I'm finished in here."*

Many experts agree that the right age to inform a child about sexual matters is when he asks questions.

Begin by answering your child's question honestly but briefly; you can always add more information as needed.

> ■ *When her four-year-old daughter asked her, "Where do babies come from?" Jenny, a thoughtful mom, said just the right thing: "A baby grows inside a warm, special place in a mother's body." Her daughter did not ask any further questions. Jenny chose to give a simple answer at first and refrained from going into any further details. That was enough for the time being.*

When your child asks a difficult question, respond by asking him, "What do you think?" When you know where he's coming from, you will have a better understanding of how to start your discussion or answer his question.

■ *Nicholas, a verbally precocious five-year-old, staring at his new baby brother, suddenly popped the question on his mom. "I've been wondering," he said. "How did you get pregnant in the first place?" Asking Nicholas what he thinks gives his mom a step up in how to frame her response.*

Teach your child the correct words for genitals and talk about them in the same way you talk about other parts of the body.

■ *While his son was in the bathtub, Clint would say, very matter-of-factly, "Show me where is your arm . . . your head . . . nose, toe, penis, ear, tummy."*

Be careful about giving your child "too much, too soon." The late child psychologist and author Dr. Haim Ginott explained, "While there is no reason why children's sex questions cannot be answered frankly, the answers need not be a course in obstetrics."

When you open the bedroom door and see two little bare-bottom kids playing doctor, keep your reaction low key as you stop the behavior.

■ *One expert suggests you say, "Oh, I see you're playing doctor. You must have some questions about your bodies. Put your clothes back on, and I'll answer any questions*

take heart

♥ *You're not the only parent who's ever been rendered speechless in the grocery store when your four-year-old innocently decides to chant something embarrassing. One mother reported her son's loud rendition of "Someone's in the kitchen with Dinah!" with the word "vagina" substituted for "Dinah"! At that moment, she found herself wishing that she had taught her son a much more childlike, less recognizable term, like "woo-woo."*

before we go out in the backyard to play."
(Redirect children to other physical activities.)

■ *Five-year-old Seth went through a phase of*
sneaking into the closet to "play doctor" with any
willing friends—female or male—he could find. After
reflecting upon it, his parents realized the most
embarrassing part for them was the overreaction
of his friends' parents. Realizing that such curiosity
was a normal part of growing up for some kids,
Seth's parents discussed the best approach to
take with their pediatrician. Together, they told
their son, "It's okay to be curious about other
people's bodies, but it's important to understand
that any part covered by a bathing suit is private."
After that, the parents were more vigilant whenever
their son had friends over and insisted on keeping
the bedroom doors open.

Tell the parents of the other child if there has
been an episode of "playing doctor" so they can
address the issue with their child.

Realize that two of the questions that puzzle many
preschool children are "How does a baby begin to
grow?" and "How does it come out?"

Note that many children are not ready for all the
facts and can actually be quite uncomfortable
when given too much information.

■ *The thought of her parents engaging in sex as it*
had just been explained to Carrie made her
respond, "Oh yuck! That's disgusting! I'm never
going to do that!"

■ *Billy, the youngest of four kids, told his dad,*
"Gross! You and Mom actually had to do that four
times!" To which his father cleared his throat and
loosened his tie, as he cleverly replied with a

little smirk, "Well, yes! Your mother and I did have
to make some sacrifices!"

Be patient; realize that sometimes a young child
may be more comfortable with his own ideas of
how things happen, preferring to deny "the truth"
until he is older. Parents can say, "That's an
interesting idea you have," without further
comment. If the child asks for more information or
his perception is causing a problem for himself or
confusion for others, read a book on the subject
together. (See our recommended list beginning on
page 337.)

■ *Bobby, age three, was very proud of "his
understanding" of where babies came from and
how they were born. He told quite an elaborate
tale about how the mommy swallowed a pumpkin
seed that grew into a baby in her tummy. He
added that the baby ate the foods that were in
the mommy's tummy to make him grow bigger.
When he got big enough, the mommy would say,
"It's time to go to the hospital," so the baby could
pop out of her belly button!*

Emphasize the fact that you will always make
time to listen and talk with your child. However, if
the subject is one that is confusing to you as well,
use delay tactics until you have the information to
form an easy answer.

Be aware of the tone you use when you talk
about sex. Establish respectful, matter-of-fact,
open lines of communication so your child feels he
can talk to you about sensitive subjects without
ridicule or shame, creating a trusting, caring
rapport in the early years.

Keep in mind that although your child says he
understands, he may not "get it" at all!

It's not always necessary to give an explanation.

> ■ *Having just hung up the phone, Mom suddenly got that funny feeling that it was too quiet in the house. Where was three-year-old Michael? Aha! There he was, contentedly playing next to the toilet. He had unwrapped an entire arsenal of "torpedos" (Mom's tampons) to fire at the enemy somewhere in the sea (the toilet). Mom told him simply but firmly that these things were Mommy's and could clog the toilet pipes and make water spill all over the bathroom floor. Then she took her son by the hand and led him to his toys. An explanation of what Mommy's tampons were for was neither necessary nor appropriate in this situation.*

Realize that a child may not view situations in the same sexual context as an adult.

> ■ *Right after Caroline gave her two-year-old a bath, she was a little embarrassed that he routinely escaped and exuberantly raced around the house in his birthday suit before she could dress him. When an experienced neighbor casually mentioned that her twin boys used to like doing the same thing, Caroline relaxed. She came to realize that her son was just innocently enjoying his freedom from the restriction of clothes and diapers.*

Be aware that many psychologists consider occasional masturbation normal. Child psychologist and author Haim Ginott felt that as long as the child's main satisfactions come from personal relationships and achievements, occasional "self-gratification" is not a problem.

■ *A Chicago pediatrician explained to Ted, a concerned dad, "It's excessive behavior that calls for professional help, for example, constant masturbation to the point of irritating the genitals, or if a child seems to be obsessed with physically examining even unwilling friends who visit, after being told it is not allowed."*

Discuss with your spouse your feelings about sex-role, gender-proper behavior and stereotyping in private. Consider allowing your children to pursue both "feminine" and "masculine" activities without being criticized or ridiculed. Boys playing with dolls and girls roughhousing with the boys next door are both well within the range of normal, healthy play.

■ *Jonathan couldn't stand seeing his young son Kevin playing "dress-up" with his sisters, using a pile of Mom's old dresses and high heels. A social worker assured Jonathan that this was perfectly normal behavior and suggested that he might feel better if he also planned some activities with his son, "just for the guys," that met his macho criteria.*

Think about the messages you give your child daily. Although there is no one "right" way to deal with certain issues, be aware of the consequences that go with your decisions. Do you walk around naked going to and from the bathroom, or do you always wear a robe? Do you let the kids into the bathroom with you, or is that a private time, with the door closed?

Realize that your children are learning about love, relationships, and problem solving from observing your marital relationship. Some couples are more comfortable expressing physical affection, like cuddling and kissing, in private. ("Fighting in Front of Your Kids," page 106, discusses the

importance of making up after a fight in front of
your children.)

the bottom line

Your kids are watching and listening to you daily
as they learn more about themselves and
others from your example and your explanations; if
you're comfortable with your own sexuality,
chances are you will be successful in helping your
kids understand and accept theirs too.

sibling rivalry

Q: Help! My kids are constantly at each other's throats. Do I retaliate, mediate, or evacuate?

A: Although this piece of advice is already too late for you, the only surefire way to avoid all sibling rivalry is to have only one child! Competition for your attention is often at the root of sibling rivalry, and the way you react can fan the flames of jealousy or help draw your kids closer together. Forget retaliation: after teaching the kids to mediate their own disagreements, in time you'll be able to evacuate!

immediate response

→ Intervene immediately if you think safety is an issue or an object is about to be broken.

→ Assume both kids are equally responsible for the fight if you weren't in the room when it started.

→ Give both children the same consequence. ("I see that some juice has been spilled. Here are two sponges to wipe it up, one for each of you.")

→ When your brain seems to "short-circuit," acknowledge the unacceptable behavior instantly, but give yourself some time to think of an appropriate consequence. "Uh-oh! Throwing your baby sister's bottle down the stairs was a *bad* decision. I'll need some time to figure out what to do about that."

➔ Consider letting the kids work it out themselves. (Easier said than done.)

sanity savers

Aim for just a few concrete rules regarding acceptable behavior.

> ▨ Gail laid down the rule "No hurting your brother or sister. That means no hitting, no punching, no biting each other, and no name-calling."

Save your intervention for times when someone is being physically or verbally hurt. Step between the kids, separate them, and restate the rules.

When it seems like play is getting out of hand, ask the kids to clarify the situation.

> ▨ Caroline said, "Remember, you guys can only play games together that both of you enjoy. It doesn't sound like your brother is enjoying this game anymore, is he?"

Use "I" statements to address the behavior and to express your feelings about it. (See page 15 for an explanation of "I" statements.)

> ▨ Sophie told her kids "I get mad when I see you hurt your brother" instead of "What's the matter with you, you troublemaker? Are you trying to drive me crazy?"

Bite your tongue in the heat of the moment.

> ■ *Joyce found that words like "What are you trying to do to your baby brother . . . kill him? You know there's only love in this house!" were tempting but not helpful.*

Focus attention on the "victim," not the "aggressor." (This is hard to do, but it's very effective.)

> ■ *Within earshot of both children, Jan walked over to the injured party and said, "Ooow! That must hurt. Let me rub it till you feel better."*

Express your positive expectations of the aggressor by what you say to the victim. This way, the aggressor gets the message but not the attention.

> ■ *Dad said, "It's not like your sister to scratch. She usually uses words to say how she feels. Let's go get a Band-Aid."*

Offer a few possible solutions to resolve an argument.

> ■ *"You can take turns, and each play with it until the timer rings; one of you can choose another toy; or we can flip a coin." Try to leave the ultimate decision up to the kids. Say, "You and your sister are smart. I know you can come up with something together," as you unglue the whining one from your leg.*

> ■ *One day Caroline, at her wits' end, told her kids, "Okay, this toy needs a 'time-out' until you can play nicely with it together."*

take heart

♥ *You're not the only parent who ends up taking away the toy that the kids refuse to share, only to find them fighting about something else a few minutes later.*

Notice how substituting the words "show" or "teach" for "share" or "give" can make a big difference in the way your child reacts to your prompting. (See the box on page 122 for more tips on sharing.)

■ *James got a lot more cooperation from his son when he said "I'll bet you can show your sister how to use that toy" than he did when he said "Give that toy to your sister right now!"*

■ *Caroline found that coaxing her son by saying "You're smart; will you teach your little brother how that works?" was more effective than demanding "You know better, you're the big brother! You'd better start setting a good example and share, now!"*

Use humor and other distractions to break up a fight.

■ *Mark, a dad in a good mood, grabbed for the Mickey Mouse ears, stepped between the kids, and in a high-pitched voice said, "Time for cheese and crackers in the kitchen. Everybody follow me!"*

Try using nonverbal messages to get your point across.

■ *As fists began to fly, Caroline flitted around the room, flashing the football signal for "time-out" because she just couldn't trust herself not to scream if she opened her mouth. After a couple of puzzled looks, the boys joined right in, playing charades with her, and forgot all about their fight.*

■ *Gail remembers, "After hearing one set of accusations too many, I finally realized it didn't really matter who started the fight, as long as the kids worked it out. This way, I avoided being the judge and referee. Besides, whenever I asked, 'Who started this?' each kid pointed his finger at someone else."*

■ *Instead of shouting the name of the supposed aggressor from another room, Caroline found she had a better chance of being heard when she said, "Kids, there's too much noise!" In so doing, she cleverly addressed the child who was misbehaving without having to single anyone out or assign blame. She had already learned that a child whose name is constantly called when there is a problem conveniently tunes you out.*

Encourage the kids to use words instead of fists to express themselves.

■ *Lee said to his daughter, "Try telling your brother, 'I don't like getting pushed!'"*

Help children learn to label their feelings. Feel free to use big words; even little kids will catch on. The more verbal ammunition you give them, the less physically aggressive most kids will become.

■ *Sloane spoke for her crying toddler, "I'll bet you feel frustrated when your brother hides your toys."*

Realize that the older child is not always the aggressor and the younger one may not be as innocent as she seems.

■ *Shelly often saw his sister, Fran, reprimanding her son Billy for fighting with his little sister. She'd say, "Billy, you're bigger, you're older, and you should know better!" But the smirk on little Eva's face was proof to Shelly that there was more to the story!*

take heart

♥ You're not the only parents who have foreseen the pain of little fingers about to get slammed in a bedroom door, only to blame yourselves for not being quick enough to stop the accident from happening.

Resist taking sides or placing blame.

Hold a family meeting to discuss the rivalry. Ask for the kids' ideas about rules and consequences. People in general tend to be much stricter with consequences when they set them for themselves. (Think about how critical you were in your last self-review at work.) (See page 17 for more details on holding a family meeting.)

Encourage kids to work it out on their own, especially as they get older.

■ Andy said to the kids, "Looks like you both want that toy now. I'll bet the two of you can come up with a plan," as he calmly left the room with his fingers crossed!

Separate the kids for a little while if they can't work it out.

■ Pat, a concerned dad, said, "I won't let you hit each other. Quick, you go to your room and you go to the den!"

Think about whether you are unwittingly encouraging tattling by paying attention to every little complaint and not giving the kids a real chance to work it out together.

■ Caroline realized that in her attempts to get her kids to use words instead of their fists when they were angry at each other, she had unintentionally encouraged them to tattle. When they brainstormed a list of actions the kids could

*take instead of hitting, Nolan came up with "C
and tell you, Mommy." When Caroline nodded h
approval, Nolan stopped listening to the other
suggestions and literally took it to mean that he
should come to her with every little thing.*

Save your sanity with a "no tattling" rule.

■ *Author and former teacher Barbara Coloroso
says it best in her book* Kids Are Worth It!: *"You
may come to me to get someone out of trouble
but not to get them in trouble."*

■ *Gail used to tell her three kids, "Unless someone
is bleeding, I don't want to hear about it!"*

Turn a tattling child into a problem solver.
Encourage her to go back and use words to tell her
siblings that she doesn't like what they are doing,
or that she would like to be included in their play.

Help the tattling child find the words to
negotiate with siblings. When she comes to you to
tattle, rehearse with her what she might say to the
other kids. Try role-playing with puppets at
another time. (See role-playing box on page 25.)

Answer with a neutral response ("oh," "hmm,"
"aahh," "oooh") if you are having a bad day. Simple
acknowledgement can encourage the kids to give
up trying to prove who started it.

Refuse to get caught up in their constant
complaints and accusations.

■ *Rachel whined for the umpteenth time, "It's not
fa-a-a-ir-r, Mommy! Aaron gets to go to bed later
than me! You're so-o-o-o mean. Everyone stays up
later than me!" Gail just looked at Rachel with
"that look" that no one crosses and said,
"Hmmm." There was no power struggle, and*

Rachel got the message. (You know how the kids always know when you're at your wits' end.) She had heard the real explanation a thousand times. So she repeated it: "When I'm older, I can stay up, too! Right, Mommy?"

Help develop negotiation skills with the "Couch Game."

■ *Trisha remembers, "The kids had been squabbling, I was at my wits' end, and the kids knew it! I dragged them to the couch and said, 'Adam, you may not leave the couch until your sister gives you permission . . . Rena, you may not leave the couch until Adam says so.' They both just stared at me in amazement. I finally had a few moments of peace and a good chuckle. After a while, they came up with a fair plan. They both counted to ten and stood up at the same time."*

Understand that, as family therapist Nancy Bruski says, "being fair" means meeting the unique needs of each child, not treating each child equally. No matter how hard you try to be fair and "equal," the kids will always keep score!

■ *Dottie deliberately bought exactly the same treat for her kids (or so she thought), only to be verbally assaulted by her youngest as they ripped open the bags. "It's not fair! Ricky has more blue M & M's than me."*

Set aside a special time for each child and give it a special name.

■ *After Gail's third child was born, she was busier than ever. "I told Joshua that we would have our special Mommy-Joshua Time now, then later it would be Mommy Alone Time, and then Mommy-Daddy Time. Not only did Josh look* forward to his special time with me, he began to get used to and respect my need for time alone."

■ The special time in Estelle and Jack's family was called a "2-Date." They realized how much their own two daughters looked forward to time alone with each parent. Sometimes Estelle and Debbie arranged a "2-Date" for lunch. Estelle and Michelle often enjoyed a Saturday movie together on their "2-Date." The parents would even get a baby-sitter so they could go on their own private "2-Date."

Make it clear that each child has some of his own special possessions.

■ Four-year-old Elizabeth grabbed her little brother's just-opened birthday present, causing him to break into tears. Andy, the dad, stopped the sobbing by saying, "That's your brother's new toy. He's playing with it right now. I'm sure he'll show it to you when he's ready."

Respect each child's personal "space" and the need for privacy, even if it is just a corner of a shared room.

■ When little David pounded on the door to his older sister's room and began screaming "In! In!," Dad walked over close to David and stroked his shoulder as he explained (so both kids could hear), "Karen needs some time to play alone right now. I'm sure she'll invite you in when she's ready."

Model appropriate responses to frustration.

■ Caroline said to Sean in frustration, "When you hit Nolan, I feel like hitting you, BUT I WON'T!" Pretty soon, when he was frustrated, Sean began to ball up his fist and say, "I feel like hitting you, but I won't!" instead of really letting his brother have it.

Tell your children that the sibling relationship outlasts most parent-child relationships and can develop into a long-lasting, loving connection for life.

■ Caroline says to her boys, "You two will always be brothers no matter what. You'll always have each other. You know how Daddy and Uncle Pat love to go to the Cubs games together? Daddy and Uncle Pat are brothers. When you grow up, I'll bet you guys will go to the games together too."

the bottom line

Sibling rivalry can be controlled but not banished altogether; look at the positive side— the family provides a safe place for kids to learn to negotiate as well as appreciate individual differences.

strangers

Q: I am anxiously waiting for my little girl to turn four so she can start karate lessons with her friends. I know I have to warn her that there are bad people out there, and yet I don't want to go overboard. How do I give her enough information to help keep her safe but not so much that it will cause her to become overly frightened?

A: You said it yourself: the key is to give your child the information she needs to be safe without frightening her. Remember, a child who is two to five years old must be closely supervised at all times; it is your absolute responsibility, not hers, to ensure her safety. You can gradually begin teaching her some important safety lessons by stating the rules and reminding her if an occasion arises, rather than by constant foreboding warnings and threats. You can also try using games, puppets, and stories to get your point across.

sanity savers

Rules are more helpful and less frightening than warnings and threats.

■ *When Molly had a nightmare about a stranger chasing her, her mom realized she had frightened her the day before, when she had warned Molly, "If you get lost in the store, a stranger might kidnap you and take you away!" It would have been more helpful to say, "Remember our rule, stay by Mommy's side when we go down the aisles."*

A good general rule is that children must always ask a parent first before they go anywhere. This rule takes the place of scary warnings such as "You must never walk away with, get into a car with, or accept gifts like candy from a stranger."

Make it a house rule that only grown-ups answer the door, not children.

Teach your child to yell "Help!," not just to scream, if someone is scaring him or if he is lost.

■ *Caroline remembers that as a child, her own mother told her to yell, "Help! He's not my father," or "She's not my mother," to draw attention if a stranger bothered her. However, one day her youngest son decided to turn the tables on her! During a trip to the playground, he was reluctant to leave when it was time to go meet Daddy's train. As she reached out and grabbed his arm, he suddenly mischievously screamed, "Ouch! Let go! You're not my mommy!" She remembers feeling grateful that they were at the local playground, where all the neighbors knew them well.*

Use games and activities to teach your child to be observant.

■ *The Simons attended a safety awareness program for parents and children hosted by the local police department. They stressed that parents should help kids develop the skills of staying aware of their surroundings and being observant. While riding in the car together, Mr. Simon often asked the kids to tell him the numbers, letters, or words they saw on license plates. This was a good reading exercise as well as a memory game that one day may come in handy for quick identification of a suspicious vehicle in the neighborhood.*

Start to teach your child what to do if he becomes separated from you in an amusement park, mall, or store. You might tell him to approach someone in uniform, such as a policeman, security guard, bus driver, or store employee for help. In a public place, consider establishing a meeting point when you arrive, such as the front door or gate, in case you become separated.

■ *Every time Gail and her kids went into a department store, she pointed out the cash registers in the front of the store. Then Gail explained that if she accidentally got lost, the kids should go to someone in uniform working at the register and ask for help finding their "lost" mommy.*

■ *Maddy made a point of carrying a current photo of the kids that she could show to store security if they got separated.*

Consider telling your child to go find children with their mother in the store and ask the mother to "Please help me find my mom." This technique is often helpful for small children who may have trouble seeing the cash registers but are at eye level with other children.

Notice how your child reacts when meeting new people and honor his feelings. Accept the fact that your child may never totally warm up to everyone and let him know that's okay. It's important for him to be allowed to take some time to be comfortable.

Listen carefully if your child tells you he does not want to be with someone. Ask him why: there may be a good reason.

Help your child understand that it is okay to be polite (or even helpful) to strangers when he is with Mommy or Daddy, and that the two of you will often greet strangers.

> ■ *Jack was with his four-year-old son when he stopped to help an elderly shopper. The frail lady was struggling to hold up her umbrella against the wind and rain and push her heavy cart through the parking lot at the same time. Jack kindly said, "Ma'am, may we help you to your car? I'd be happy to push the cart for you."*

Keep in mind that no matter how well you coach your young child, he needs constant supervision by a competent adult.

Teach your four-year-old how to operate the telephone. By age four, your child should know his address, area code, and telephone number. Practice making a "collect call," dialing "O" for the operator, pretending you have no money for a call, and dialing 911.

> ■ *One day Sharna's daughter interrupted Mom's shower with a demand that she immediately refill her cereal bowl. Sharna told her she'd get a second helping as soon as she got out of the shower. Well, that just wasn't quick enough! The next thing Sharna heard was the police ringing the doorbell! It seemed her "little angel" had*

called 911 and told the operator that she was starving!

Practice what your child will say to callers if you decide to allow him to answer the telephone. Consider teaching a child to say, "Hello, my dad is coming to talk to you."

the bottom line

Find the middle ground that enables you to protect your child without unduly scaring him with threats and warnings; remember, although the word "stranger" rhymes with "danger," it can also be defined as a friend you haven't met yet.

tantrums

Q: I just don't know what to do about my child's tantrums. Is this a permanent problem or just a phase she's going through?

A: Most two- to five-year-old children experience tantrums in varying degrees as part of a normal phase of development. Some tantrums can be prevented with prior thought and preparation, whereas others are unavoidable. Recognize the two types of tantrums; one battle is against the child's own developmental inability to do something, the other is a battle to get his own way. Keep in mind that when kids are tired, hungry, dealing with transitions, or overstimulated, they can become frustrated or overloaded and break down (this is the first type). The second type of tantrum occurs when your child attempts to manipulate someone into giving in to his demands by screaming, foot stomping, and other "Sarah Bernhardt" dramatics. Tantrums can cause *both* parent and child to experience feelings of anger, confusion, frustration, or embarrassment.

immediate response

→ Ignore the tantrum. Sometimes, without an audience, it will stop.

→ Get down on the floor and whisper calm words into your child's ear until she feels better. Say, "Daddy's here with you . . . Daddy's here." Pat her back as you speak.

→ Sometimes humor with a touch of reverse psychology will work. Say, "Oh, honey, whatever you do, don't smile. Remember, don't smile . . . Uh oh, I think a see one coming . . . Yes, there it is . . . A great big, laughing smile!"

→ Guide your unhappy child to the "tantrum room," a room you have designated during a family meeting for this purpose. In a calm voice, tell the child, "You may come out when you're done."

→ Express empathy when your child does not get what he wants. Say, "I know you're mad when you can't have what you want right now. You know, sometimes I get angry too when I can't get what I want."

→ Allow yourself and your child a "quick exit" every time the child loses it in public, even if it's extremely inconvenient to leave. When you follow through with an appropriate consequence, your child will realize you mean what you say.

sanity savers

Approach your child's tantrum according to his own unique personality and temperament. What works for one child may send another into an even worse state.

Be prepared with ways to "keep your cool." When *you* can stay calm, your youngster sees that his whole world isn't out of control if he loses it. (See "Anger," page 19, for more strategies for parents and kids.)

Touch your child if it comforts him. Try holding him securely, rubbing his back, hugging him, rocking him, or stroking his hair.

Remove yourself from the scene. This will work for some children and is worth trying.

For some children, being left alone with strong emotions can be frightening. Stay close by those children and go about your business; on a bad day, a set of headphones comes in really handy!

Choose to let your child "cry it out" until he regains his own control, if that's a good match for his personality and temperament.

Consider relocating the child to a place he finds safe and comforting.

■ *When Beth threw a tantrum, her dad told her it was time to turn off the television. Then he picked her up and said, "Daddy's plopping you on your favorite beanbag chair to compose yourself."*

Redirect your child's mounting tension with running, jumping, or dancing to music (feel free to join in) to nip a tantrum in the bud before it becomes full blown.

Try to put an end to a tantrum that seems to be simmering down, and redirect.

■ *One day at the park, Melanie told her tantruming toddler, "It's time to stop now. Let's breathe deeply together so you can feel calmer. Then we can go home and eat lunch."*

Help ease your child's transition out of his tantrum by providing him with supportive suggestions for what he can do next.

> ■ *Stan calmly told his three-year-old, "I'll be in the kitchen, making pancakes. When you feel like it, you're welcome to come and help me."*

Set up some boundaries for tantrums with your child.

> ■ *During their weekly family meeting, Jesse said calmly, "Jason, you can cry, lie on the floor, and stamp your feet, but it's not all right to pinch, scratch, kick, punch, or scream at the top of your lungs. The next time you have a tantrum, try to remember our rule: no hurting people or things."*

> ■ *When Debby's son went into a full-blown tantrum in the supermarket, she asked the supermarket manager to hold her half-loaded cart until she returned, and carried the screaming youngster outside. The fresh air helped the child calm down, and they finished shopping. (Sometimes it's necessary to go out to the car for a time-out to regain composure.)*

Try preventing tantrums by telling your kids ahead of time what to expect.

> ■ *Ron discussed his plan repeatedly with his daughter. "Katie, going to the circus is your special birthday present from me and Mommy. We won't be buying anything in the gift shop, but if you see something you would really like, you could put it on your wish list for Christmas, which is coming very soon."*

Use fantasy to grant a child's wish that you cannot carry out in reality.

> ■ On a long, hot drive, with no rest stop in sight, Caroline's son started whining loudly for a drink. Caroline averted a full-blown tantrum by saying, "Boy, we're all so thirsty! I wish I could fill up the whole car with root beer right now and we'd slurp it up with enormous straws." "Oh, no!" was the kids' response, but they continued enthusiastically, "Let's make it a root beer float and fill the car with ice cream and cherries!"

Curb your kids' demands for everything in sight by offering a limited choice.

Remember, your young child is going through an intense inner conflict between the need for dependency and the drive toward independence. Preschoolers generally have short attention spans, are by nature self-centered, and are controlled by their impulses. Brush up on what exactly those "age-appropriate" expectations are.

Develop an awareness of the types of situations that seem to trigger tantrums in your child. Look for patterns so you can prevent them by avoiding certain scenarios.

take heart

♥ *You're not the only parent who stops a full-scale tantrum by "giving in" once in a while. Let's not sweat the small stuff.*

Accept your child for who he is; be realistic in what he can handle without a meltdown. If your child's temperament is very active, high-strung, and impulsive, then long shopping trips, restaurants, and movie theaters may not be a sensible match in the preschool years.

Appreciate your child's ability to "hold it together" around others and understand when he "falls apart" with you.

■ *Elaine remembers, "My mother-in-law occasionally watched my two-year-old while my husband and I had an evening out alone. Without fail, each time I picked him up, he immediately let loose with a huge tantrum. Then my mother-in-law said the words that drove me crazy! 'He was so good the whole time he was with me. He only acts like that because he knows you let him get away with it.' I took a deep breath and managed to recall what a counselor had told me. 'Some children let down their guard when they see their parents after holding it in all day.' The counselor further explained that it was actually a compliment to my parenting, because my son felt comfortable expressing his feelings around me. However, I wondered: If it really was a good thing, why did it make me feel so bad? Another conundrum of parenthood!"*

Give your kids positive attention; acknowledge progress, big or small.

■ *Martha said to her daughter, "I know you were very angry when Tracy grabbed your toy without asking. That really took a lot of self-control not to hit. I'll bet you're really proud of yourself."*

When your child is being "difficult," remind yourself that he is really special and focus on what he *can* do correctly!

■ *Zoe, an exasperated mother of a difficult child, changed her approach. After a long and trying day, she met her husband at the door. Instead of rattling off a list of what had gone wrong in earshot of her son, as was her habit, she chose instead to share the one nice thing he had done that day. The mood in their home that evening was much improved!*

Consider consulting with a counselor if you're feeling out of control or if your child becomes so out of control that you feel he could be a danger to himself or others. A counselor can provide an objective opinion and can suggest various approaches to the situation.

the bottom line

Tantrums are simply no fun; the key is to hang in there and keep from having one yourself as your child gradually masters self-control.

television, video, and computers

Q: Should I be concerned about how much of my son's free time is spent watching TV and videos and playing video games?

A: While some experts believe that occasional exposure to even questionable shows and games won't harm an otherwise stable child, it's important for parents to find the time and the courage to monitor both the quantity and the quality of their children's exposure to today's technology. Keep in mind that those responsible for TV shows, videos, and electronic games are often more focused on ratings and profits than on the educational value or the ill effects of visual violence on children. As members of a TV-watching American society, we can't always just shut off the TV. We can, however, discuss the confusing or controversial issues and the feelings of fear or concern that may arise when our children are inadvertently exposed to images that could be upsetting. And remember, moderation is the key; even the best programs can become addictive. Although many TV programs are educational, entertaining, or relaxing, Betty Weeks, a well-respected kindergarten teacher, often reminded parents in her daily conversations as well as in her professional lectures that none can ever truly take the place of a child's need for social interaction with his family and friends.

sanity savers

Decide what's acceptable in terms of both content and viewing time; encourage your child's participation in making these decisions. Many experts feel that one to two hours total screen time per day is enough for young kids. Expect some resistance from your kids; it takes a while for them to learn to use discretion.

■ *The Gleason family decided to quit watching TV "cold turkey" for a week, discuss how it went, and then come up with new rules together.*

■ *Every Sunday morning, the Van Winkle family goes through the weekly TV program guide with their kids and together they select shows that the kids can watch.*

■ *Caroline told her five-year-old that he could watch TV for only one hour per day, but that he could decide which shows he wanted to watch from a list approved by Mom and Dad. Giving him some control in the matter made him much more cooperative when it was time to turn off the TV.*

Movie Resources for Parents

Nell Minow's book *The Movie Mom's Guide to Family Movies* is helpful in choosing quality rental videos for kids ages two to eighteen. The author has identified hundreds of movies whose stories encourage children to think, feel, and question—and to share those thoughts and feelings with their parents. Some examples of movies and their thought-provoking themes include:

→ *Pinocchio:* Striving for honesty

→ *Sesame Street Presents Follow That Bird:* Tolerance

→ *Babe:* Courtesy

→ *Mike Mulligan and His Steam Shovel:* Problem-solving

→ *Sleeping Beauty:* Jealousy

→ *The Sword and the Stone:* Finding the hero within

→ *Ferdinand the Bull:* Peace

→ *Willie Wonka and the Chocolate Factory:* Making moral choices

Another book parents will find helpful in monitoring and choosing programs is called *Stay Tuned! Raising Media-Savvy Kids in the Age of the Channel-Surfing Couch Potato,* by Jane Murphy and Karen Tucker.

Make a point of turning off the TV during meals and talking with your kids instead.

take heart

♥ *You're not the only parent who's ever parked your kids in front of a video so you could catch a little well-deserved time for yourself. In fact, this book never would have gotten written without one of the authors occasionally plunking her young kids down in front of a carefully chosen (and rather lengthy) kids' video.*

Make available a few carefully selected videos, placed on a designated shelf that the kids can watch any time (young children like to watch the same things over and over). This can replace the laborious daily process of monitoring, debating, and deciding what to let your kids watch.

If you purchase educational software, keep it light and fun for your child. Your child can become very turned off if you insist he use a certain program for a certain length of time. Let your child's natural attention span guide you.

Sit and watch TV *with* your children whenever possible, so that you can explain sensitive or confusing subjects when necessary. Sometimes shows and games that do include violence, casual sexual conduct, or racial and gender stereotyping can still be worth viewing with your children five and older. They can help you initiate discussions and teach valuable moral lessons when the consequences are sensitively and honestly portrayed.

Keep in mind that many young children cannot distinguish make-believe from fantasy; what they see on the screen is real to them. (See "How Does a Two- to Five-Year-Old Think?," page 181.)

Be aware that a show during prime time (or a so-called children's movie) may not be appropriate for your child.

Check the guidelines related to safety and children's health in a book titled *Failure to Connect: How Computers Affect our Children's Minds—for Better and Worse,* by Dr. Jane M. Healy, internationally known brain-research psychologist. Physicians and developmental optometrists caution parents to pay attention to possible physical effects such as nearsightedness, postural and musculo-skeletal problems, repetitive stress injuries resembling adult carpal tunnel syndrome, and exposure to electromagnetic emissions. (Studies show that seizures caused by the flashing lights on video games are actually rare.)

Know that your child may catch a case of the "gimmes" from commercials. Discuss commercials with your children and explain how advertising works in terms that they can understand. (See "'Gimmes,'" page 130, for more tips.)

■ *One of the older neighbor kids got three-year-old Michael "hooked" on a popular cartoon show. It was the constant commercials for toys that bothered Michael's mom, Judy, the most. She decided to approach the situation by asking, "Do you know there are evil forces at work during the commercials?" Judy had her son's attention, so she continued, "They are beaming down commercials to try to get us to want all this stuff and spend all our money!" She noticed that many times after that when a commercial appeared, Michael would roll his eyes and say, "Oh no, here they go again, Mom, trying to take all our money!"*

Be aware that your child may pick up negative, insulting language from some TV shows.

Realize that the daily TV news can be one of the most visually violent and scary shows of all for young children. Psychologist Bruno Bettelheim felt that it is visual violence that is the most harmful. He explained that children will conjure up images only as gruesome as they can handle in their own minds as they listen to stories, fables, and fairy tales. Television doesn't offer them the same level of control.

Take note that many experts are questioning whether graphically violent games are a factor in desensitizing children to violence.

■ *Caroline and Gail were concerned when they read in* Time *magazine that the U.S. military has used games like the violent video game "Doom" to improve so-called fire rates—encouraging soldiers to pull the trigger in battle. They also heard on the news that Disney had decided to remove all violent video games from its arcades at both Disney World and Disneyland in the aftermath of several school shooting incidents.*

Keep in mind that true creativity is often stimulated by boredom. TV shows and games supply children with instant images, instead of letting them use their own imaginations. It can also prevent them from social interaction, and real "hands-on" experiences.

Consider offering your child "quiet time" playing in his room, rather than always turning on the TV when you need a break. Taking the few extra minutes needed to bring out the wooden trains or blocks or to start a game of make-believe may really pay off in the long run.

Realize that excessive screen time can rob a child of time for physical activities and start him on the road to being a "coach potato."

Place the TV and video screens so that you can monitor them—for example, in the family room rather than in the child's bedroom.

Note that some families choose to do without TV and video games completely. Dr. Burton White, renowned child psychologist, says, "Rest assured that if your child never sees a single TV program he can still learn language through you in an absolutely magnificent manner." However, socially your child may feel left out of the popular subculture rooted in children's TV shows and games.

Be aware that kids don't always learn as much as you think they are learning from educational software. Dr. Healy points out, "Just because your computer is stimulating your eyes and ears, it doesn't necessarily mean it's doing the same for your intellect!"

> ▪ *Caroline realized that her son was learning very little from his computer game. Instead of working out the math problems himself, he kept begging her to just tell him the one right answer that would make the buzzers ring and the cartoon figure jump up and down!*

On the other hand, computers can be helpful tools, especially for children who have trouble learning with more traditional methods; some are more visual, while others are more auditory or kinesthetic (touchy-feely) learners.

Recognize that computers are particularly good for strengthening some specific skills. Patricia Greenfield, a psychology professor at UCLA, actually attributes a worldwide increase in nonverbal IQ (spatial skills, the use of icons for problem solving, and the ability to understand things from multiple viewpoints) to the spread of video games (for example, Tetris and Marble Madness). So it's not *all* bad!

Be aware that, used with discretion and in moderation, TV, videos, and electronic games can give us all a chance to relax, be entertained, or just "veg out"!

> ■ *Denise recalls that it was hard for her five-year-old to adjust to a full day at school. He often rolled in the door too pooped to do anything but sit on the couch. Instead of rushing him into his homework, discussing his day, or sending him out to play, she realized that letting him relax in front of the TV for half an hour really refreshed him.*

the bottom line

Moderation is the key; it's your job as parents to use your heads and guts to determine your own comfort level with your child's use of today's technology. Once you come up with the rules that feel right for your family, the trick is to enforce them.

thumb sucking

Q: My daughter has sucked her thumb since she was a baby. Not only does it look unattractive, but I'm starting to worry that it could damage her teeth. Now that she's three and I don't see her friends sucking their thumbs, isn't it time for me to step in and stop this habit?

A: Many professionals regard thumb, finger, and pacifier sucking by children under age six as a common, harmless habit. The baby who learned to suck her thumb as a physically soothing mechanism has now learned to rely on it for psychological comfort. Thumb sucking alone is usually neither a sign nor a cause of emotional distress or dysfunction. Intermittent thumb sucking throughout the day, (as opposed to continuous sucking) is usually not harmful to either your young child's teeth or her speech development. (And even when such problems do occur, they are treatable.) If your child is generally well adjusted, relax. Many children naturally outgrow this habit gradually, without parental intervention, often around the time they start school.

immediate response

→ Ignore occasional daytime thumb sucking.

→ Try giving your child a nap. Many kids start sucking their thumbs when they are tired.

→ Offer other means of physical comfort to a child who's sucking his thumb. Pick him up, rub his back or cuddle him, or sit him in your lap and read him a story.

→ Give your child a special toy to cuddle or play with (preferably one that requires two hands).

→ An older child (five or more years) may be indirectly prompted to remove his thumb from his mouth. Try gently saying "Can I see your smile?" or "Show me your new teeth."

sanity savers

Notice when your child sucks his thumb—is he tired, upset, nervous, facing a new situation, or simply relaxing?

Realize that scolding, teasing, parental pressure, and other negative attention may hurt your child's feelings and damage his self-esteem. And teasing ("Only babies suck their thumbs!") may actually reinforce your child's habit—the exact opposite of the result you are trying to achieve.

■ *Looking back on her childhood, Sandra remembered how her uncle Jerry teased her for sucking her thumb. Even though he meant no harm, Sandra was embarrassed by the teasing and never knew how to respond. "Gee, Sandra," he would say, "that thumb looks delicious. What flavor is it anyway? Chocolate, strawberry, or* vanilla? I hope it's chocolate. That's my favorite flavor. Can I have a lick? Come on . . . please!" Though the teasing was intended to discourage her from thumb sucking, Sandra remembers that it made her feel so uneasy, she wanted to suck her thumb even more!

Resist the urge to reach over and physically pull that thumb out of your child's mouth.

Realize that thumb sucking can comfort a child and help her "hold it together" in a difficult situation. It can provide her with a means of feeling comfort and security when she can't rely on her parent or caregiver.

take heart

♥ You're not the only parent who's "turned off" by the sight of a thumb in your child's mouth. Who knows? Maybe a subconscious tape from your own childhood is playing in your head . . . "NO, NO, NO! Take that thumb out of your mouth right now!"

■ Caroline was talking to a teacher outside preschool when she noticed for the very first time that her son's friend Kayla was sucking her thumb while twirling a lock of hair with her free hand. It seemed that Kayla's mother was late picking her up from preschool and Kayla was the only child left. Although Francine, the teacher's aide, reassured Kayla that her mom was on her way, she also kept looking around anxiously and checking her watch as she spoke. Caroline understood that Kayla was using the thumb sucking to help her cope. The sucking and twirling helped her relax and wait patiently for her mom. Instead of clinging to Francine, breaking down in tears, or anxiously looking around for Mom, Kayla was handling the situation quite well all by herself.

Realize that your child's ability to comfort himself is actually a step toward independence.

Respect your child's choice of self-soothing techniques and let the habit run its course.

> Gail recalls how her son Joshua developed his own comfort ritual even before he was a year old. It included a cloth diaper that he carried with him everywhere. Wanting to avoid the many stressful scenes they had experienced with their other kids and their smelly and tattered but beloved "blankies," Gail and her husband took a different approach with Josh. They would say, "Josh, here's a nice fresh one to use." That's how his "lovey" became known as his "fresh"—and he had a stockpile of an even dozen. The twelve diapers were rotated, so that they all smelled just right to Josh. One day when he was nine years old, as he was leaving the house to go to a friend's for a sleepover, Gail noticed that he had left his constant nighttime companion on his bed. She knocked on the window and held it up, but Josh shook his head, indicating he did not want it. That day marked the end of his ritual.

Go with it. Cuddle, rock, and sing to your child while he sucks his thumb, and learn to appreciate thumb sucking's natural ability to soothe you *both*!

Respect your child's ability to gradually decrease thumb sucking all on his own.

> Jill's four-year-old daughter, Kira, refused to go to school without her pacifier "binky." Although Jill was a bit embarrassed by this, she decided it was not a daily battle she wanted to fight. For nearly four months, Kira took her "binky" to school and sucked on it. She managed to talk to her classmates by simply holding her pacifier in

her hand while she spoke and placing it right back in her mouth when she finished. Interestingly, the teacher never heard the kids make fun of her. If she happened to set it down, one of her friends would pick it up and hand it back to her. Then, one day during Christmas vacation, Kira just threw the pacifier into the garbage can, telling her mom, "It doesn't taste good anymore." And that was the end of "binky"!

Let peer pressure help discourage your child.

■ *Big brother Sean was sitting on the couch beside five-year-old Nolan, who was sucking his thumb. Sean watched Nolan for a minute, then said, "You know, Nolan, when you start kindergarten next week, if you suck your thumb, the other kids will make fun of you." Nolan continued sucking his thumb while he considered this. Then, suddenly pulling his thumb out of his mouth, he confidently answered, "Well, the kids won't see me because I'm not going to suck my thumb when I'm in kindergarten. I'm only going to do it when I'm at home." True to his word, Nolan stopped sucking his thumb whenever he was around other kids from school.*

Help your thumb sucker wash periodically during the day to ensure that his thumb stays as germ free as possible, to cut down on the chances of catching colds, ingesting dirt, and spreading germs.

Discuss the downsides of thumb sucking in private with your five-year-old and ask your dentist for advice.

■ *Marla relaxed when her dentist told her that her preschooler would probably stop sucking his thumb all by himself; he added that he didn't know for sure why this happened. His guess was that once the four front baby teeth fell out, there was an open space where the thumb used to rest; sucking probably just didn't feel the same anymore.*

Help your child practice speaking clearly. Put your arm around her as you say, "Honey, I couldn't understand you. Try taking your thumb out of your mouth, and tell me again."

Turn it into a game. If you decide to help your child give up sucking his thumb, set up a little challenge ("Let's see if you can stop sucking your thumb in the kitchen, before school"), rather than giving an order to stop "cold turkey."

Consider working out a withdrawal plan by gradually setting limits on thumb sucking. Try putting certain rooms off limits for thumb sucking. Or allow only certain times of the day for thumb sucking—while watching a favorite TV show, in the car seat, or at bedtime, for example.

Try setting a timer to limit thumb sucking to certain amounts of time. Start at thirty minutes and decrease the time by five minutes every couple of days.

Use a special signal that only you and your child understand to secretly remind your child to remove his thumb from his mouth when he starts sucking it.

■ *When Sally wanted to remind Max, her thumb-sucking five-year-old, to take his thumb out of his mouth, she borrowed the signal Carol Burnett had used when she said goodnight on her TV show. She established eye contact with Max and then gently pulled her own ear.*

Involve your child in daytime activities that involve two hands.

> ■ *Alexia saw that when her daugter Kaylee was busy with Play-Doh or her Magic Markers, she didn't even think about sucking her thumb.*

When your child achieves even a small degree of success in decreasing his habit, be generous with your praise. (See page 240 for more about praise pointers.)

If your child is receptive, ask him to establish his own goal for when he will give up sucking his thumb.

> ■ *Miriam sucked her thumb, and her twin, Mark, sucked a pacifier. After discussing it with Mom and Dad, the twins both decided they wanted to quit. However, they seemed to have a hard time remembering their vow. Dad encouraged the kids and decided perhaps what they needed was a goal to shoot for. He was planning a big family vacation, and the twins were excited about it. He took out the calendar, and together the family counted the days until they would leave. Dad then asked the twins if they thought they could leave Mark's pacifier at home when they went on their trip. Mark said he could do it, but only if Miriam promised not to suck her thumb. Miriam agreed. As they crossed off the days on the calendar, each child was reminded of the goal. To Dad's surprise, when the time came, they had no problem kicking the habit.*

In order for it to work, your child must want to stop. Try offering a reward or using stickers or a chart with stars for thumb-free days.

If your child seems to be obsessed with thumb sucking, depressed, or withdrawn much of the time, consult your pediatrician. The child may need help in solving an underlying problem.

the bottom line

Instead of regarding your child's thumb sucking as a bad habit, consider it a step toward independence; she is learning how to comfort herself.

time-out

Q: My friends suggest that I try giving a "time-out" when my son misbehaves repeatedly. What is involved? Do I have to drag a chair around with me?

A: "Time-out" is literally the pause that interrupts inappropriate behavior. For some, it refreshes as well, giving the kids (and you) a chance to cool down. Many parenting experts recommend a rigid procedure, including the use of a specific location and a set time period. Others have adopted a more flexible approach that can be used anywhere. There's really no need to "schlep" that chair, since there's no one right way to do it; tailor your time-out approach to what works best for your child. When your child breaks a rule, immediately and matter-of-factly stop the dangerous or inappropriate behavior by saying "Time-out."

sanity savers

Define which behaviors warrant a time-out and use it each time the behavior occurs. Many parents reserve time-out for hitting and hurting others, destroying property, using "bad words," and out-of-

Tips

...e-out simply as an acceptable
...at serves to stop the dangerous
...te behavior immediately.

→ Does a child have to be relocated for a time-out? That depends on what works for your child and you. Some children are better able to calm down and regroup in a designated place. Others fall apart at the thought of sitting on a "time-out" chair for the purpose of calming down or of contemplating their poor behavior.

→ A time-out can be brief; it's not meant to be a punishment or "doing time for the crime." Some experts recommend using one minute per year of age as a general time frame for "cooling down." However, many kids need only a few seconds to regroup.

→ Use time-out for only the most serious of offenses; otherwise, it will lose its effect.

→ If time-out is not comfortable for you to implement, or if it isn't effective with your child, stop using it.

control behavior. Other methods, such as distraction, work for less serious offenses. (See "Discipline," page 82, "Sibling Rivalry," page 261, "Anger," page 19, and "Tantrums," page 276, for additional ideas.)

Use the words "Time-out for . . ." as you immediately identify the bad behavior verbally for the child.

■ Sally calmly told her son, "Whoops! Time-out for punching your sister."

Remember, time-out as we define it does not teach your child anything; it only mandates a STOP to an undesirable behavior, while preserving the dignity of both you and your child.

Give your child the words he needs to use next time something similar happens.

> ■ *After giving four-year-old Sammy numerous time-outs for hitting, Eric, his dad, modeled the correct response for his son: "Michael, Sammy is upset. He wants to tell you that he would like a turn now."*

Note that some parents and teachers call a time-out *before* the aggressive or dangerous behavior happens. If you have a very active, distractable child, watch for the signs that the bad behavior is brewing and call a time-out to allow the child to cool down and regroup before he gets in trouble.

Decide whether you will remove your child to an isolated location, away from toys and the attention of family members. Is it helpful for your child to spend some time alone cooling down, or does he just become more furious and uncooperative in isolation? Consider letting your child decide when he's ready to join others.

> ■ *Tina had read so much about "time-out," she came to believe it was the "be-all, end-all" solution to just about every parenting dilemma— until she had to put it to the test! Her son, Vic, absolutely refused to go in the designated kitchen chair, and she literally had to drag him there, kicking and screaming. Then she found herself standing over him, anxiously praying for the sound of the kitchen timer, while he kicked, squirmed, and eventually fell out of the chair. One day, in exasperation, she simply put him in his*

*room, closed the door, and hoped he would calm
down. Without all the exciting negative attention
from Mom, he did just that. Alone in his room, he
played quietly with his toys and calmed down.
That was so much more effective!*

Praise your child for staying in the designated
time-out location if you use one.

Realize that time-out can be flexible; it doesn't
have to be limited to one chair, one location, or
even a "place" at all. While one designated time-
out place at home may work best, you may need to
use time-out at Grandma's, or even in the bank.

> ■ *One day at the grocery store, three-year-old
> Andrea had a full-blown tantrum in the cereal
> aisle. Lynn, her mom, had already told her that
> they were not going to buy sugared cereal today.
> However, Andrea could not be consoled, and all
> eyes were on Lynn, wondering what she would do.
> Since this had happened before, Lynn was all
> ready with a plan. The manager had designated a
> spot where she could park her half-loaded cart.
> So Lynn picked Andrea up and said, "Time-out in
> the car for tantrums." Andrea was able to calm
> down in a few minutes, and they returned to the
> store. Intentionally avoiding the cereal aisle, they
> finished the rest of their shopping as quickly as
> possible.*

Consider giving a quick hug or a smile to
welcome your child back after a time-out.

Guide your preschooler away from trouble when
time-out is over. After time-out, five-year-olds often
can go right back into the original situation and
behave appropriately, but sometimes they need
your help. Many younger kids don't do well going
back to the scene of the confrontation; distraction
works better for them.

■ *Gail recalls, "I used time-out in my preschool class to immediately stop aggressive behavior. If a three-year-old began punching his best friend, I'd quickly step behind him and gently but firmly give him a 'hug hold' as I whispered in his ear, 'Time-out for hitting.' A few seconds later, I slowly released him as I said, 'Time-out is over. Let's go to the block corner.' Then I would talk to him about it later that day or even the next day, when he was calm. Often, as in this case, I didn't even use a time-out chair."*

Remember that young children have little understanding of the passage of time; instead of saying "Time-out for three minutes," try using a timer, bell, or whistle as a signal.

Try to keep an eye on your child and "catch her" being good. Then reward her with a compliment. "I notice how nicely you're sharing your puzzle, Laura. Doesn't it feel good to be kind?"

Use time-out, like a strong spice, sparingly. If used for every offense, time-out can lose its effectiveness (while you lose your mind).

Discuss time-out together as a family; consider including when and why it will be used, where it will take place, and how long it will last. Invite your kids' participation in the discussion.

Continue to teach the lesson outside the heat of the moment. Talk with your

take heart

♥ *You're not the only parent who's asked yourself, "Why did I call this time-out, again?" You may find yourself physically battling your way to the time-out chair as your child kicks, screams, bites, punches, and swears at you. Then you ask yourself, "Now, how long should he stay in time-out for all of that?"*

children about their behavior again during bath time, bedtime, story time, or in a more formal family meeting.

Remember that unacceptable behavior does not change instantly.

Use the word "time-out" in various ways to reinforce the meaning; it may catch on sooner than you think!

■ *Donna told the kids, "Mommy needs a time-out in her room. I'm too angry to talk to you right now."*

■ *When Sally's boys were fighting over the same toy, she quickly stepped in and said, "Time-out for the fire truck. This toy needs a break until we can figure out how to take turns."*

■ *Three-year-old Nolan was annoyed when the cat kept grabbing the string on his new pull-along toy. Caroline was amazed that instead of kicking and screaming at the cat, he took control of the situation and assertively said, "No, no, Kitty! Time-out for pulling on my toy. Go under the bed until the buzzer rings." (Then he quite carefully set the timer halfway around, having no idea that was a full thirty minutes! Of course, with a typical three-year-old's attention span, Nolan wasn't in the room even five minutes later!)*

the bottom line

Kids need you to help them put the brakes on bad behavior until they learn to do it themselves; time-out is one way to immediately stop bad behavior and help everyone regroup. The trick is not to let the time-out itself lead to a power struggle.

traveling with the kids

Q: My wife and I agree that our whole family needs to get away together. It actually has been a monumental task of rearranging five daily schedules, but we finally accomplished it! Now the pressure is on to make it perfect—a dream vacation come true, and nothing less. Any tips on how I might help guarantee a fun and memorable trip for all of us?

A: Plan, plan, plan, and don't forget to pack your patience, a sense of humor, and a positive attitude. Keep in mind that the term "vacation" takes on a totally different meaning than it did before you had children, mainly because you and your wife may be away, but you're both still working—on duty twenty-four hours a day, seven days a week. So try to limit the number of expectations you have, and involve the kids in planning the trip. Most of all . . . lighten up! Try to relax, and enjoy; after all, that's the purpose of the trip!

Checklists for Safe Travel

Before You Leave

Place the following in your first aid kit:

- Your pediatrician's phone number

- Your insurance information with preapproval telephone number.

- Thermometer

- Medicine spoon

- Syrup of ipecac or liquefied activated charcoal to induce vomiting. (Use only with the recommendation of the Poison Control Center or your child's doctor.)

- Wet wipes

- Tweezers (precision tip) to help remove splinters, ticks, and insect stingers

- Band-Aids (assorted sizes)

- Ice packs to help reduce swelling or bruising

- Elastic bandage to help secure an ice pack on "boo-boos"

- Antibiotic ointment to help prevent infection from cuts, scrapes, and bruises

- A nonaspirin pain and fever reducer and dosage measure

- A tummy settler for diarrhea or constipation (ask your doctor for a recommendation)

- An antihistamine to stop allergic reactions

- Calamine lotion or 0.5 percent hydrocortisone cream (with doctor's permission) for rashes and itchy bites.

- Sunscreen

- Adhesive or masking tape (to secure disposable diaper tapes that won't stick)

- Small scissors

- Small flashlight

Also consider the following to keep in your car:

- A small pillow, blanket, and light sweater for each child

- Plastic bags (Ziploc and garbage)

- Disposable toilet seat protectors

- A roll of toilet paper

- A roll of paper towels

On the Way

Take the following precautions to curb motion sickness:

- Keep the child safely secured in place by buckling up properly according to the child's weight and age.

- Circulate fresh air. In the car, crack open a window; in a plane, direct the overhead air vent for more comfort.

- Drive during off-peak times of the day to allow a steadier pace, thereby avoiding frequent starts and stops that contribute to motion sickness.

- Arrange travel in the wee hours of the morning or at naptime (providing the driver is well rested). Sleeping or resting with eyes closed for a good portion of the trip reduces the chances of feeling ill.

- If your child shows signs of motion sickness, discourage activities that require focusing close up, such as looking at books, coloring, and playing with handheld games.

- Try distracting the child from feeling queasy by singing songs, offering him a cracker, or playing a tape recorder with some favorite recorded stories.

- Draw attention to sights in the distance on the horizon, to help the child avoid gazing at fast-moving objects alongside the car, which will exacerbate motion sickness.

- Feed your child light, frequent snacks to avoid an empty tummy, which often contributes to a queasy feeling while traveling in the car (whole-grain breadsticks, crackers, and pretzels work well).

- Avoid fatty foods like greasy fries, chips, burgers, ice cream, and other rich desserts that add to motion-sickness discomfort.

- Offer water, nonacidic fruit juices, and ginger ale that has gone flat to avoid upsetting sensitive tummies on the move.

- Wear "Sea-bands," elastic bracelets designed to be placed on the pressure points of the inner wrists and said to stop nausea associated with motion sickness on land or at sea. They can be purchased at camping supply stores, some pharmacies, and health food stores. Although they do not come in sizes, you can sew a few stitches to ensure a snug fit on a small child's wrist.

When You Get There

Take the following precautions to avoid accidents:

- Never leave a young child alone in a hotel room or the pool area, even for a short period of time.

- Tie or tape the drapery cords out of the reach of the children to avoid possible strangulation.

- If you find the bathroom tap water runs scalding hot immediately when you turn the handle, place a decorative child's sticker on the cold water faucet handle and tell the kids they can turn only the handle with the happy face (or whatever it is) on it.

- Check to see if heavy objects like televisions are secured so that a curious child will not suffer the crushing consequences of climbing up on the furniture.

- Ask the hotel management to tape any exposed electrical cords or wires from the air conditioner, refrigerator, or floor lamp to avoid tripping or shocking a child.

- Keep a young child from locking himself in a hotel bathroom by placing some masking tape over the door-locking mechanism (thereby depressing the metal protrusion until it is flush with the edge of the door). The door will close but not lock.

- Keep a two- to five-year-old out of the whirlpool or hot tub. Their bodies are too small for the hot temperature of the water, and the child could pass out.

- If you are visiting a friend's or relative's house, assuming that it has been childproofed is a mistake. With permission from your hosts, when you arrive, take a walk through the house and address anything that you feel poses a danger to your child.

sanity savers

Schedule some family meetings preceding the vacation to plan the trip, including the behavior that is expected and the consequences of misbehavior. (See page 17 for more on family meetings and setting consequences.)

Have older children help collect pictures, state guidebooks, maps, and brochures. Good resources include the library, a travel agency, and the American Automobile Association (AAA). Check the travel section of your local newspaper as well as the state Web sites, which may even include information about highways undergoing construction, travel coupons, and other helpful hints. Some popular vacation destinations also have their own Web sites.

Sit down with the family and look at the travel materials you've collected and discuss all the options.

Plan a vacation that stays in one spot—the beach, the mountains, a theme park, etc. (Once you're there, you're there!) Although some toddlers don't mind a Paris today, Rome tomorrow type of trip, it's probably not right for most.

Once you've chosen the spot, get the kids involved. Tell them where you're going, how long you're staying, what they'll be doing, and so on. Show pictures if possible.

Get input from the kids—their likes and dislikes, hopes and expectations, and tell them yours. (It is a valuable life lesson for children to learn that we all make compromises for each other and that no one can do everything he or she wants, not even Mom or Dad!) Include all family members in as many decisions as possible. Although a preschooler is usually not going to choose the destination, talking about what you're going to do and see in advance increases her anticipation. The planning becomes part of the excitement.

Consider "practicing" with a mini-getaway. Try a short camping trip close to home, an overnight or weekend at a city hotel with a pool, or just an all-day trip somewhere fun, like a local beach.

Let the kids decorate their car seats with stickers to make them look special and ready for the trip.

Before your vacation begins, take your child to visit the airport, the train, or the bus station so he will have been introduced to the hustle and bustle of the new place. This can minimize fears and bad behavior on the day of departure.

take heart

♥ *You're not the only parents who are completely overwhelmed by the thought of the preparations necessary to get away with two or three young kids. Just laying out the amount of stuff you have to take is enough to make you want to cancel the trip on the spot!*

Create a daily "trip routine" and follow it; structure and predictability help promote cooperative behavior. Try to follow the same routine and time for naps and meals that you use at home, whenever possible.

Bring along some favorite items from home— a pillow, a blanket, a favorite book, or a teddy bear—to help your child feel secure.

■ *Adina remembered to bring a kid's portable tape recorder to play her daughter's favorite lullaby tape, which helped her fall asleep in a strange place.*

Encourage each child—even a two-year-old—to pack her own backpack. Let your kids choose a few of their own toys—small stuffed animals, books, tapes, and colored pencils, prepackaged snacks, paper, stickers, and games without small pieces. (A noisy choo-choo train or talking doll may drive you crazy, so use your parental veto power!)

take heart

♥ *You're not the only parents at the airport "schlepping" a diaper bag, a double stroller, two car seats, two dolls, two "blankies" and two dawdling toddlers with backpacks. Do you find yourself ever guiltily longing for those spur-of-the-moment romantic getaways that required only one carry-on bag for the two of you?*

Make getting there fun; ask your kids interesting questions, sing their favorite songs, and play games to avoid boredom and the inevitable, oft-repeated question "Are we there yet?"

Offer snacks—munching travelers are less likely to fight.

■ *Sherry came up with a great idea for serving a variety of small quantities of cereal, raisins, granola, and croutons. She put the snacks into a plastic vitamin container that has seven doors that little fingers can easily open, each compartment holding a different treat. The rule was that only one door at a time could be opened. In this way, if there was an unexpected jolt, everything wouldn't spill out onto the floor.*

■ *Jim unpacked two of his army canteens, one for each of his sons to use every time they went*

on a long car trip. They each hung their canteen
on the hook above the window in the backseat
and knew that was the "ration" of juice they had
to drink for a few hours. The kids really liked
drinking out of their daddy's canteens, and it
remained a special treat year after year because
they were never used at any other time.

Set reasonable limits, tailored to your youngest
traveler, on how far you can comfortably drive in a
day.

Rotate the seating arrangement from time to
time. (It's a bit of a hassle to move the car seats,
but sometimes it's worth it.)

■ *Even after many planned pit stops for food and*
fun, once in a while Carla and Cassidy started
bickering in the car and needed to be separated.
That's when Mom took the wheel and Dad moved
into the backseat with his daughters. They played
a special game at times like this. Dad and the
girls teamed up against Mom in a game of "I Spy."
Mom always lost, as Dad cleverly united the
formerly quibbling siblings into victorious
teammates. Because the parents chose not to do
this very often, it worked like a charm to turn the
mood around!

Reserve accommodations in advance. Avoid the
nightmare of driving late at night in a thunder-
storm from hotel to hotel, only to be greeted
repeatedly by flashing "NO VACANCY" signs.

Make frequent pit stops for young children who
need to run around. Carry an inflatable beach ball
to kick around at the rest stop. (You can store it,
deflated, in the glove compartment.)

Let a timer help you and your children know when it's time for lunch or another pit stop. Remember, young children have little understanding of minutes or hours.

Have a change of clothes (or two) handy for a young child. Kids' outfits take up so little space, and accidents are bound to happen.

■ *Caroline remembers her frequent flights to Florida to visit her son's grandparents when he was a toddler. After Sean began to experience motion sickness, Caroline patted herself on the back for always bringing a change of clothes on board. Then came the time Sean threw up all over the new outfit Grandma had sent him. No sooner had Caroline changed his clothes than he had another loud bout of "the heaves." They finally arrived at the airport, greeting Grandma with Sean clad only in a diaper and wrapped in a stained blanket!*

Pack an outfit for each day (plus a couple extra for emergencies), including underwear and socks, in a two-gallon-size zipper top plastic bag so the kids can get dressed without your help.

When you arrive at your destination, realize that it's not a sin to not do everything together as a family.

■ *Monica and Russ realized that when their two-year-old was in the midst of an inconsolable tantrum, no one was going to enjoy miniature golf. So Monica went back to the room, put the child down for a nap, and took a bubble bath herself in peace. She later rejoined the family with a rested "happy camper." Next time the two-year-old showed signs of fatigue, Russ volunteered to go to the room, where he caught a quick nap himself with the toddler.*

For two- to five-year-olds, keep activities simple. One or two activities a day is often all they can handle. Treat yourself to room service or rent a video when your child needs some "downtime."

> ■ *Caroline's family took a trip to a popular family vacation spot in northern Wisconsin. When they arrived, Caroline was impressed with the wide variety of activities geared to tots and preschoolers, from elaborate water playgrounds to mini-golf. But after a couple of days of sightseeing in the heat, she came to share her kids' appreciation of simpler pleasures. Four-year-old Sean delighted in skipping stones across the lake with Dad, while one-year-old Nolan squealed happily as he took his first steps chasing a duck.*

Find out what special accommodations or "time-savers" are available at amusement parks.

> ■ *When visiting an amusement park with his toddler, who was too short for or afraid of many of the attractions, Pat learned to take advantage of a real time-saver. Called "Switch-off" at Disney and "Trade-off" at some other amusement parks, it works like this: at the point of embarkation, one parent waits with the toddler, in the Trade-off area, while the other parent and the older children go on the ride. Then the parents "trade off" and the parent who has been waiting gets to go on the ride without waiting in the hour-long line!*

Save souvenirs and remembrances from the trip. Kids love to collect things that don't even cost anything, such as matchbook covers, napkins, postcards, small stones, ticket stubs, and autographs from the waiters and other people they meet.

Make the most of your vacation: arrange a family meeting after you've returned to talk about it and to make scrapbooks, picture albums, and video presentations.

Realize that your perception of the trip's highlights may be very different than those of your child.

■ *Doris was looking forward to an educational trip to Washington, D.C., with her kids, ages four through eight. The kids were actively included in the planning process, and it promised to be a fabulous learning experience. When they returned home after a busy, successful trip, Doris couldn't wait to ask the kids, "Now, what was your very most favorite thing about the trip to Washington, D.C.?" Without hesitation they all agreed, "The ice machine in the hotel!" Those perfectly formed, clear, tiny cylinders with a hole in the middle that fell in abundance with a grinding bang whenever you pressed the button! This was not exactly the answer she had hoped for! But Doris acknowledged that kids don't always learn what you think they are learning but are, nevertheless, making fond memories of their own.*

Accept the fact that you may not be able to make "quality time" happen, no matter how much money you spend or where you go, and realize that quality time seems to blossom naturally out of spending "quantity time" together as a family, loving and laughing at what tickles your children's fancy.

the bottom line

Try to let go of the guilt and pressure associated with achieving perfection, and accept the fact that your trip will be an interesting adventure for the whole family, complete with many memorable moments—some of which may challenge your sanity!

values

Q: These days it seems as if respect, empathy, honesty, and gratitude too often take a backseat to an everyone-for-himself attitude. Is it too early to start teaching my three-year-old some good old-fashioned values?

A: Not only is it not too early, you are already doing it whether you realize it or not! No matter how hard you try to say the right thing, it's what your kids see you do that will stick with them. So it's important to take a deep breath and try to be at least semiconscious of what you are doing as much of the time as you can. Have patience—while you can lay the groundwork early on, it takes a long time for values to fully "kick in."

sanity savers

Identify and list the values that are important to your family. Visual, concrete models help children deal with abstract concepts, even if they can't read yet. You can also look for pictures that illustrate values.

■ *When Caroline taught Sunday school, her preschool class made a "values tree." Each leaf had a value written on it and a simple example. The Conservation leaf had on it: "We recycle newspapers to save the trees." For Courage: "I'll sleep without the lights on tonight." For Empathy: "I can imagine how it would feel if that happened to me." Forgiveness: "That's okay—I know it was an accident." Generosity: "I can share my cookie with you." Honesty: "I'm sorry I broke this." Justice: "Let's take turns." Kindness: "Let's ask the new kid to play with us." During the year, the class continued to reinforce positive values by taking a picture of each child doing something good (sharing, hugging, taking turns) and pinning it to the matching leaf.*

State "the Golden Rule" simply and often to reinforce its importance. (For many families, it becomes their only rule.)

■ *Gail repeatedly reminded her children, "Treat others as you want to be treated." Her children practiced daily what she preached, though not always easily or successfully, by sharing toys, waiting in line for the slide, and being kind to others.*

■ *Jim Fay, education consultant and author of* Parenting with Love and Logic, *says: "we influence our kids by the way we treat them. A corollary to the Golden Rule applies here: Kids will do to others as their parents do to them. Treating our kids with respect teaches them to go and do likewise."*

Explain to your children *why* **we do what we do,** including our underlying feelings and reasons.

■ *Barbara told her kids, "Take turns so both of you have a good time. If you are having trouble, we can flip a coin to pick who goes first, and who can go first next time."*

■ *When Tony found a toy in the hotel lobby, his dad said, "What a neat toy you found! I'll bet somebody's looking for it. Let's bring it to the 'lost and found.' Remember how bad you felt when you couldn't go to the pool because someone took your water wings?"*

Catch kids "being good," and praise with words that specificallly convey your values. (See box on praise pointers in "Self-Esteem," page 240.)

■ *When Richie took his three kids for their annual dental checkups, he noticed that his middle child volunteered to go first. "Wow!" he said. "It takes a lot of courage to be the first one in the dentist's chair."*

■ *Sally told her grandson, "Thanks for telling me the truth about how the pitcher broke. It's not easy to admit when you make a mistake."*

■ *When three-year-old Ryan picked a minuscule crumb off his cookie and slyly held it out, although his mom could barely see it, let alone taste it, she decided to focus on the positive, exclaiming, "Thank you for sharing."*

take heart

♥ *You're not the only parent who has ever had to lower his or her expectations a bit. (Well, okay, maybe even quite a bit!)*

Resist the urge to nag, bribe, or berate your kids in the name of teaching values . . . it just may backfire!

■ *Caroline was embarrassed the time she yelled across the playground, "It's rude to cut in line!" In front of everyone, Sean boldly shouted back, "It's rude to yell, Mommy, and you do it all the time!"*

Encourage empathy by discussing hurt feelings with everyone present, rather than singling out the "wrongdoer."

Admit when you have made a mistake, and say "I'm sorry."

   ■ *After losing his temper, Brad confessed, "Daddy was really in a bad mood. I'm sorry I yelled at you. Next time, I'm going to try to calm down before I talk."*

Let your children see you take responsibility for your actions.

   ■ *One mother reported that when her son Lucas said, "Mommy, the speed limit is thirty-five and the needle says forty," she replied, "Oops! My mistake. Thanks for noticing. I'm breaking the law, and I'd better slow down."*

Give kids simple chores to help them develop a sense of responsibility, pride, and their special role in the family. (See "Chores," page 57.)

   ■ *When Gina and Matt attended an open house at nursery school, they couldn't wait to see what five-year-old Austin had drawn for his assignment, "Why I Am Important." Imagine their amusement at the picture of a little boy holding a huge shovel with several mysterious clumps by his side. Of course! Austin was the family's chief pooper-scooper, and proud of it!*

Give your child some chores relating to the entire family in order to develop compassion and feelings for others. Asking kids to pick up their own toys will only get them tidy bedrooms (if you are lucky). Asking them to help you set the table can help them learn to consider other's needs. ("Does Baby need a soft spoon? Does Daddy need a knife?")

Take some time out of your planned schedule to do something good in the presence of your child, such as calling 911 when you see a car accident, giving directions to an out-of-towner, opening a door for a handicapped person or someone laden down with packages, or struggling with a stroller. It may make you late for an appointment, but it will be well worth it! (Calling ahead to say you're sorry that you'll be late presents another opportunity for modeling responsible behavior.)

■ *Malcolm and his four-year-old daughter, Ellen, were leaving the store with a few items in the middle of the afternoon. Spying an elderly woman having some trouble negotiating the curb with her wheelchair, he stopped and helped her. After helping the woman, Malcolm pointed out to Ellen that when he takes time out to do a good turn for someone in need, it makes him feel very good!*

Demonstrate kindness by putting money in the Salvation Army kettles—explain to your child where the money goes and how it makes you feel good inside to help others. Gradually, your child will internalize the positive feelings that come from being respectful, kind, and helpful to others.

Include children in performing acts of kindness (the less abstract, the better). Young children are able to feel more compassion for someone they know, or at least can see, than for an orphan halfway around the world. (After all, didn't you ever wonder how cleaning *your* plate was going to help "the starving children in China"?)

■ *Gail made a fresh batch of chicken soup, bundled up all three kids, and they all trudged together through the snow to visit their sick neighbor. They all felt great when her face lit up at seeing them on her doorstep and even better when she ate the soup and said, "Thanks so much. That's just what I needed, some good old-fashioned 'penicillin'!"*

Recognize that young children think and reason differently from adults. Preschoolers are happy to help you shop for a present or food for the needy. However, for most four-year-olds, being asked to give away one of their own toys or use their own money to buy a child a gift may cause feelings of resentment. (This is a perfectly age-appropriate response.)

If relatives or friends demonstrate values different from the ones you want your children to adopt, talk in a positive way to the children about what's important to *you*.

■ *Millie got sick of hearing her kids ask Grandma, "Whadidya bring me?" before she could even get in the door. Millie told them, "I know it makes Grandma happy to buy you things, but in our house we are grateful just to have her company, because people are more important than things."*

Teach the difference between compassion and lack of assertiveness to a child who seems "wimpy" or too nice.

■ *Payden said to her daughter, "I see how well you are waiting your turn, but you don't have to let others push in line ahead of you. They wouldn't like to be treated that way. How about if you use words and tell them to wait their turn at the end of the line?"*

Summon the courage to let your kids know what's important to you even if it's not popular. Having clear limits and following through with positive discipline strategies when those limits are challenged or tested helps children feel secure. Selfish, bossy kids are often raised by very permissive parents.

■ *When four-year-old Sean lamented, "I don't want no church today. It's so boring!" Caroline said, "I understand it's not lots of fun for you, but it's important to me that we go; I would appreciate your sitting still, to show respect to God. Today I want to thank God for Grandma's getting out of the hospital. What do you want to thank God for?" Sean smiled and said, "I'll thank God that tomorrow's not Sunday!"*

■ *When one of the five children in Margaret's family really wanted to do something that simply wasn't allowed, her father would sound the familiar family refrain: "You say everyone is doing it, eh? What's our name?" The child would respond quickly and proudly, "Jackson!" Then Dad would add, "And the Jacksons are not doing it!" And that was that!*

Teach your child to value things that can't be bought in stores. (See "'Gimmes,'" page 130, for more ideas.)

■ *Gail recalls, "Ever since my daughter Rachel was little, we both enjoyed taking the time to make unique handmade gifts and cards for special occasions. She is now an adult and is quite well known for her one-of-a-kind customized cards and gifts."*

Involve your child in volunteer opportunities such as visiting nursing homes, raking leaves for a sick neighbor, or putting together a holiday basket for a needy family. Discuss with her how fortunate your family is, as well as your responsibility to help others in your community.

> ■ *One Sunday afternoon Caroline and her five-year-old spent a couple of hours in their church's soup kitchen, where they chopped up a lot of fruit and made a huge salad. Later, Caroline was amazed at how much work Sean was capable of doing. His little face beamed when he received compliments and thanks as he served his salad to the people in line.*

> ■ *Tom was careful to schedule family volunteer activities when the kids were well fed and well rested. He found out the hard way that trying to work in a soup kitchen with two crabby, hungry kids glued to his leg was not the best way to model empathy.*

Realize that the process of teaching values can be challenging, difficult, and often inconvenient, but it's well worth it! Kids who have strong values often also develop a high sense of self-esteem and can better resist peer pressure. Studies show that kind, compassionate kids are not only successful but also well liked.

the bottom line

When you take the time to talk with your children about how the values you are modeling relate to your everyday life, they will more easily internalize them.

whining

Q: My daughter has started whining every time she wants something. If I don't give in, the whining escalates to screaming and crying. Just the pitch of her voice is driving me crazy! What can I do to discourage this?

A: Many young children go through a whining, shrieking phase. Sometimes whining may be the only way your child can express herself when she is feeling tired, frustrated, cranky, hungry, or ill. At other times, she may be trying to get your attention or whittle down your resolve. The unrelenting tone can certainly feel like torture to even the most patient parent! The key is to stand your ground and not give in to whining and other annoying behavior—or you may find *you're* actually encouraging it to continue.

immediate response

→ Refuse to give in to those annoying tones so the child learns he will not get what he wants by whining.

→ Use an "I" statement to express your feelings. Say, "I cannot listen to that voice, it hurts my rs." (Then, with your hands over your ears, leave the room.)

→ Try some humor, and whine right back! The child will often get the message and will begin talking in his regular voice again after a good laugh.

→ Take a deep breath, then ask yourself if your child is frustrated because you have become inappropriately demanding due to *your* very bad mood. If so, try to restore good feelings and consider apologizing to your child.

→ Try giving your child a quick hug or cuddle (while ignoring the whining); this won't work for every child, but for some it's just enough of the right kind of attention to reset the mood and enable you to mollify "the whiner."

→ Treat your child as if he were speaking a foreign language—and if you know one, consider responding in a foreign tongue. Your child will wonder what you're saying and, for the moment, may stop whining!

sanity savers

Acknowledge your child's feelings without attacking her character.

■ *When Daniel was little, he hated the way his father attacked his character and made threats to get his point across, "You big baby, you'd better stop whining this instant or I'll really give you something to cry about!" he'd say. That's why Daniel consciously chose to tell his daughter, "Samantha, that's enough! I can see how tired you are, but I still don't like whining and I simply won't listen to it!"*

Ask your child to speak in his "big boy" or "big girl" voice.

■ *Mom told Caitlin, "I can't understand you when you whine. I'll bet you can make a really big voice and talk to me. Take a big breath and tell me like this," Mom puffed up her chest and deepened her voice, which Caitlin seemed to enjoy imitating.*

Praise your child when she speaks in an acceptable voice.

■ *"I'd be happy to get you a glass of juice since you ask so politely," Mom told Cody.*

When your child is caught in a cycle of whining, be absolutely consistent in your refusal to reward the whining. It's not always easy to hold your ground, but it is necessary in breaking bad habits. Be forewarned, your kids will test you to the "*n*th" degree. And on a bad day, you may feel like a broken record!

Tell your child that you will ignore him when he chooses to whine. Even scolding him for the whining serves as a form of attention he may be seeking. Adopt a "neutral" facial expression, avoid direct eye contact, and direct your attention elsewhere.

Distract the child by directing her attention to something else. As you walk to the window, pretend to be a little bird in the tree and start "talking" to her in your best bird voice: "Dana, come and see my nest. I have two little baby birds in here. I wonder if you can see them?"

take heart

♥ *You're not the only parent who's ever found it impossible to ignore something that nearly drives you crazy!*

Admit when you've simply "had it!" Tell your child that you just can't stay in the same room with him while he's whining. Either *you* take a time-out by leaving the room yourself or give a time-out to your child. (See "Time-Out," page 299, and "Wits' End," page 331, for helpful strategies.)

Try taking a breather when your child is whining in public. Tell him that you are both leaving for a little while, until he gets control of his voice.

Use humor to jog your child out of his whiny mood.

■ *When Nolan ran into the kitchen whining about getting another cookie, something in his dramatically contorted face struck Caroline as funny. She whined right back, "Oh, no-o-o-o, not you-o-o-o again! I just started washing these dishes and there's so-o-o-o-o many of them." Nolan looked startled for a second. Then, to Caroline's amazement, he put his hands on his hips, wagged his finger in her face, and firmly said, "Mommy! You know I can't understand you when you whine!"*

Tape-record your child whining so he can hear how he sounds. This is often surprising to the child and often gets a big laugh! You might also tape-record your child asking for something in an acceptable way, though this isn't quite as much fun.

Practice ways to ask for something without whining with your child. (Try role-playing, using puppets, or telling stories to make your point. See the role-playing box on page 25 for more ideas.)

■ *While Manny was on the phone, his three-year-old daughter, Christa, rudely interrupted him by whining incessantly for a cookie. The next day,*

*Manny had some one-on-one time with his
daughter. He chose to discuss the previous day's
incident as they gathered her dolls for a "picnic."
Manny said, "You know, yesterday, I couldn't listen
to you when you were whining for a cookie. Here's
how I like to be asked: 'Excuse me, Daddy, may I
please have a cookie?' I'll bet you can make one
of your dolls ask for a cookie just the right way."
When Christa complied, Manny complimented
"the doll" on how politely she had asked, without
whining.*

Expect your child's whining to actually increase
temporarily when he doesn't get his way. Hold your
ground! Thankfully it will lessen as he realizes you
won't give in.

Go all out and if you can't beat 'em, join 'em!
Declare an "all-whining" day.

■ *Gus and Jan tried an idea suggested by author
and parent educator Fred Gosman. They called the
kids together and organized an all-whining
Sunday! Gus and Jan started out the day by
painstakingly demonstrating the annoying decibels
and shrill tones that were required. Any pleasant-
toned conversation was strictly forbidden. Although
Gus and Jan had great fun with their little charade,
the kids soon grew tired of it. They called everyone
together in exasperation and begged, "Please, no
more whining!" Everyone in the family got the
point, and there was no more whining in their
house for a while.*

Help your child come up with "non-whiny" ways of
expressing herself. Brainstorm ideas outside of the
heat of the moment, perhaps in a family meeting
or "quiet time."

■ *Chelsea came up with a nonverbal signal that only she and her shy child understood. Instead of interrupting Chelsea with her familiar whine, Melissa came right up to her mother and pulled twice on Mom's little finger to get her attention.*

Periodically "check in" with your child during times when you're particularly busy with a project, so she won't be as tempted to use annoying behavior to get your attention.

See if you can determine an underlying problem when your child is whining that is easily addressed. Is she tired, hungry, sick? Some children resort to whining only when they are overtired; a little more sleep just might do the trick!

Take an honest look at your own behavior; are you modeling the correct way to speak and minimizing your own complaining? Remember, children tend to do as you do, not as you say.

Develop the patience you need to "stay cool" by remembering to take the time to address your own needs. A good mood promotes tolerance. Rest assured that even a two-year-old who seems to whine for just about everything he wants will pass out of this stage as his verbal/language skills develop.

the bottom line

Discourage persistent whining by giving your child the clear message that it will never get him what he wants. Remember, children continue to do only what works.

wits' end

Q: Just when I think I've got things under control and I'm taking a well-earned five-minute break, one of my kids suddenly, but very skillfully, pushes me to the edge of my sanity. How can I best handle the situation?

A: It seems children know just which "buttons" to push to get your immediate attention. Often they don't really seem to care if it's positive or negative attention; as long as they get a rise out of you, they've accomplished their goal. In addition, so many parents deal with an incredible amount of work stress, leaving them little time to think and order their priorities. You owe it to yourself to first take a deep breath and focus on restoring your self-control as well as your sanity.

sanity savers

Realize you can do it all, but not all at once! And sometimes you need to ask for help to get it all done.

■ *Caroline remembers, "One day, I had three kids in the car and four errands to complete before lunchtime. When our first appointment took*

*longer than expected, the kids got antsy waiting
and started to squabble. I could see everything
was starting to go downhill. So I calmly told
them, 'Only one more stop, at the dry cleaner's.
You know he's going to ask you if you've been
good, and if we can honestly say yes, everyone
gets a lollipop.' Then I phoned my husband and
begged him to finish the errands for me on his
way home from work."*

Give yourself permission to be "less than perfect."
The "perfect family" is an unrealistic media-
created myth with which we torture ourselves.
Instead of reaching for the impossible, aim for
what pediatrician Marianne Neifert, author of
Doctor Mom's Parenting Guide, calls "consistently
adequate."

■ *Tanya usually couldn't relax until the house
was spick-and-span. However, one day when her
three-year-old daughter had stopped napping and
was begging her to play outside, instead of
saying, "After cleanup!" Tanya said, "That's it! . . .
No more chores today. Let's just hang out
together!" Tanya got a big smile from her
daughter and gave her one right back. Outside
they went, leaving all the guilt behind, where it
belonged—with the dirty dishes in the sink!*

Lighten up! Try to keep your sense of humor.

To get more accomplished, focus on only one
thing at a time.

Assess your current emotional state before you
take on a problem. Sometimes, by just stepping
back and admitting (to yourself, if no other adult
is around) that you've had a bad day at work,
you're angry at your neighbor, or something

unrelated to the kids is really bugging you, can help put things in perspective. After all, what parent wouldn't be in a better mood with the kids right after he'd had a massage than when he'd just gotten news of a new deadline at work?

Give a warning before you totally "lose it."

> ■ *Helen used to tell her two boys, "The big voice is coming . . . The BIG VOICE is COMING . . . Oh, no! I can feel it . . . THE BIG VOICE IS ALMOST HERE . . ." before she really started yelling at them.*

Avoid pushing yourself "just one more time" when you don't have an ounce of strength or patience left. Admit to your own imperfections; tell your family when you've "simply had it!"

> ■ *"Look, honey, I just sat down and I'm really pooped," Gail told her five-year-old. "Mommy's going to rest, and when the next commercial comes on, I'll go get your juice." While this strategy wouldn't work with a whining toddler, some things really do get easier as your kids get older.*

Replenish yourself with the things that give you pleasure. When you're in a happy place emotionally, you can "be there" more effectively for your children.

> ■ *A "full-time, stay-at-home" mother of four gave Caroline a priceless little gem of advice right before her first child was born, "Never for one moment underestimate the power of a play date or a baby-sitter to give yourself a well-deserved break!"*

Engage in activities that reinforce your sense of competence as well as those that are just plain fun, such as volunteer work, playing bridge, gardening, golfing, or going to the gym.

Beware of becoming a "wimpy" mom or dad; in other words, put aside your fears that your kids won't like you, and just do your job!

■ Pam shared something with the play group moms she had heard in a parenting class: "Loving and setting limits are the two most important parts of a parent's job. Children need limits to bounce off of. Remember, they will do their job as children and frequently test those limits." (You can count on it!)

■ Caroline remembers, "My cousin's mother-in-law used to say, 'You can't let children run your life; you have to show them who's in charge.' You know, I've come to believe she was actually right on target!"

Resist catering to your child's moods. Many parents are afraid to disappoint their children; others give in to their demands in order to avoid public embarrassment.

■ Vivienne started making a conscious effort not to let anyone else's moods influence her own. "When my five-year-old came home from school after a bad day, I realized that it simply wasn't my fault. While I sympathized, I let him know in no uncertain terms that picking on his brother or saying mean things to me was not acceptable. Before, I would have overlooked his griping and teasing until it started to get to me. Then, after I'd blow up, it would seem he'd suddenly feel better, as if we'd cleared the air, but I'd be the one still in a lousy mood."

take heart

♥ *Although you love your child, there will be times when you don't like your own child and vice versa.*

Love your "imperfect" child just because of who he is, not for what he does. Each child has his own particular strengths and weaknesses, just as you do. Celebrate the strengths often.

Become aware of and try to minimize self-critical thought patterns; it's simply not helpful to get into blaming yourself. (Seek help if necessary.)

Look for solutions; let go of guilt and blame. Ask yourself such questions as: What *is* working? What do I like about myself? How can I get closer to where I want to be?

For a better chance at success, plan ahead. Many hair-raising moments can be totally avoided by having prior discussions with the kids, clarifying the rules, or practicing the behavior expected for an upcoming event.

Develop some strategies ahead of time for what you will do next time you find yourself at your wits' end and about to lose it. Try putting on some soothing music, cuddling up with a good book with your child or without (she can watch her favorite video in another room), lying down for a couple of minutes, or fixing a snack to restore your energy level. (See "Anger," page 19, and "Tantrums," page 276, for more suggestions about how to soothe yourself.)

Make the time to sit down and decide what really counts in your life. Then follow through on those priorities. This may require making some difficult decisions, like how much money you realistically need as a family. It may require changing your job or the hours you work to make more time available to be with your family. These things are not "beyond

> **take heart**
>
> ♥ *You're not the only parent who feels a bit guilty that you lost your temper with your child earlier when, out of the blue, she presents you with a "bootaful" bouquet of freshly picked dandelions and reaches up to bestow a loving, sticky-fingered hug around your neck!*

take heart

♥ You're not the only parent who, on a very bad day, momentarily questions why you chose to have a child in the first place . . . that is, until you catch a glimpse of your little one lying so adorably and innocently in bed sound asleep. How could this "little angel" (you can almost see a halo) have caused you so much trouble earlier? Not to worry; with some new strategies to try along with a good night's sleep, you'll be ready to better handle the challenges tomorrow is sure to bring.

your control," though they may seem so in the rush of day to day. And remember—it's your life, no one else's!

Jot down a list of those things you really enjoy and that relax you. Think of two or three things you would do if you suddenly had a week off without the kids, spouse, or house to take care of. (Note: Cleaning up the house and doing the laundry don't count. Sitting in the sunshine with a good book, attending a sporting event, getting a massage, going fishing, or doing yoga does!) Once you identify what gives you pleasure, figure out how you can fit it into your schedule, an hour a week or even just ten minutes a day.

Apologize when you lose it. Say, "I'm sorry I screamed at you when I walked in the house; it wasn't your fault. I came home from work with a bad headache and had trouble listening to you. Now I feel much better; let's go do that puzzle that you have been wanting to do together. Okay?"

the bottom line

Bag that stress and guilt as you identify your priorities and honestly acknowledge what you need in order to be replenished; you'll be in better shape to do your job as you make it ap*parent* exactly who is the *parent!*

recommended children's books

Reading books together can be a wonderful way for you and your child to revisit a variety of issues away from the heat of the moment or to prepare ahead of time for a situation. When you are having trouble finding the appropriate words, a book can often get the point across to a child in just the right way. Sometimes, the text or pictures encourage the child to ask questions, thereby giving you a clearer sense of his or her understanding. Then you can focus further discussion as needed.

We compiled the following list of excellent children's picture books (as well as a few video- and audiotapes) that address issues raised in each of the chapters in *THE POCKET PARENT*. A few of the books are currently out of print, but they are available at many public libraries and on the Internet. Additionally, we suggest you ask your librarian to recommend her favorites, including any brand-new titles that address your concerns.

anger

Feelings, by Aliki, can be a useful tool in helping children to articulate their anger and other emotions. The short stories in the book can be read over the course of time to keep the discussion going.

How Are You Peeling, by Saxton Freymann and Joost Elffers, is an unusual and creative book to help you and your child identify and talk about feelings. Full-color photographs show different fruits and vegetables, each designed with an expressive face that portrays an emotion such as anger, sadness, joy, or fear.

Mean Soup, by Betsy Everitt, is about Horace, a little boy who feels very mean at the end of a bad day. With supervision and humor, his wise mother encourages her son to work through his angry feelings by making mean soup.

My Many Colored Days, by Dr. Seuss, was actually written in 1973, but it was first published nearly 20 years later. Illustrated with impressionistic full-color art as requested by Seuss, this book is a terrific tool to encourage discussions of emotions.

Today I Feel Silly, by Jamie Lee Curtis, shows that everyone has moods that can change each day, from silly to angry to sad. The zany, touching verse and the fun mood-wheel that lets kids change a character's facial expressions can help you and your child identify and discuss both good and bad feelings.

When Emily Woke Up Angry (out of print), by Riana Duncan, tells how when Emily wakes up grumpy, she imitates the angry movements of several animals, thus illustrating different ways kids can express their anger.

new baby

Be Gentle, by Virginia Miller, can help toddlers understand what it means to be gentle, a phrase they often hear when approaching a baby. In this story, Bartholomew learns to be gentle with his new kitten after she hides because he was too rough.

Big Like Me, by Anna Grossnickle Hines, shows how eager big brother is to teach his new baby sister all the joyous things he knows about the world. The easy format can be enjoyed by even a two- to three-year-old.

Big Panda, Little Panda, by Joan Stimson, describes the feeling of wanting to stay little even though you're suddenly the "big" brother.

"Hey, What About Me?" is a VHS video produced by Kidvidz that focuses on the older child's perspective and is very helpful in exploring how it feels to be the sibling of a new baby.

I Wish My Brother Was a Dog, by Carol Diggory Shields, portrays the naughty fantasies that spring from the everyday frustrations of dealing with a pesky, younger brother.

Something Special, by Nicola Moon, tells how Mom seems too busy to pay attention to Charlie since the new baby arrived. So, all by himself, Charlie has to come up with something special to bring to school. The ending delightfully illustrates the growing bond between the new siblings.

When the New Baby Comes, I'm Moving Out, by Martha Alexander, illustrates how a little boy expresses his fearful and angry feelings about the impending birth of a new sibling by fantasizing doing naughty things.

bad words

Andrew's Angry Words, by Dorothea Lachner, reveals how Andrew's angry swear words are passed on to the people and animals around him. They anger everyone, until a wise woman replaces them with kind words that ripple back positively through the characters.

Elbert's Bad Word, by Audrey Wood, shows how replacing a bad word with a child's own fun, made-up expressive word works better than punishment to curb the use of inappropriate language.

The Meanest Thing to Say (part of a series of *Little Bill* books), by Bill Cosby, illustrates a response to teasing that can empower a picked-on child and perhaps open up a discussion of ways to help your child defend himself, all by himself.

My Name Is Not Dummy: A Children's Problem-Solving Book, by Elizabeth Crary, tells how a young girl's friend won't stop calling her names. Your child can make choices about what the main character might do and then explore the consequences of those actions.

bedtime

Good Night Baby Bear, by Frank Asch, is a simple story for toddlers about a baby bear who doesn't want to go to sleep for the winter.

Goodnight Moon, by Margaret Wise Brown, is a classic bedtime book. For many families this is a "read-every-night book" as the young bunny says good night to everything inside and outside the window. This story is also told on a VHS Video called *Goodnight Moon and Other Sleepytime Tales (2000)*, which includes some "wind-down" tunes sung by celebrities as well as real kids' answers to a variety of bedtime questions.

Night Shift Daddy, by Eileen Spinelli, tells about the special bond between a daughter and her dad, and their ritual of tucking each other in bed at their different bedtimes.

When Mama Comes Home Tonight, by Eileen Spinelli, shows how hard it can be for a child to wait for her favorite time of day, when Mama comes home from work. This soothing book celebrates the routines and rituals that mother and child perform together each night at bedtime.

biting

Bootsie Barker Bites, by Barbara Bottner, makes the point that when a child acts aggressively, other children will not want to play with him or her.

No Biting, Horrible Crocodile (out of print), by Jonathan Shipton, handles the biting issue with great care and understanding, demonstrating that other children are wary of biters.

chores

Amelia Bedelia, by Peggy Parish, is a humorous reminder to adults that, like Amelia, children need simple, easy-to-understand directions. Five-year-olds will laugh at Amelia's disastrous propensity to take all directions literally.

Curious George Takes a Job, by H. A. Rey, is a timeless classic that will make kids laugh as George, the monkey, deals with some childlike struggles, such as following directions and paying attention.

comparing and labeling children

Harry and Willy and Carrothead, by Judith Caseley, beautifully portrays how Harry, born without a left hand, has the strength to stand up for his friend when some kids label him "carrothead."

I Love You the Purplest, by Barbara M. Joosse, reassures each child that he is special and loved in his own unique way when competing siblings ask their mom who is the best.

Shy Charles, by Rosemary Wells, tells how being painfully shy does not stop a young mouse from heroically rescuing his baby-sitter.

death

Circle of Seasons, by Gerda Muller, is a nice way to begin discussing the circle of life with your child. The delicate paintings show the special joys of each changing season.

The Fall of Freddie the Leaf, a Story of Life for All Ages, by Leo Buscaglia, helps explain permanent loss in a way understandable to children.

I'll Always Love You, by Hans Wilhelm, deals with the sensitive subject of the death of a boy's beloved dog. Kids learn the importance of telling loved ones how they feel about them, and will find this book a celebration of love rather than a mourning of loss.

Nana Upstairs & Nana Downstairs, by Tomie dePaola, is a quietly touching story depicting the loving relationship between a boy and his two grandmothers. It will help kids think about what it means to be young, to be old, and finally to die.

discipline

Elizabeth, Who Is Not a Saint, by Kathleen C. Szaj, is a humorous book about impulse control for children. Elizabeth's grandmother helps her spirited granddaughter channel her strength into more creative and socially acceptable activities.

Mama, Do You Love Me?, by Barbara M. Joosse, tenderly tells the story of a child testing the limits of her independence and of a mother who reassuringly proves that her love is unconditional and everlasting.

Mommy Go Away, by Lynne Jonell, provides a fun role reversal for a frustrated little boy named Christopher. Tired of his mom always telling him what to do, he magically shrinks her down to a very small size. He reassures her that he'll take good care of her because he knows what it's like to be small.

No David!, by David Shannon, uses large expressive illustrations to show what it's like to hear the word "No!" over and over again from a child's perspective.

doctor and dentist visits

Barney and Baby Bop Go to the Doctor, by Margie Larsen, introduces young children to the routine doctor's visit when Barney takes Baby Bop for her yearly checkup.

Barney Goes to the Dentist, by Linda Cress Dowdy, helps allay any fears your toddler may have regarding a dental visit. Many good pictures explaining what will happen during the visit are included.

Curious George Goes to the Hospital, by H.A. Rey, portrays the discomfort of getting a shot without making a big deal about it.

My Little Friend Goes to the Dentist, by Evelyn M. Finnegan, tells the story of how a child with a wiggly tooth brings along her special doll from Grandma when she goes to the dentist.

A Shot for Baby Bear (out of print), by Dorothy Corey, is a simple picture book in which Baby Bear gains courage for a visit to the doctor, which includes getting a shot, by watching his big brother go first.

fears at night

Tell Me Something Happy Before I Go to Sleep, by Joyce Dunbar and Debi Gliori, tells how little sister rabbit can't get to sleep because she's afraid of bad dreams. Her big brother comforts her by helping her think of happy things.

There's a Monster Under My Bed, by James Howe, is the story of a boy who sets aside his own fears in order to comfort his younger brother.

There's an Alligator Under My Bed, by Mercer Mayer, is the humorous story of a boy who uses food to lure an imaginary alligator out from under his bed and into the garage.

fighting in front of your kids

The Quarreling Book, by Charlotte Zolotow, tells the story of a typical family that bickers all the time.

When They Fight, by Kathryn White, shows how a small badger feels when he witnesses his parents arguing, and how, when they make up, the world becomes sunny again.

first days of preschool

Annabelle Swift, Kindergartner, by Amy Schwartz, takes a perceptive look at the "ups and downs" of a beginning kindergartner whose big sister told her to do some things that were not quite right.

Edward Unready for School, by Rosemary Wells, tells how Edward's classmates are all happy and busy at school—but Edward, a late-blooming bear, would rather be happy and busy at home. This author touches on many topics, such as being shy, making comparisons, bolstering self-esteem, and respecting your child's temperament and developmental readiness.

Timothy Goes to School, by Rosemary Wells, talks about the one or two kids at every school who seem extra popular and talented but aren't kind to others. Kids will enjoy reading about Timothy's ability to overcome his insecurities.

friends

The Brand New Kid, by Katie Couric, tells your five-year-old about Ellie, who wonders what it's like to be Lazlo, the new kid in class. She decides to get to know him, risking her friends' ridicule. Through rhyming text, Ellie reports to her friends that Lazlo isn't that different from the rest of the kids.

Edward's Overwhelming Overnight, by Rosemary Wells, stars Edward, the late-blooming bear, who has fun on a playdate until an unexpected sleepover freezes Edward in his tracks.

Everybody Takes Turns (out of print), by Dorothy Corey, is a simple book that illustrates for the two- to three-year-old child how everybody, even an adult waiting at a traffic light, needs to take turns.

How Humans Make Friends, by Loreen Leedy, shows aliens observing children who make each other feel good by keeping secrets and promises, sharing, telling the truth, and being considerate. It also illustrates how it's best to resolve conflicts between friends by talking rather than resorting to physical aggression.

How to Be a Friend, by Laurene Krasny Brown and Marc Brown, features cartoonlike green dinosaurs who speak to your five-year-old about the ups and downs of friendship.

I'm Sorry, by Sam McBratney, illustrates how even the best of friends fight occasionally and that by saying, "I'm sorry," although it's sometimes hard to do, they can patch things up.

It's My Jumbo (out of print), by Claude K. Dubois, is a wordless picture book that illustrates for your toddler the attachment of two siblings for the same toy and how they learn to share by taking turns playing with it.

Take Turns Penguin, by Jeanne Willis, shows how on his first day at school, Penguin learns the hard way what happens when you don't give others a turn on the slide.

"gimmes"

The Berenstain Bears Get the Gimmies, by Jan and Stan Berenstain, teaches the lesson that everyone suffers when kids get the gimmies.

Giving Thanks: A Native American Good Morning Message, by Chief Jake Swamp, explains that Iroquois children are taught to greet the world each morning by saying thank you to the wind and the stars and all living things, which we often take for granted.

Red Fox and His Canoe, by Nathaniel Benchley, tells the story of an Indian boy who wants the biggest canoe his father can make. The bottom line is made very clear—bigger is not always better.

grandparents

Grandma's Smile, by Elaine Moore, tells how Grandma smiles her special smile whenever her granddaughter comes to visit, and they enjoy different activities in each passing season.

Grandpa's House, by Harvey Stevenson, beautifully portrays the special love between the generations. Woody loves going to his Grandpa's, where everything is different.

Little Bear's Visit, by Else Holmelund Minarik, is a timeless classic depicting the fun, security, and unconditional love Little Bear experiences when visiting his grandparents.

Thanksgiving Treat, by Catherine Stock, shows how Matt, the youngest member of the family, feels left out when he's told he's too little to help prepare for the holidays. Grandpa is the only one with plenty of time to spend with his grandson. Together, they come up with a surprise that enriches the whole family's celebration.

hitting and hurting others

Hands Are not for Hitting, by Martine Agassi, Ph.D., provides simple words and warm illustrations to reinforce the concepts that violence is never okay and that toddlers and preschoolers can learn to manage their anger.

Hershel and the Hanukkah Goblins, by Eric A. Kimmel, illustrates the theme of brains outwitting brawn. Five-year-old children of any religion will admire a hero who uses his wits rather than violence to stop the hobgoblins from ruining a joyous holiday celebration.

Make Someone Smile and 40 More Ways to Be a Peaceful Person, by Judy Lalli, is an ideal read-aloud book containing clear and understandable ideas for promoting peaceful thoughts and behavior.

We Can Get Along: A Children's Book of Choices, by Lauren Murphy Payne and Claudia Rohling, teaches essential conflict resolution and peacemaking skills—think before you speak or act, treat others the way you want to be treated—in a way that children as young as three can understand.

"I hate you!"

Angel Child, Dragon Child, by Michele Surat, tells the story of a Vietnamese girl trying to adjust to life in the U.S.A. and the teasing she gets from the other children.

The Hating Book, by Charlotte Zolotow, sympathetically portrays how young children think and act, by focusing on a hurt little girl who talks about a misunderstanding with her friend.

Let's Be Enemies, by Janice May Udry, is a great book for four- and five-year-olds. It realistically depicts how young children are constantly making, breaking, and renewing friendships, all in the process of self-discovery.

Lilly's Purple Plastic Purse, by Kevin Henkes, tells what happens when Lilly's beloved teacher takes away the purse she just can't stop playing with. This book accurately portrays how fast a child can go from love to hate to love again.

interrupting

Be Quiet, Parrot, by Jeanne Willis, tells the story of Parrot's first day at school where he definitely has no trouble talking. In fact, he talks too much and needs to learn not to interrupt.

Dawn and the Round To-It, by Irene Smalls, is a lovely story that illustrates the importance of spending some one-on-one time with a child.

How Long?, by Elizabeth Dale, shows how a child's concept of time differs from an adult's. This book provides concrete ways to help your child understand how long it will be until you can spend time with him or her.

I Am Not a Pest (out of print), by Marjorie & Mitchell Sharmat, is a humorous book from a pest's point of view.

listening

Come Along, Daisy, by Jane Simmons, teaches a simple lesson in listening and following a basic and important safety rule: staying close enough to your mom or dad so they can see you when you're out together.

Dinofours: I'm The Boss, by Steve Metzger, shows what happens when the main character acts very bossy and doesn't listen to his friends' point of view.

The Tale of Peter Rabbit, by Beatrix Potter, is the classic story of a young rabbit who experiences the scary consequences of ignoring his mother's instructions when he enters a tempting but very dangerous garden.

lying

Armadillo Tattletale, by Helen Ketteman, is the story of Armadillo, who loves to hide and spy on the other animals and tell tall tales about what he hears. Through lyrical text and vivid illustrations, children learn that it is important to respect the privacy of others and avoid telling lies that hurt feelings.

Chicken Little and *The Boy Who Cried Wolf* are two classic tales that can help your child understand the consequences of lying. A popular retelling of the "Chicken Little" story is *Henny Penny*, by Paul Galdone.

The Emperor's New Clothes: An All-Star Illustrated Retelling of the Classic Fairy Tale (with audio CD), published by Harcourt Brace, is a wonderful, humorous version of the classic story with narration by Robin Williams, Madonna, and Dr. Ruth Westheimer.

The Empty Pot, by Demi, recounts the story of a young boy whose courage to tell the truth is rewarded when he becomes the heir to a great kingdom.

manners

Grover's Guide to Good Manners is a Sesame Street picture book that's useful for introducing preschool children to the basics, such as when to say "please," "thank you," and "excuse me."

It's a Spoon, Not a Shovel, by Caralyn Buehner, teaches etiquette in a fun way. Parent and child can answer the quizzes or search the full-page color illustrations for the subtly hidden letters of the correct multiple-choice answers.

Manners, by Aliki, uses simple words and colorful illustrations to help a four- or five-year-old distinguish between appropriate and inappropriate behavior.

Me First, by Helen Lester, is a funny story with a surprise play on words. Pinkerton Pig is pink, plump, and pushy, but he overcomes his selfishness and greed to learn that being first isn't always the best.

Pass the Peas, Please: A Book of Manners, by Dina Anastasio, features rhymed text and illustrations that model the most appropriate behavior for many different situations.

mealtime

Bread and Jam for Frances, by Russell Hoban, tells the story of little Frances the badger, who refuses to eat her mother's food. So, her mother lets her eat her favorite thing—bread and jam— at every meal. Frances soon learns that eating the same thing over and over doesn't taste so good after a while.

D.W. The Picky Eater, by Marc Brown, shows how a tantrum in a restaurant results in D.W. having to stay home with a baby-sitter the next time the family goes out. In the surprising, funny ending, D.W. realizes that eating can be a fun, social experience and decides to give it another try.

I Will Never Not Ever Eat a Tomato, by Laura Child, deals with a long list of foods that are simply inedible for Lola . . . that is until her creative big sister comes up with a plan.

No Carrots for Harry! (out of print), by Jean Langerman, is a charming story about a rabbit who won't eat carrots and the dilemma he faces when he goes to his aunt's house for dinner and cannot have dessert until he eats his carrots.

The Sensational Samburger, by David Pelham, is a three-dimensional book shaped like a hamburger! Sam and Samantha decide to try to entice the bun burglar to steal the world's worst hamburger— complete with shampoo mayonnaise and bugs galore! Simple, zany food fun!

morning "crazies"

Froggy Gets Dressed, by Jonathan London, will appeal to toddlers as well as second graders because of its humorous ending. While dressing to play in the snow, Froggy forgets essential items and must get undressed and dressed a few times before getting it right.

Hurry Up, Harry!, by Kathleen C. Szaj, tells the story of Harry, who like most children, thinks he has no need to hurry until he experiences the "not so fun" consequences of being late.

Jesse Bear, What Will You Wear?, by Nancy White Carlstrom, is a rhyming picture book for toddlers that illustrates a young bear's joy in his independence.

picking up toys

The Berenstain Bears and the Messy Room, by Stan and Jan Berenstain, adeptly illustrates a mother's frustration over her children's messy room and the kid-friendly solution she comes up with.

Everything Has a Place (out of print), by Patricia Lillie, is a book that teaches with few words: "In the best of all possible worlds, everything has a place." Even a two-year old should be able to confidently understand the concept.

potty training

Everyone Poops, by Taro Gomi, can be used to introduce your child to the concept that pooping is a natural process. Written and illustrated in a straightforward manner, it will satisfy a preschooler's interest in bodily functions. Follow up with a book explaining the potty.

It's Potty Time is a VHS video in The Duke Family Series. Set at a child's party, it illustrates how preschoolers discreetly go to the bathroom during the celebration.

Once Upon a Potty (choose the boy or girl version), by Alona Frankel, tells what happens when Grandma brings over a potty.

To Pee or Not to Pee, by Linda Johns, respects a child's point of view as it tells the story of little Will, who decides not to pee in the new potty Mom brings home. He finds many other uses for it until he finally decides he's ready. Stickers and tattoos are included to use as potty-training rewards.

Uh Oh! Gotta Go! Potty Tales from Toddlers, by Bob McGrath, humorously depicts the challenges of toilet training.

What Do You Do With a Potty: An Important Pop-Up Book, by Marianne Borgardt, uses humor, cartoonlike illustrations, and flaps and tabs to engage your child while introducing him or her to the idea of a potty.

power struggles

Contrary Mary (The Giggle Club Series), by Anita Jeram, tells how one day Mary simply refuses to cooperate and decides to do everything backward. Instead of letting a power struggle ensue, her patient mom sympathizes by tucking Contrary Mary into bed upside down at the end of this difficult day.

Harriet, You'll Drive Me Wild!, by Mem Fox, shows the tension rising as Harriet goes from one mishap to another, always claiming she's sorry, until her mother yells at her. Once the pent-up anger is released, Harriet cries, her mother says she's sorry, and they hug each other and laugh.

Pookins Gets Her Way, by Helen Lester, is about a little girl who always tries to get her way. Everything is a power struggle until she meets a gnome who grants her every wish. She soon discovers that getting everything she wants isn't always the formula for happiness.

self-esteem

A Bad Case of Stripes, by David Shannon, tells the story of Camilla Cream, who loves lima beans but won't eat them because she's worried that the kids at school will make fun of her. Camilla comes to accept the idea that it's okay to be different from everyone else.

The Biggest Nose, by Kathy Caple, tells how Eleanor Elephant overcomes her self-consciousness and stands up for herself after being teased by her classmates about having the biggest nose.

I Like Me, by Nancy Carlson, is a simple book in which the main character, a pig, shows how she's her very own best friend. She demonstrates all the reasons kids can feel good about themselves.

The Little Engine That Could, by Watty Piper, is the classic children's story that illustrates how even difficult tasks can be accomplished when you have the inner strength to believe in yourself. The book is available in an engaging pop-up version. Preschool kids will enjoy spinning the train's wheels and making the toys pop up and down.

Olivia, written and illustrated by Ian Falconer, does a great job of enabling kids to see themselves in a talented little pig who knows she is good at many things, especially at "wearing people out, including herself."

Yoko, by Rosemary Wells, tells the story of Yoko the cat, who is teased when her mother sends her to school with sushi for lunch. Her teacher tries to help by creating an International Foods Day, but no one will sample Yoko's sushi except for a very hungry little raccoon, who learns to appreciate how special and delicious another culture's food can be.

separation anxiety

Alfie Gives a Hand (out of print), by Shirley Hughes, deals with young children's anxious feelings at birthday parties. One little boy overcomes his own by helping a friend who is even shyer than he.

Daddy, Will You Miss Me?, by Wendy McCormick, illustrates how waiting for a parent to return home from a trip can seem like forever to a child. A father and son create rituals for each passing day, so love can span the distance between them.

Oh My Baby, Little One, by Kathi Appelt, describes how sad Baby Bird and his mama feel when they part each morning. But, as Mama says, the love they share is with them always, keeping them close until they can be together again.

What to Expect When the Baby-Sitter Comes (What to Expect Kids), by Heidi Murkoff, helps prevent separation anxiety *before* it happens. The child learns exactly what is going to happen when you go away and the baby-sitter takes over. This is part of a series of helpful books.

Who Will Pick Me Up When I Fall?, by Dorothy E. Molnar, tells of a little girl with two working parents who feels anxious and frustrated about her ever-changing schedule and about being picked up by different people every day.

You Go Away, by Dorothy Corey, uses soothing, repetitive text to address a toddler's separation anxiety. The child learns that when Mom and Dad leave, they do come back.

sexuality

What to Expect When Mommy's Having a Baby (What to Expect Kids), by Heidi Murkoff, is for kids ages two to five. It features Angus, the Answer Dog, who helps to answer questions about this important event in an appropriate, easy-to-understand manner.

William's Doll, by Charlotte Zolotow, addresses gender issues and notions about what are appropriate toys for each gender in a gentle, reassuring manner. More than any other toy, William wants a doll. His grandma buys him one and reassures William's father that William needs a doll to practice taking care of a baby as all good fathers do.

You Were Born on Your Very First Birthday, by Linda Girard, provides a good introduction for talking about babies with older siblings. Rather than focusing on how they got here, the author approaches the subject by explaining how babies grow inside the mother, how they might feel, and what they might hear.

sibling rivalry

It's Not My Fault (out of print), by Franz Brandenburg, is a simply illustrated book that does a great job of portraying family life. Although the mice family siblings quarrel and blame each other, they miss each other terribly when apart.

Katie Did It, by Becky Bring McDaniel, portrays how Katie, the youngest, gets blamed for all her siblings' mishaps until one day she takes credit for doing something wonderful and loving all by herself.

Noisy Nora, by Rosemary Wells, is a rhyming story that addresses the emotions of a middle child. Nora feels left out and jealous of her siblings, a baby brother who needs constant care and a big sister who gets to do all the fun things.

A Place for Ben, by Jeanne Titherington, demonstrates the frustrations that older children sometimes feel when pestered by younger siblings.

strangers

The Berenstain Bears Learn About Strangers, by Jan and Stan Berenstain, recounts how Mama Bear taught her cubs how best to deal with strangers.

Never Talk to Strangers, by Irma Joyce, is a lighthearted rhyming book that points out situations where children should and should not talk to strangers.

The Visitor, by Patrice Aggs, tells the story of two kittens, Cosy and Posy, who are a bit apprehensive at the thought of meeting a guest—the giraffe who is coming to dinner. It turns out that everyone has a lot of fun together, and the giraffe becomes a new friend.

Where Did My Mother Go?, by Edna Mitchell Preston, uses role-reversal between a cat mother and child to reinforce the rule that you don't go away without checking with a loved one and telling them where you are going.

Who Is a Stranger and What Should I Do?, by Linda Girard, helps to put the issue into perspective by stressing that most strangers are nice people. She recommends reassuring your child by reminding her that harm from strangers is rare. The book also contains some "what-if" situations you can role-play and practice with your child.

tantrums

Tiger and the Temper Tantrum, by Vivian French, introduces us to Tiger, who's fond of saying "No!" all the time. When he throws a temper tantrum in public, his mother puts her paw down and Tiger learns that there are more agreeable ways to get what you want.

Tristan's Temper Tantrum, by Caroline Formby, tells the story of Tristan the volcano and what happens when he lets loose.

television, video games, and computers

Arthur's TV Trouble, by Marc Brown, tells how Arthur does chores to earn the money to buy something he sees advertised on TV. This book deals with the effects of TV commercials on kids and provides an eye-opening lesson about how some products aren't exactly as advertised.

The Berenstain Bears and too Much TV, by Stan and Jan Berenstain, depicts how Mama Bear bans TV for a week after she decides the family spends too much time in front of the tube. Everyone is pleasantly surprised by all the fun activities they find to do instead.

thumb sucking

David Decides About Thumbsucking: A Story for Children, a Guide for Parents, by Susan Heitler, is written from a child's point of view and invites young readers to join David as he decides whether to give up his thumb-sucking habit. The book also includes information for parents about thumb- and finger-sucking.

Harold's Hideaway Thumb, by Harriet Sonnenschein, tells about Harold the bunny, who is having a hard time giving up his thumb-sucking habits. Harold experiments with a few different

ways to solve the problem and eventually finds one
that works.

time-out

Dinofours: It's Time-Out Time, by Steve Metzger, is
the story of Brendan, who winds up in the time-out
chair at school. Brendan learns from his
experience how to control himself better. This
helpful book is one of a series that includes topics
such as friendship, getting ready for school, and
separation.

traveling with the kids

Arthur's Family Vacation, by Marc Brown,
recounts how Arthur's family tries to make the
best of their summer vacation even though it rains
every day. In a happy ending, the weather on the
very last day turns out to be perfect for the beach.

Curious Kids Go on Vacation, by Ingrid Godon,
illustrates various vacation scenes and the things
you might find there to help parents prepare their
toddlers for traveling experiences. This is one in a
series of helpful word books.

A Fun Weekend, by Franz Brandenberg, about the
Bear family, who decide to go on a weekend
getaway to a lodge in the country. Although the car
trip doesn't go exactly as planned, the family has a
true adventure and a lot of fun just being together.

Mr. Bear's Vacation, by Debi Gliori, reminds us
that even the most meticulously planned and
eagerly awaited vacation is not without humorous
mishaps, especially with a toddler in tow.

values

The Children's Book of Virtues, by William J. Bennett, provides a collection of stories, poems, and fables to read aloud with your five-year-old. The selections illustrate such virtues as courage, honesty, compassion, and faith.

Dragon's Merry Christmas, by Dav Pilkey, is a heartwarming tale of a simple, funny dragon that shows us how good it can feel to share with those who are less fortunate than ourselves.

Fables, by Arnold Lobel, features 20 stories, each only one page long. There is a simply stated moral at the end of each story to reinforce its lesson.

Kids' Random Acts of Kindness, with a foreword by Rosalynn Carter, describes how kids from around the world spontaneously demonstrated kindness by reaching out to a stranger, helping out at home, or giving of themselves in other ways.

Reach for the Sky: And Other Little Lessons for a Happier World, by Allison Stoutland, can be used to initiate conversations with your child about cooperation, dedication, empathy, humor, and love.

Native American Stories, told by Joseph Bruchac, illustrates many of the lessons Native Americans teach their children (respect for others, conservation, cooperation) in simple, easy-to-understand stories for the four- or five-year-old.

whining

A Children's Book About Whining, by Joy Berry, is one in a series of "Help Me Be Good" books. Although these books tend to lecture children (so, hopefully, you don't have to!), they also include some practical alternatives to misbehavior and can serve as a good way to open a discussion.

How to Lose All Your Friends, by Nancy Carlson, provides a tongue-in-cheek lesson in reverse psychology. It looks at the negative consequences of behaviors like never smiling, never sharing, and whining when you don't get your way.

wits' end

Alexander and the Terrible, Horrible, No Good, Very Bad Day, by Judith Viorst, is a humorous story written from the perspective of a little boy who gets no sympathy or help from anyone and considers escaping to Australia. But Mom explains that all kids, even in Australia, have days like this.

Five Minutes' Peace, by Jill Murphy, tells how a mother elephant named Mrs. Large seeks just five minutes of solitude away from her kids, who follow her *everywhere* and make a mess *everywhere!* Adults will enjoy this witty and oh-so-true tale as much as their kids.

The Seven Silly Eaters, by Mary Ann Hoberman, portrays a mom at her wits' end when each of her seven children will eat only one of her homemade dishes and nothing else. Of course, none of the picky eaters likes the same thing, but just when Mom is feeling really unappreciated, they get together and make her a special birthday surprise.

index

A

Abstract words, 181–82
Accidents, avoiding
  during travel, 308–9
Action, replacing words
  with, 175
Address, forms of, 195
Advertising, 133, 287
Advice, 177
  expert, 3
  from grandparents,
    139, 141–42
  to help children solve
    problems, 20
Affection, taking away,
  87–88
Age:
  mixed, play and,
    125–26
  socialization and,
    124–25
Aggressive behavior:
  biting, 50–56, 341
  hitting and hurting
    others, 155–62,
    347–48
  new baby and, 31
  time-out for, 299–304,
    360
"Agreeing to disagree,"
  141–42
Allergies, 127
Allowances, 64–65, 132
Amusement parks, 273,
  315
Anger, 19–29, 337–38
  acceptable physical
    outlets for, 21
  acknowledging
    children's feelings
    of, 20, 234
  bad words and, 37, 41
  hateful outbursts and,
    147–54, 348–49

modeling appropriate
  responses to, 28–29,
  33
toward new sibling,
  31–32
not responding to, 28
parents' feelings of,
  19–24, 27–29, 89,
  109, 110, 154
separating yourself
  from source of
  irritation and, 22–23,
  233–34
tantrums and, 276–82,
  281, 358–59
triggers of, 24
Apologies, 23, 41–42, 194,
  320, 336
Appetite, 200, 202, 204
Appropriate
  consequences, 13,
    86–87, 239
  choosing, 14–15
Assertiveness, 322
"As soon as you . . ."
  requests, 84
Attack ("you") statements,
  16, 108, 173, 174
Attention:
  children's seeking of,
    30, 31, 32, 37, 53,
    152–53, 235
  negative vs. positive,
    given by parent, 235
  withdrawing, as
    response, 38
Auditory cues, 174–75,
  213
Awareness training,
  272–73

B

Babies:
  new, 30–36, 228, 338–39

E

Eating. *See* Food;
  Mealtime
Egocentricity, 124–25,
  163, 181
E-mail, 167
Embarrassments:
  sexual matters and,
    255, 256, 258
  see also Public
Empathy, 6, 53, 153–54,
  181, 277, 318, 320
Equality, fairness vs., 268
Etiquette. *See* Manners
"Excuse me"s, 165
Expectations, 263
  explaining to children,
    192
  placed on children,
    72–73, 188
Explanations, 258
  minimal, for requests,
    84, 174, 208–9
Eye contact, 173, 192, 210

F

Failure, 67, 90, 243
Fairness, 268
Family bed, 48
Family history, 143, 245
Family meetings, 17–18,
  27, 90
  aggressive behavior
    and, 159
  chores and, 58–59,
    63–64
  listening in, 177
  planning trips and, 310
  sibling rivalry and, 266
  travel and, 315–16
Fantasy, 151–52, 183, 210,
  233, 279–80
  distinguishing reality
    from, 179, 182,
    185–86
  television or videos
    and, 286
Fay, Jim, 318

Fears:
  of child,
    acknowledging, 101,
    248–49, 326
  about death, 80
  about doctor and
    dentist visits, 93, 94,
    96
  at night, 43, 100–105,
    344
Feelings, 281
  of children,
    acknowledging, 18,
    20, 32, 76, 83, 96,
    149, 176, 187, 188,
    208–9, 211, 231, 234,
    237–38, 248
  egocentric thinking
    and, 124–25
  helping children
    with verbal
    expression of, 6, 16,
    54, 158, 265
  human, given to
    objects, 182
  "I" statements and,
    15–16, 19–20
  of parents, explaining
    to children, 19–20,
    318–19
  parents' expression of,
    6, 16, 79, 110
  "Use words" requests
    and, 16
  see also Anger; Fears
Fighting:
  between children, 5,
    128
  "fair," ground rules
    for, 107
  of parents, in front of
    kids, 106–13, 344
First aid kits, 306–7
First days of preschool,
  114–19, 345
  see also Preschool
Food:
  children's likes and
    dislikes and, 202–5
  fun with, 207
  new, introducing to
    children, 201

N